INTRODUCTION TO THEORY OF MIND

Children, Autism and Apes

Peter Mitchell

Lecturer in Psychology, University of Birmingham

ARNOLD

A member of the Hodder Headline Group
LONDON • NEW YORK • SYDNEY • AUCKLAND

First published in Great Britain in 1997 by
Arnold, a member of the Hodder Headline Group,
338 Euston Road, London NW1 3BH
175 Fifth Avenue, New York, NY 10010

Distributed exclusively in the USA by
St Martin's Press, Inc.
175 Fifth Avenue, New York, NY 10010

British Library Cataloguing in Publication Data
A catalogue record for this book is available from the British Library

Library of Congress Cataloging-in-Publication Data
A catalog record for this book is available from the Library of Congress

ISBN 0 340 64590 3 **(hb)**
ISBN 0 340 62497 3 **(pb)**

Typeset in 10/12 Palatino by
Saxon Graphics Ltd, Derby
Printed and bound in Great Britain by
J W Arrowsmith Ltd, Bristol

For my son Andrew – the light of my life

CONTENTS

ACKNOWLEDGEMENTS

I would like to thank my wife, Rita, not only for making an important contribution to the artwork, but also for being so patient over the countless weekends and evenings that went into the writing of this book. I also thank my son, Andrew, for his wizardry with computer graphics. I am always indebted to my friend and colleague, Elizabeth Robinson, for providing an eternal source of inspiration as well as moral support and understanding. I thank my students for making life so lively and for contributing substantially to my thinking – they are Kristina Cole, Rebecca Saltmarsh, Emma Steverson and Laura Taylor. I am grateful to Naomi Meredith for suggesting that I should write this book, and for her remarkable patience over the time it has taken to produce the goods. Finally, but certainly not least, thanks are due to all the children who have participated and all the teachers and headteachers who have been so tolerant of intrusions into their schools.

Figure 4.1 is reproduced with the kind permission of the National Autistic Society, 276 Willesden Lane, London NW2 5RB, UK.

1

WHAT IS A THEORY OF MIND?

INTRODUCTION

Suppose an alien on a mission to document life in our local galaxy paid a visit to earth. They would see the diversity of life, noting how beautifully adapted each species was to its habitat and lifestyle. They would report in their journal some of the highlights of evolved life form, and in doing so would admire the mastery of flight by birds. The aerodynamic shape permits soaring, whilst the musculature is suited to a beating of the wings that allows directional and purposive flight. An alien would compare and contrast the respiration of animals that live on dry land with that of those which inhabit the oceans. They would note the evolution of sensory perception and take delight in the refinement of muscles and general physique, as for example in the cheetah.

What might not be obvious to an alien, however, is the remarkable case of humans. Apart from the curious artefacts, such as buildings and transport vehicles, that surround us, humans would appear to be very mundane creatures indeed. We are not especially agile, large, strong or ornate (unless we decorate ourselves), yet we dominate our planet and most other life forms on it.

What we have that other creatures do not, of course, is a massive brain which has heralded the blossoming of intellect. We were not born with wings, yet we can invent a machine that carries us through the air faster, higher and further than a bird could ever fly, even beyond the confines of our own atmosphere in space flight. We do not have gills, yet we build machines that can navigate oceans deeper, further and faster than a fish could ever swim. Are there no bounds to human intellectual feats? Yes, so we invent a machine, known as a computer, that can process information more efficiently for us. We should take time to pause for a moment and dwell upon our discovery and mastery over the natural world, which has been made possible by our dazzling intellect. We are now exploiting our intellect so efficiently that some recent technological advances would have been unimaginable to a generation of people just a few decades ago.

Despite our astonishing technological prowess, it sometimes appears that we are perpetually seeking a more spiritual vision. Aldous Huxley's novel *Brave New World* (1950) touched on a common anxiety in his depiction of a futuristic world in which people had unwittingly become slaves to an insidious technological domination. B.F. Skinner wrote of a Utopian future in a novel called *Walden Two* (1976), in which his 'technology of behaviour' had eradicated crime and all other undesirable by-products of civilization. What both novels had in common is that they portrayed a soulless existence, intentionally in Huxley's case but inadvertently in Skinner's. It is as though we are frightened of losing a spirituality that feels like a meeting of souls when we are in the company of someone we like and with whom we have an affinity. We fear a life that revolves around technology and which excludes human emotional contact and bonding.

The humanistic psychologist Maslow (1954) noted that we could never experience satisfaction and fulfilment in career or professional spheres if we did not first have a secure emotional bond with at least one other person. Why is social contact and bonding so important? It is rooted both in evolutionary history and in our childhood, probably much more so than any technological orientation or aptitude. It seems that our massive intellect emerged in the context of a challenging social environment, given that we evolved from and continue to be social creatures who live in groups and depend on others for survival and well-being. We achieve social co-ordination *par excellence* thanks to our flair in dealing with others, which might involve charm, altruism or, on the darker side, a calculated betrayal.

Perhaps it is a myth that intellect blossomed largely from a human quest to be master of the physical and animal world. Yet a widely held assumption remains that the pinnacle of intellectual achievement is to be seen in mathematical and scientific endeavours. Accordingly, Humphrey (1986) sought a clue to the evolution of a technological intellect on an expedition to African rain forests where he observed gorillas. He expected to find the apes living on their wits in order to solve problems of how to forage and hunt for food and how to protect themselves from the natural elements and from predators. To his enormous surprise, he discovered that the apes seemed to live a tranquil existence, apparently free from the potential difficulties just listed, in a setting resembling the Garden of Eden. On prolonged observation, however, it became obvious that the idyllic and trouble-free life that the apes seemed to enjoy was in fact just an illusion.

The gorillas lived in groups composed of individuals united by emotional bonds of attachment of varying strength. These bonds were not static, but required servicing to ensure that harmony without one-sided exploitation prevailed. Smart individuals would achieve popularity and high status within the dominance hierarchy, whilst socially incompetent individuals might be banished. Smart and popular individuals might also be the ones who are physically strong, resourceful in seeking protection from the elements and wise in their foraging for food, but this need not necessarily be the case. Humphrey concluded that every ounce of intellect had to be marshalled in the ape's fight to achieve social harmony and satisfy social ambitions. Hence, it seems that the evolution of intellect owes as much to the social challenge as to any technological conquest of the natural world. The arrival of our technological tool-using ancestor *Homo habilis* was an important milestone in our history, but perhaps we exaggerate its significance compared with the evolution of social intellect.

Apes and humans evolved from the same ancestor, and it is not surprising that we have a good deal in common. We see a parallel between an ape hierarchy and the kind of corporate hierarchy that typifies many companies. Those who are best paid and hold highest office are not necessarily the people who have a record of being most competent at their job. Fulfilling career ambitions can have as much to do with impressing superiors and damaging competitors as to working efficiently at the job in hand. Some of us channel an enormous intellectual effort into planning how to interact and influence others to satisfy our own goals. This investment can pay dividends in the kind of social environment that has evolved. Some of us have intellects eminently suited to this kind of process, even if we are not well suited to making widgets, or whatever it is that our company manufactures. Others might excel in making widgets, yet be socially inept. Guess who gets the most pay and enjoys highest status!

Although most of us are immensely insightful in dealing with other people, there is in principle scope for further evolution in this respect. At present, we have to make educated guesses about the mental life of others. We have no direct access to others' thoughts and feelings, and if extra-sensory perception (ESP) were to evolve, those who had this ability would have a massive selective advantage over those who lacked it. Alas, the physical universe might be such that extra-sensory perception is impossible, so we must make do with our ordinary senses, coupled with a powerful intellect, to evaluate evidence about people and then formulate a hypothetical model of the content of their minds. That is, we are not capable of ESP, but we do have an ability to form a conception of mind that tells us more about what is inside other people's heads than we could gather just from a surface impression of the data supplied via our senses.

According to Dennett (1978), the minimal justification for crediting an individual with a theory of mind is that they should be able to acknowledge that people hold beliefs of a simple factual nature. For example, if I present my friend Rebecca with a box of candies on her birthday, she will believe that the content is as proclaimed by the exterior of the box. I know that the box contains candies, and I also assume that she thinks the same. Hence, I possess a conception (or 'theory') of her mind because, at the very least, I understand that Rebecca (and everybody else for that matter) holds simple factual beliefs. How could I then check whether you also have a conception of (Rebecca's) mind? This seems like a silly question, because surely all I have to do is ask you to say what you think Rebecca thinks is inside the candy box. If your reply is 'candies', then presumably you too have a conception of (Rebecca's) mind. However, that would not necessarily follow. For all I know, your understanding of the word *think* is completely different. What if you have no conception of mind, you fail to comprehend the word *think* as a consequence, and you just guess wrongly that I mean 'What is in the candy box?'. In other words, when you give the right answer of 'candies', I can't tell whether you are correctly reporting what you understand about Rebecca's belief, or just reporting what the box really contains.

I require a more sensitive test that could identify whether you had genuine insight into people's simple factual beliefs. Specifically, I require a test which indicates whether you are using an aberrant strategy of reporting reality when asked about belief. If so, then I would have no evidence to suggest that you possess a conception of mind according to Dennett's (1978) minimal criterion.

A test of your ability to acknowledge false belief satisfies the requirement. Unknown to Rebecca, prior to presenting the candy box you and I carried out a practical joke by swapping the usual content for crayons. Rebecca is unaware of this because she was absent when we carried out the deed. This scenario permits me to check whether you have a conception of mind, because if you do, then you ought to realize that Rebecca would falsely think that the candy box contains candies. If you did not possess a conception of mind, then you would judge that Rebecca thinks the box contains crayons – what it actually does contain. In other words, when asked to comment on Rebecca's belief, you would instead just be reporting reality. A test of false belief dissociates belief from reality and hence is capable of revealing whether an individual possesses the basis of a conception of mind.

An ability to impute beliefs, including false ones, is easy for us, and so easy that it is difficult to imagine anybody having the slightest problem with the concept of belief. However, there is some evidence to suggest that most children below approximately 4 years of age are unable to acknowledge false belief, with the result that some theorists claim that a conception of mind is something we acquire during childhood, following a radical shift in our thought processes (e.g. Perner, 1991). There is also evidence to suggest that people with autism have substantial difficulty with the concept of false belief (Baron-Cohen *et al.*, 1985). Intriguingly, we might be tempted to conclude from this that people with autism are socially debilitated and isolated because they lack the insight into mind that the rest of us take for granted.

Although we normally assume that psychological theories are exclusively the property of academics, when it comes to being perceptive or intuitive about other people, those with training in psychology probably fare no better than people without such training. This is likely to be because (almost) everyone has an understanding of mind, an understanding that is so highly sophisticated and evolved that a century of psychological investigation has not advanced knowledge beyond what we know intuitively in some (but not all) respects. The ordinary human understanding of mind thus becomes a fascinating topic for investigation itself. Where does this remarkable insight into mind come from? Why do we have it? Do we have our own personal and informal 'theory' of mind?

In answer to the last question, there is a vague sense in which we have a 'theory' of mind, where the word *theory* could serve as a useful metaphor. It seems that we possess notions about how the mind governs actions. The two central concepts standing at the heart of this 'theory' are that people act to satisfy their desires, but that their actions will be guided by how they believe the world to be, rather than how it really is (Wellman, 1990). Like a formal theory, there are processes of induction and deduction associated with the 'theory'. Through a process of induction, we entertain the supposition that Rebecca will think a candy box contains candies if she has not witnessed the usual content being exchanged for something atypical (e.g. crayons). We certainly cannot be sure what she thinks, but it is reasonable to assume that she thinks the box contains candies. Then suppose we are presented with the condition that Rebecca wants candies. Now, from our 'theory' we can deduce a testable prediction. If Rebecca believes the candies are in the candy box, then that is where she will look for them – in which case she will look there in vain because the candies are actually in another place. Hence, our 'theory' of mind has some of the qualities of a real theory in the sense that we construct theoretical knowledge through a process of induction and can then deduce testable predictions. Like a real theory, the knowledge that we construct is not directly accessible but remains hypothetical (i.e. beliefs and desires cannot be perceived directly). If the knowledge were directly accessible, then it would qualify as fact rather than theory.

UTILITY OF A CONCEPTION OF MIND

I have already touched upon the utility of a conception of mind in suggesting that it helps individuals to gravitate towards the top of a social hierarchy. I have suggested that it has primitive origins by mentioning that apes also have social hierarchies. I shall now flesh out my thoughts on utilities.

If we did not take into consideration other people's thoughts and feelings we would become very unpopular indeed, and might even acquire the stigma of a social outcast. Sometimes, however, despite good intentions we might face conflict with another person. It might not be our own fault, but arise because the other person in question aims to subjugate those around him or her. If this adversary could not be appeased without loss of face, we would be well advised to inform others of our plight and try to persuade them that we are the good guys and that we have to combat evil (which we would claim is epitomized in our adversary). If we succeeded, our adversary might then have second thoughts about persevering with his or her unpleasantness.

Regrettably, suppose we fail to secure allies and an emergency is imminent with the prospect of a physical clash. The winner will probably have skill and strength in battle, but these are not the only or perhaps even the most important qualities required. We need to outwit our opponent. For example, to avoid being attacked we need to hide and so scramble behind a bush. Our hiding would be more effective if we had predicted correctly that our adversary would search for us not behind the bush but behind the wall. We might even lay a false trail to the wall to lead our opponent off the scent.

If we wish to mount an offensive rather than be evasive, an attack that was dispatched with surprise would be much more effective than one anticipated by our adversary. If the latter, the attack could be neutralized if our adversary prepared counter-measures. In this emergency an individual who knew the thoughts of his or her opponent would almost certainly triumph.

In fact, we cannot know with complete certainty what other people think, but we can make an educated guess by noting what other people have seen or not seen, and assume that what they think will be based on this. We might even intervene, to supply an opponent with misleading clues such that he or she would draw incorrect conclusions. In this rather gross example we see that having a conception of mind confers enormous advantages on an individual. Most interactions are a good deal more subtle and less threatening of course, and handling these with skill requires an equally refined conception of mind. The hypothetical scenario I have presented was conceived with primitive humans in mind – the social intellect evolved under such primitive conditions. Even so, the example could almost be an allegory of twentieth century diplomacy and warfare.

Having a conception of mind is also vital in forming friendships and love. First, we need to judge who is a suitable partner, worthy of our attention. An old saying maintains that love is blind, yet it is surprising how common it is for people who are similar to fall in love and go on to have a family. It remains uncommon that people of widely different age, social status or culture strike up a partnership. However, being the right category of person still is not sufficient to ensure a harmonious relationship. It might be that we make judgements about who is suitable by guessing what kind of ideals they hold, and generally what thoughts they have. Once we have set our sights on a person we then face the task of making ourselves appealing to him or her. The better we are attuned to the minds of those around us, the more likely we are to select wisely and, having done so, the more chance we stand of doing and saying things that will impress a potential partner. Obviously we would not feel that we were calculating these things, but our impressions of a person might stem to a large extent from an automatic process of making judgements.

If we are on the receiving end of attention from an admirer we would feel inclined either to encourage or discourage such attention. This is a very serious matter, and perhaps even more important for females than for males. As in finding a target for attention, once again we make judgements about character and content of mind. The reason I suggest there might be an asymmetry in males and females in being selective about a partner is that an error of judgement has much more profound consequences for the woman. In the event of pregnancy caused by an unsuitable man, the woman might face the burden of solo child-rearing. The man involved might judge, quite wrongly, that he has less responsibility for the child, and so feel inclined to escape from the situation. Moreover, if the man is unsuitable for more deep-seated reasons, e.g. because he suffers from a genetic defect, the woman could face the potential hardship of rearing a genetically defective child.

In essence, perhaps women make much more of an investment in choosing their partners wisely than men because it is primarily they who bear the enormous costs (in time and energy) of pregnancy followed by years of child-rearing. Consequently, a woman has only a few opportunities for procreation, whereas a man, in principle, has almost unlimited opportunities. Hence choosing a partner requires shrewd judgements of character and mind, especially for women. Again, the process of making a judgement would normally be largely automatic rather than calculated.

Another use of a conception of mind is that it allows us to interpret each other in communication. Communication is not just about deciphering literally what people say to us and reciprocating with unambiguous utterances. We show a contextual sensitivity that allows us to interpret idioms, irony and metaphor. We question such things as why a speaker tells us what they tell us, and interpret what they say accordingly (Grice, 1975). For example, if asked, 'have you any sugar?' in one context you might respond 'Plenty!', while in another you might remain silent but pass a bowl of sugar to the speaker. In the former context you were being asked to check which groceries need to be restocked prior to a shopping expedition, whereas in the latter your guest had been served coffee and wished to sweeten it. In these examples an appropriate interpretation hinges on correct assessment of the speaker's motives, and in the process making use of clues available in the context.

In another example we can see how an explicit understanding of a speaker's factual beliefs allows us to interpret correctly what is said. Elizabeth Robinson and I (Robinson and Mitchell, 1992) devised a sketch in which John makes a request for Susan to fetch an item from a location, but John actually holds a false belief about where the item he desires is stored. John has two bundles of crayons, puts one under his bed and the other behind the dressing table, and then leaves the room. In his absence, Susan gets out the crayons and returns them later on, but inadvertently swaps the bundles round. Unknown to John, the bundle he put under his bed is now behind the dresser, whereas the bundle he put behind the dresser is now under his bed. Later, John needs one of the bundles (and it is very important that he receives the right bundle), and he asks Susan to fetch the bundle from under his bed.

We can infer that the bundle John really wants is actually the one behind the dresser. We take into account John's belief about the situation and understand that the bundle *under the bed in his outdated belief*, is at present behind the dresser. In making a correct interpretation of what John says, we should take into account his distinctive beliefs about the world. If we did not, then sometimes we would make inappropriately literal interpretations of what John or anybody else says. Hence, having a conception of mind allows for a meeting of minds via the medium of verbal communication.

I have outlined some obvious uses of a conception of mind, and it should be apparent that this is just the tip of the iceberg. The ramifications of having a conception of mind evidently penetrate most spheres of mental life, and accordingly this topic deserves recognition as a central issue in psychology.

EVOLUTIONARY HISTORY OF CONCEPTION OF MIND

Because it is dedicated to understanding how we acquire a conception of mind, most space in this book is devoted to how a conception of mind develops during childhood. However, we should remember that development also occurs by evolution via the process Charles Darwin described as natural selection. Before proceeding, then, we should pause to speculate about how the kind of intellectual processes underlying a conception of mind might have evolved. For a more detailed account of my speculations, see Mitchell (1994). Povinelli (1993) also presents a stimulating account of the evolution of mind.

Somewhere in the murky past of our ancestry, cognition apparently blossomed as the use of tools evolved. This could have taken the form of expansion of imagination and insight, for example, insight into how an item normally associated with one situation could be used to good effect for a novel purpose in a completely different situation. A small branch may usually serve as a handle while we eat the fruit from it, but could subsequently serve as a device for poking, measuring or construction in another situation.

With augmented powers of imagination we might refrain from discarding a stick once it has been stripped of food, owing to foresight that it could be exploited in a forthcoming situation. We might go on to cogitate over the detail of its potential uses. For example, it might form part of the roof-frame for a shelter, but would it be sufficiently robust to withstand strong wind? Perhaps a more rigid stick or bone would be more suitable.

We can see from this example that as imagination occupies more of the individual's time, so their behaviour would become more a product of the individual's thinking and planning. To know the individual's thoughts is to know their future actions. To know their future actions is to achieve a selective advantage over individuals who lacked this kind of insight.

It seems, then, that the advent of an ability to understand minds would confer an evolutionary advantage upon the fortunate individuals concerned, giving us our deserved place at the intellectual pinnacle of the evolutionary tree. Because we are social creatures, our survival depends upon smooth social co-ordination, which in turn depends on our ability to prophesize the behaviour of others. To achieve this, we create a selection of abstract conceptions including 'desire' and 'belief'. As behaviour becomes more the product of imagination and planning rather than of trial and error, so there will be increasing pressure for the mind to understand itself and other minds.

We learn from this account that there would be no selective pressure for the evolution of a conception of mind in a species that did not engage in much planning prior to executing behaviour. For example, the behaviour of a rat is predictable from external stimuli and the principle that prior behaviour which is followed closely by reward is more likely to occur in the future. Therefore, to anticipate the rat's next move we do not require a conception of mind but a theory of behaviour of the kind described by the behaviourist B.F. Skinner (1957). In essence, there is no pressure for a simple creature like a rat to evolve a conception of mind, but there is in more sophisticated social creatures such as the higher primates (including humans).

Another piece in the jigsaw is the arrival of language in our species. Once language has evolved, there is further evolutionary pressure for us to treat verbal messages as expressions of thoughts. The other side of the coin is that we would anticipate that people who display a severe lack of understanding of mind would be poor communicators. Children with autism supposedly lack a conception of mind (e.g. Baron-Cohen *et al.*, 1985), and perhaps it comes as no surprise that they are also notoriously poor at communication (Frith, 1989). In particular, unlike clinically normal children aged 4 years and above, they do not take account of a speaker's false belief when interpreting his or her message (Mitchell and Isaacs, 1994).

In summary, initial expansion of the brain may have resulted from the advantage given by increased imagination and language. It is perhaps no coincidence that these abilities are located largely in the frontal cortex, which has expanded more than other cortical regions in our recent evolutionary history. This increase in cognition would then make the social environment predictable more from people's thoughts and less from any external stimuli that impinge on them. Increased imagination necessarily engenders accompanying evolutionary pressure for even further expansion of the brain in developing a potential to understand itself. The same is true with regard to the emergence of language. These pressures would be less prominent in other species, because their behaviour is more predictable from external stimuli, and they lack language. Thus it follows that humans would have the most impressive conception of mind in the animal kingdom.

WHY A CONCEPTION OF MIND RATHER THAN A THEORY OF BEHAVIOUR?

If so inclined, we could successfully anticipate most of the actions of those around us without giving any consideration to their thoughts. For example, suppose Jane deposited chocolate in her kitchen cupboard for consumption at a future date. Later, unknown to Jane, Steve moves the chocolate to the refrigerator. We know that Jane's belief about the location of the chocolate has become a false one, and because of that she will search for her chocolate in the wrong place, at least initially. However, we need not bother ourselves with such imponderables as Jane's beliefs in order to predict that she will search in the wrong place. Instead, we could apply a behavioural rule that people search for things where they left them. In other words, because Jane's last association with the chocolate was at the kitchen cupboard, on that basis alone we could predict that she would look there.

If all problems that tax our conception of mind were of this kind perhaps we could dispense with the concept of belief altogether, but in fact they are not. First, people comprehend the word *think* and they do not treat it as a synonym of *behave* or *search*. Jane does not have to search the cupboard for us to judge that she thinks that is where the chocolate is. She would think the chocolate was in the cupboard if she had seen someone else put it there, or was told by someone else or read a label on the door saying 'chocolate cupboard'. Having said that, there is some affinity between behaving and thinking in the sense that, if we witnessed Jane searching in the empty kitchen cupboard for her chocolate, we might interpret this as a clue that she falsely believes the chocolate is stored there.

Another reason for saying that we have a conception of mind rather than a theory of behaviour is that we are able to be introspective about our own beliefs. In the absence of behaviour, we are able to reflect that we once held certain simple factual beliefs that were subsequently falsified. For example, we might assume that Piaget was a woman, having the Christian name of Jean, only to learn subsequently that this is the French equivalent of John. If we only had a theory of behaviour, presumably we would not be able to code any of our own beliefs as false, and accordingly we would be unable to introspect and discuss them.

Some of the problems that we solve with our conception of mind could equally be handled by means of a theory of behaviour. However, our ability to comment upon a whole plethora of mental phenomena, including some that are detached from behaviour and other external stimuli, shows that we must have more than just a theory of behaviour at our disposal. What we have is a conception of an intervening variable that takes the form of a selection of thematically interrelated mental states that link input to output. For example, observing that a protagonist is exposed to the input of seeing chocolate in the cupboard will be linked with the protagonist's subsequent search in that location via an attribution to the protagonist of the mental states 'desiring to eat some chocolate' and 'believing that the chocolate is in the cupboard'.

CONCEPTION OF MIND ENCAPSULATED IN CULTURE AND LITERATURE

A fascination with mind and psychological states is reflected in our love of such things as drama, gossip and sport. This fascination is apparent in the massive increase in the number of people applying to study for a degree in psychology over the past few years; the popularity exceeds that of almost every other subject, perhaps with medicine and English remaining as exceptions. The enjoyment of reading literature could actually have a great deal in common with enjoyment of psychology: both putatively explore the mind – one discipline through systematic observation, and the other through fiction.

Fiction held in the highest esteem, such as that written by Shakespeare, is typically concerned with people's motives, ambitions, attitudes, beliefs and other states of mind, and how these influence the actor's behaviour, especially towards others. There is also exploration of the impact of this behaviour on others, and how they interpret it.

Psychological issues are so intriguing to us that even the most mundane story can become fascinating when it concerns a character's psychological state. This could account for the popularity of certain television soap operas. Sometimes these can be trite or amateurish, yet viewers in their millions become enthralled by the opportunity to explore the characters' minds. The real-life parallel to this is the gossip which so many of us indulge in and enjoy, although few of us admit it! This is an activity we both love and loathe. We love a communal contemplation of others' intentions, motives, beliefs and attitudes, yet we loathe the prospect of becoming the subject of such scrutiny ourselves, presumably due to a fear of hidden psychological secrets being divulged.

In contrast, things which lack human interest, such as computer games, are regarded by many as boring. Interestingly, however, these games do hold the attention of children, adolescents and young adults, and perhaps it is no coincidence that these people are also typically unsophisticated in understanding psychological states, and apparently lacking in awareness that topics interesting to oneself might be perceived as uninteresting by another person (e.g. Elkind, 1967; Lapsley, 1985; Lapsley and Murphy, 1985). Computers are none the less useful tools to have at our disposal, but perhaps their greatest fascination lies in the prospect that eventually they could simulate a mind electronically. Once again, this points to our deep interest in psychological matters.

Participation in sport might be another symptom of our addiction to grappling with the mind. Sport provides an opportunity to exercise not just our body but also our mind's ability to understand mind. Just as the cat plays at chasing non-existent mice, so we joust with non-serious rivals. Perhaps many games appeal to us because they provide a non-threatening opportunity to outwit our opponents whilst trying to avoid being outwitted ourselves. This is obvious in cerebral games such as chess, but the point can also be made for games such as football. Winning requires not just brawn and fitness, but also trickery. These sessions are bound to sharpen our faculties in playing the more serious game of life.

One need not participate in sport in order to experience the psychological drama surrounding it. Spectator sports create an arena in which one person or a group of people seek to dominate and dishevel their opponents. Granted that the interest could partly be in the skill, technique and fitness of the participants, the primary intrigue could still arise from the spectacle of one person trying to 'outsmart' another, where we witness a clash of minds. For example, in a game such as tennis, the beauty of the contest can often reside in observing the wielding of psychological tools of deception and intimidation, which both participants strive to use to their advantage.

These examples suggest that human culture could be the product of our passion for contemplating psychological matters. It is perhaps no mere coincidence that humans are unusual in the animal kingdom both in their generation of a culture and in their expertise in contemplating the psychological (see Crook, 1980, for a detailed sociobiological view of the emergence of culture). In summary, above all we are interested in people. We are interested in what they get up to, what motivates them and what they believe. In other words, we contemplate the mind and in doing so we adopt the role of the 'intuitive psychologist' (Humphrey, 1986).

One might now protest that if we are so attuned to psychological matters, then why is it necessary to spell out the psychological significance of culture and warfare – surely this should be self-evident if we have expertise in understanding mind. However, that does not necessarily follow. Indeed, it is perhaps because we are so familiar with the concept of mind that it is hard to distance ourselves from it and to reflect upon our abilities. Likewise, we are expert at handling the rules of language, yet this is so close to us that it is virtually impossible to distance ourselves sufficiently to specify the rules of language. Similarly, we are expert at walking, but again it would be difficult for us to specify how we do this. These are abilities that we unreflectingly take for granted, along with contemplating the mind. The aim of this book is to shake us out of our complacency and question the fundamental components of a conception of mind and how we acquired them.

A VERY BIG MYSTERY

We live in a remarkable world where biological organs that we call 'minds' have developed (through evolution and through childhood) to understand themselves and each other. It is a very big mystery indeed as to how this development takes place. What is the evolutionary history of our special ability? What kind of understanding of mind is evident in our cousin species, the great apes? To what extent are we born with an insight into mind? What kind of experiences are necessary for the healthy development of an understanding of mind? What happens when development goes wrong? What are the clues or symptoms that mark the child's negotiation of developmental hurdles in getting to grips with the concept of mind? Having stated the importance and versatility of an understanding of mind, it is now time to explore where this understanding comes from and how its development progresses. In doing so, we shall examine a variety of theories that suggest the character of our conception of mind and its origins.

Some (e.g. Fodor, 1992; Leslie, 1994; Mitchell, 1994) have discussed innate factors that might feature in our development of a conception of mind. Others (e.g. Perner, 1991; Gopnik, 1993) regard our conception of mind as an informal 'theory' that the child constructs during childhood following the integration of new experiences into existing conceptual structures. This constructivist account proposes that a theory of mind emerges in the child at approximately 4 years of age in the form of a radical conceptual shift. Still others (e.g. Dunn, 1994; Lewis, 1994; Siegal and Peterson, 1994) stress the role of social interaction and communication as the vital experiences for nurturing a conception of mind, in which the child might be viewed as an apprentice receiving tuition from older and wiser people.

The rest of this book details evidence that points to the character of the conception of mind held by apes, children, adults and children with autism. We shall look at the findings in some detail and explore the theories that compete to explain the findings.

EVOLUTION AND A MEETING OF MINDS IN APES

WAR AND PEACE

It is a massive advantage to know what your allies and adversaries are thinking and scheming. Picture two armies in conflict. The army with the detailed and accurate intelligence has a considerable advantage over the one without such information. Generals who are blind to the plans of their enemy are forever at the mercy of a surprise attack, and can only deal with their enemy's tactic once it is under way. In contrast, a general who is privy to the enemy's future actions will have mobilized forces to the required region and in appropriate concentrations. He may even go so far as to mount an ambush. It is for this reason that nations at war place so much emphasis on obtaining intelligence. An individual spy thus stands to shift the balance of the conflict one way or the other.

Because spies are so influential, they are likely to be dealt with in the most severe way if caught. However, a sensible way to respond on identifying a spy is to allow them to believe that they remain undetected. Then it would be possible to feed them systematically with false information. To the enemy, this information would be much worse than useless, because they would formulate an image of what you believe and plan to do, an image that is actually a total fiction. For example, in the D-Day landings, the Allies allowed the Nazis to believe that an invasion was imminent around the ports of Calais and Dunkirk, when in fact the strike was to be at the weakly defended beaches in Normandy. Consequently, the Nazi forces were in concentration and on alert in a place where they were destined to be idle. Meanwhile, the actual invasion zone in Normandy was under-defended. 'The rest is history', as they say.

Now picture a group of apes living naturally and in harmony with their environment. Just as generals strive to obtain intimate knowledge of their enemy's plans, so it is vital that individuals have a good intuition about those around them. In this respect, it seems that a specialized 'social' intellect has evolved in apes, which has provided a legacy in the form of a cognitive aptitude handed down to humans. It is not the case that the apes are in a permanent state of hostility towards each other, unlike warring human factions. On the contrary, their social groups seem to be especially harmonious for the great majority of the time. None the less, the apes do compete with each other to an extent – or at the very least they have to contend with each other. They are not in overt conflict for the simple reason that it is actually advantageous to them as individuals to co-operate in social groups. Foraging for food, rearing young, fending off predators and navigating to new territory are all tasks that are made much easier by the combined effort of many hands. Presumably it is for this reason that apes have evolved into social and co-operative creatures. However, we should not lose sight of the fact that they have adapted in this way because it is of advantage to them as individuals. Consequently, while there is a pervasive semblance of co-operation, and even altruism, the apes still have to compete and contend with one another; they certainly cannot take support, co-operation and general altruism of their peers for granted. Effectively, these are prizes that the individual has to earn.

Like humans, apes live in a social hierarchy. This means that one ape is pre-eminent in the groups and all others are subordinate to him (it is usually a 'him'). Other individuals in the group will vary in the authority that they wield and the esteem that they enjoy. One's place in the social order is not fixed but flexible. Positions of status are open to conquest and individuals can promote themselves or be supplanted by another. Status confers special privileges in terms of feasting and mating. Hence Darwinian fitness, or the capacity to survive and reproduce successfully, could be measured indirectly in terms of prowess in climbing the social ladder.

Apes are cerebral creatures, and in this respect are not at all like animals with a simpler nervous system, such as rats and pigeons. Several decades ago, the behaviourist B.F. Skinner set out to discover the principles of learning, which culminated in his account stating that behaviour is the product of reinforcement history. Accordingly, the concept of mind seemed to become redundant within the behaviourist tradition. There was no longer any need to explain behaviour by invoking desires, intentions and beliefs. One need only say that the rat pressed the lever because it had been reinforced previously for doing so, and not because it was hungry and believed that lever-pressing was causally linked to the delivery of food. To predict the rat's actions we need only consider the principles of behaviour and we need not consider the content of mind.

Apes are different, however. The large intellect of the ape allows a selection of different actions – and their outcomes – to be simulated in imagination, perhaps similar to the thinking that goes into a chess game where we consider the hypothetical state of the board several moves in advance. Ape behaviour is undoubtedly under the influence of reinforcement history, but surely there is much more to it than this. Surely apes are capable of more thoughtful and creative planning, with the consequence that their behaviour is going to be less predictable just because they know about external contingencies and stimuli. To begin to understand the ape's behaviour, we need to know something about how the ape's mind works. More specifically, we need to be endowed with an aptitude for making educated guesses as to what the ape might be wanting or thinking at any given time. To understand the ape we need not so much a theory of behaviour as a conception of mind, given that the ape's behaviour is governed by a sophisticated mind. That is the challenge presented to the members of an ape hierarchy.

Competition for the various positions in the ape hierarchy involves a great deal more than posturing. It is seldom the case that individuals within a band engage in mortal combat, and so strength and aggression are not necessarily the qualities that contribute to good prospects. Indeed, it would not be surprising if an overly aggressive ape found himself facing not others as individuals, but groups of adversaries operating as a team. In this eventuality, the overly aggressive individual would be subdued and then perhaps expelled from the hierarchy altogether. The individual who is destined to go far is probably one who is socially wise. An ape who is firm at just the right time but who is not 'pushy' will probably thrive. He is almost certainly an individual who finds favour with more senior members of the group, and he will be attuned to the general psychology of others, especially their moods, desires, and perhaps even their beliefs in some primitive sense. His current status will be pretty much invulnerable because an underling who challenges him will be met not only with a resolute defence but also with the wrath of more senior members of the hierarchy. In other words, the individual who is to prosper depends greatly on the patronage of those with power and authority.

Now the analogy between apes and generals begins to make more sense. The general's prospects depend on being able to understand the enemy's mind – to achieve insight into his plans. The ape's prospects depend on being able to understand the minds of other apes in the hierarchy – both superiors and subordinates. Any individual who had insight into mind would have a great advantage over one who could only observe and then react to the behaviour of others once it occurred. To predict behaviour in rats we need only know about the history of the environment, whereas to predict the behaviour of an ape we need to understand the mind. We need some insight into what they desire and what they think. Any individual endowed with the potential to 'read' a mind would have a great advantage over those who did not.

We can go a step further, to suggest that not only would it be an advantage to be able to decipher messages emanating from minds, but also it would be useful to be able to transmit messages to the mind. Darwinian fitness is augmented not only when an individual enhances his or her own prospects of survival and reproduction, but also when he or she enhances those same prospects in close relatives such as offspring. If they could be

1

Keep this card in the book pocket
This book is due on the latest date stamped

Keep this card in the book pocket
This book is due on the latest date stamped

2

tutored in the games of life, then surely this would be a tremendous advantage. It so happens that many or all of the games of life in apes require some understanding of others' minds, as I have suggested above. An individual who could transmit information about her own mind to her offspring would be equipped to provide a vital lesson in how to thrive in the social group. Instead of having to invest much time and toil in understanding the psychology of elders in the group through the direct experience of personal interaction, the young could learn a great deal from their mothers.

COMMUNICATION BETWEEN MINDS

Being able to transmit messages from one mind to another also offers a more sinister benefit. If I were well in control of the thoughts I transmitted to you, then there might be occasions when it would be tempting to communicate my thoughts falsely. I could signal that I believe something to be true when in actual fact I believe it to be false. You would become a victim of my misinformation, which would almost certainly be to your disadvantage and therefore to my advantage if we were in competition.

Apes stand to benefit if they have some understanding of minds. This could be manifested both as an ability to read minds and as an ability to transmit thoughts to other individuals. I am effectively saying that the capacity for extra-sensory perception (ESP) would confer an obvious and massive selective advantage. Strictly speaking this is probably physically impossible. However, we might say that a kind of compromise faculty has evolved. This is the ability to communicate with language. Without language, to a considerable extent we are confined to an understanding that is bound to be on or close to the level of the stimuli that bombard our senses. We would know about physical reality and little more. Language allows us to break free and consider a past, future or hypothetical world. It offers a channel of communication between minds, such that we are no longer just a passive receiver of information about reality.

When I hear you speak, effectively I am hearing your thoughts. Whilst you are reading this book, effectively you are reading my thoughts. There is an affinity between the language of speech and the language of thought. This affinity actually runs in two directions. The obvious one is alluded to here – that you can know my thoughts pretty much directly by listening to what I have to say. It is not ESP, but it is the next best thing. The opposite direction is one in which an ability to use language supports an ability to think. Thus speech is not just a vehicle for communicating preformed ideas, but the capacity for language that can become internalized, as thought, might actually support the development of ideas. I shall say more about this shortly.

To say that speech opens a window on the mind requires a qualification. I can look in through a window in most cases when I choose and gain an accurate impression of what is inside the room beyond. The window on mind that opens through speech is entirely at the prerogative of the person doing the articulating. Moreover, this person can choose to withhold information or to utter misinformation. So we should say that the window of speech is paned with frosted glass.

Once language as a means of communication has evolved, secondary benefits emerge. Language can be used not only for communication between individuals, but also as a vehicle for enhancing a meeting between minds in which ideas are not merely passed from one to the other, but actually created within the dialogic exchange. Language also confers benefits on the individual in isolation. Because language involves the creation of category concepts, this can serve as a useful system or mental notation at the individual's disposal. This use comes most clearly into focus when we write. Writing creates an environment in which ideas can be tried out and monitored by reading back. The writer can read what he or she is thinking in order to check whether it makes sense – not just grammatically, but as a constellation of ideas that are being assembled. This is also possible with thought, but the limitation of conscious space imposes a constraint on how elaborate or complex ideas to be contemplated can be. Writing effectively expands the conscious space.

A further benefit of language is that thinking in a symbolic code, in place of the more canonical images of reality, surely allows for a more objective view of nature – one that is not locked into the individual's current perspective. An individual who is unable to think in an abstract code once removed from reality is perpetually at risk of being seduced by current but misleading appearances. For example, the individual would be condemned to thinking only about reality itself and not about the possibility of the multiplicity of interpretations that different minds might impose on reality. In that case, the individual could not be credited with any understanding of mind.

A study conducted by Boysen (1993) neatly illustrates this point. She taught a pair of chimpanzees to play a competitive game against each other. One of the chimps had the task of pointing to one of two plates of food. On one of these the quantity of food was large, while on the other there was only a small amount. Because both chimps were rather hungry, they both desired the plate containing the larger amount of food. Which chimp ended up with which plate depended ultimately on where the chimp playing the role of communicator gestured. Whichever plate this chimp pointed to first was promptly offered to the chimp playing the role of receiver. Effectively, then, the chimp doing the gesturing was being rewarded more heavily for pointing first to the plate with the smaller quantity of food.

Curiously, the chimps doing the gesturing persistently frustrated themselves by pointing to the plate with the larger quantity of food. It seems likely that this larger mound of food was so tempting that they could not resist gesturing toward it. What they meant, ironically, was that they wanted it, not that they wanted their partner to get it! The appealing image of the food seemed to exert a magnetic effect on their attention which actually thwarted their quest to obtain that food.

The chimps who were participating in this study had been trained extensively in a previous programme of research to recognize numbers appropriately in connection with various quantities. For example, if shown three objects, they would respond by selecting a card that showed the number 3 from a large set of number cards. Alternatively, if they required five blocks to complete a puzzle, they would reliably select a card showing the number 5, following which they would be issued with the five blocks. It seems that the apes had acquired a simple and general concept of number.

Boysen proceeded to substitute the quantities of food on the two dishes for numbers (see Figure 2.1). Miraculously, the chimps doing the gesturing were liberated from the attentional pull of the larger quantity of food. They now successfully pointed to the dish that had a card with a low number on it, and accordingly the experimenter promptly handed the smaller quantity of food to the receiver and the larger quantity to the gesturer. When the game returned to the version with actual food on the dishes, the gesturing chimp once again reverted to pointing first of all to the plate with the large quantity, and in doing so frustrated her own desire for the larger amount.

This example shows that objects that you see directly can be so attentionally salient and compelling that it is difficult to step back and make a more measured and considered response. It is easy to fall into the trap of responding impulsively and imperatively (pointing to mean 'I want it!') in

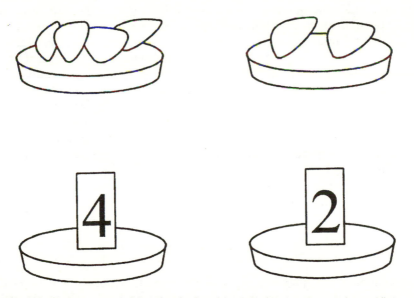

FIGURE 2.1 Under one condition (top), the chimps had to gesture to the smaller quantity of food in order to receive the larger quantity. Under another condition (bottom), they had to gesture to the card showing the smaller value to get the food. They succeeded much more easily when gesturing to numbers.

this context. However, when the judgement is made about symbols that represent real objects, then that judgement is on a more abstract, detached and therefore objective level.

The moral of these findings is that thinking on a symbolic level, a mode of reasoning made possible by the faculty of language, is bound to confer massive advantages when contemplating such an abstract concept as the mind. The mind has no existence in reality, although obviously it is created by the physical organ of the brain, and it is therefore not something that can be seen, touched or heard, although we come close to hearing minds when we hear people speak to us. Paradoxically, however, the mind is often thinking about reality. That is, minds hold beliefs about reality, e.g. how many steaks are in the freezer, who is president of the USA, or what is the rate of inflation. Because these beliefs *model* reality, any of them can actually be untrue. The criterion for checking their truth is whatever prevails in reality itself. Because minds are about reality, then, it is very tempting simply to think only about reality and not to think much at all about minds in most contexts. None the less, as I have said previously, an aptitude for thinking about mind as distinct from reality confers great advantages on the individual. Yet to realize this potential, we have to override a default to reality.

It is difficult to override a default to reality because our senses are perpetually bombarded with what is going on in the world. In contrast, the mind remains invisible, and we can only infer its existence. However, if we resist thinking on a level of sensory images, and instead think on a higher level once removed, a level that relies upon symbolic encoding, then contemplating mind and contemplating reality can perhaps compete on an equal footing. Expressed at its simplest, perhaps it is because 'mind' is an abstract concept that thinking about it is made easier by having an abstract symbolic code at our disposal, a code that we call language. In that case, it makes eminent sense in particular that Boysen's chimps could resist pointing to a larger quantity of food when that was encoded symbolically. More generally, it is reasonable to suppose that any species capable of understanding the sophisticated symbolism of language might also show a glimmer of insight into the concept of mind. Apart from that, surely a primitive ability to understand communication via language would depend on an attitude of receptivity where other minds are concerned. Surely a willingness to communicate implies some awareness that other minds exist and that one could connect with them.

LINGUISTIC APES

In questioning the linguistic capacity of animals, whether with regard to speech production or comprehension, we must proceed with great caution. It is easy to be fooled into thinking that the animal has sophisticated understanding when in fact it has responded appropriately on a very low level. This point is illustrated by 'Clever Hans', a horse who attracted a great deal of publicity at the turn of the twentieth century for his spectacular numerical feats. Gullible Edwardians were astonished to witness Hans reliably give the correct responses to sums presented to him verbally. Hans gave his answer by tapping his hoof on the ground the appropriate number of times. For example, if asked to calculate three plus five, he would tap on the ground eight times. People marvelled at Hans' apparent numerical competence, but it is at least as amazing that he could interpret their verbal presentation of the problem. Seemingly, the horse was linguistic as well as numerate!

Eventually, the mystery was dispelled on discovery that Hans solved the problems by means of a low-level strategy that required neither linguistic nor numerical competence. It seems that when he reached the correct number of taps, the people who were crowded round him unwittingly shifted their posture slightly. Hans stopped tapping on this inadvertent cue and was promptly rewarded with a sugar cube by his owner. When a screen was erected between Hans and the onlookers, he no longer stopped tapping at the correct point but continued aimlessly until he became fatigued. Many of us are so excited at the prospect of being able to communicate with animals that it is easy to overlook more simple explanations for apparent competence.

The story of Clever Hans serves as an allegory for the vain attempts to teach language to apes in the 1960s and 1970s. The seminal work was conducted by Alan and Beatrice Gardner, who trained their chimp Washoe in American Sign Language for the Deaf. Earlier attempts to teach chimps to speak had proved futile because the vocal tract of these animals is not adapted to articulating the combinations of vowels and consonants necessary to form speech sounds. In other words, apes can grunt but not much else.

The impasse seemed to end with the recognition that the fine manual dexterity of chimps should afford them sufficient skill to communicate using sign language. Over a period of 5 years, the Gardners taught Washoe to use a vocabulary well in excess of 130 words. Washoe was able to ask for things she wanted and to respond appropriately to requests. However, this modest success was entirely eclipsed by the severe limitations in Washoe's communicative abilities, which actually began to challenge the entire concept of what it means to be linguistic. At this particular period in the history of psychology, a dominant theme was behaviourism. Only a few years before the Gardners embarked upon their imaginative enterprise, Skinner (1957) had published his treatise laying out an account of language acquisition via trial and error learning. Skinner had assumed that the baby's spontaneous babble, which first occurs at the age of about 10 months, is shaped into speech by selective reinforcement from the parent. Any sounds which approximate to words would be greeted warmly by the parent, while articulations which did not meet this requirement would go unacknowledged. Hence, babble would gradually come to approximate speech more and more until finally we might say that the child is able to speak.

There are at least two serious problems with Skinner's account. The first is that children, and indeed adults, generate novel yet grammatical sentences. It is difficult to reconcile this with claims that speech is the product of reinforcement history. Rather, it seems that combinations of words are assembled in a sequence strictly according to the rules of syntax. Secondly, there is ample evidence to suggest that in fact parents do not reward children greatly for the correct use of grammar, but instead focus on meaning. For example, if a child said, 'Look, Mummy, sheeps!', the mother would probably say 'Yes dear' if they were sheep, but 'No, cows' if they were cows. The mother would probably not correct the child for using a deviant plural form of 'sheep' (Brown, 1973). More generally, the behaviourism account of language acquisition is naïve and facile (Chomsky, 1975; Bruner, 1983).

In essence, then, the Gardners attempted to teach language to a chimp according to a programme based on fallacious theoretical dogma. Accordingly, critics alleged that Washoe had no deep understanding of language, but could merely respond appropriately in a stimulus–response manner like a rat pressing a lever in a Skinner box. In particular, it was alleged that Washoe had no understanding of syntax. From then on, the criterion for crediting a linguistic competence hinged on the understanding of grammar. Terrace *et al.* (1979) published a critique of studies reporting the linguistic abilities of apes, including Washoe and those who followed her. He concluded that there is no evidence to suggest that any ape has ever demonstrated a grammatical proficiency. Although some apes do generate strings of signs, these do not appear to be ordered according to rules of grammar. It seems that the only thing the apes had learned was to respond appropriately according to stimulus contingencies, which is not surprising because their trainers had explicitly used Skinnerian conditioning as a technology for making them linguistic. The trouble was that the resulting 'language' was remote from anything we might see in humans. Accordingly, it was never possible to hold a conversation with a chimp, or to have any meeting of minds through the medium of language.

This negative evidence does not necessarily mean that apes have no linguistic capacity whatsoever. It only means that using the principles of conditioning for teaching language, whether to apes or to humans, is doomed to failure. It seems that an impasse had been reached once again. However, this was circumvented by adopting a radically new but disarmingly simple approach to the problem.

Savage-Rumbaugh and her colleagues (Savage-Rumbaugh *et al.*, 1993) focused not on what an ape can achieve in language production, but on what he might achieve in language comprehension. She reared a bonobo (see Figure 2.2) called Kanzi in a natural linguistic environment without any deliberate attempt to teach him language. For the first two and a half years he was reared by his natural mother, but he was then separated from her when she began mating. This was done to protect Kanzi from the courting male, since it would be natural for this animal to be aggressive towards the

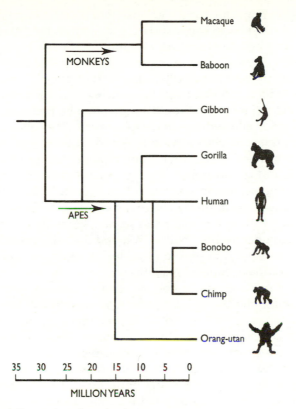

FIGURE 2.2 Evolutionary tree for primates.

young of another male. Kanzi's mother had been trained to recognize symbols, and it became apparent that Kanzi had picked up some knowledge in this department. However, there was no deliberate attempt to teach him language. Instead, his caregivers simply talked to him in the way adults would speak to small children. The researchers made a serious attempt to recreate the linguistic environment of a human family home for Kanzi, who was 8 years old at the time of his participation in the study.

The purpose of the study was to investigate Kanzi's ability to comprehend human speech. Even though he was unable to speak or to use sign language, he might have had sufficient linguistic competence to comprehend verbal utterances. Indeed, casual interaction with Kanzi seemed to confirm that he understood much of what was being said. He not only wore an attentive expression when people addressed him, but he actually responded appropriately to many requests. For example, if asked to fetch a teacup, he would do so (providing that he was so inclined).

The lesson that researchers have learned from the case of Clever Hans is a lasting one, and Savage-Rambaugh *et al.* did not wish to be fooled into attributing linguistic competence to Kanzi when he was achieving apparent comprehension on the basis of a low-level strategy. Although ordinary interaction was compelling and persuasive of Kanzi's linguistic insight, it might be that he responded appropriately to requests by acting upon visual or other cues that people unwittingly emitted. To find out whether this was the case, Savage-Rambaugh *et al.* cajoled Kanzi into wearing headphones, and then communicated novel utterances to him directly in the absence of any visual or other incidental cues. Presumably, if Kanzi responded appropriately to these requests, this would suggest that he had a genuine linguistic competence that allowed him to decipher verbal messages.

Kanzi was presented with a wide range of requests. For example, 'give Liz some pine needles'. Kanzi took some pine needles nearby and handed them correctly to Liz and not to another person present. Another request was, 'Put the pine needles in your ball'. Kanzi had a basket ball with a hole in it, and on request he dutifully inserted some pine needles in through the slit in the basket ball. The researcher also said, 'give the ball a shot'. Kanzi took a syringe, punctured the ball with it and then depressed the plunger. Another request was, 'knife the toothpaste', to which Kanzi responded by stabbing the toothpaste tube with a knife.

Altogether, Kanzi's ability to comprehend novel and even bizarre sentences is nothing short of remarkable. The novelty of the sentences is important in showing that Kanzi's comprehension is more than a mere enactment of familiar routines. On the contrary, the acts provoked by the requests were ones that Kanzi had never carried out before in many cases, suggesting that he was genuinely able to understand the sentences. That said, there were limits to what Kanzi understood. I have presented examples of his success, and have not listed his many failures to comprehend or to act only partially correctly. Savage-Rambaugh *et al.* concluded that Kanzi's linguistic comprehension was at least comparable to that of the human child aged two and a half years who they also tested.

It is very tempting to conclude that Kanzi was attuned to other minds sufficiently to adopt the appropriate attitude for interpreting speech. To an extent, it was possible for a human to connect with a bonobo through the medium of speech. In a small way, the minds of two individuals from different species were united by language, where Kanzi was receptive to another mind as a mind.

Maybe that seems to be a rather extravagant claim. Perhaps it would be possible to treat utterances not as though they originated from another mind, but rather to treat them as information that emanates directly from reality. Surely we should only say that Kanzi was receptive to another mind if there was evidence that he interpreted utterances according to the spirit of what was intended by the speaker, rather than literally according to the letter of what was said. Savage-Rambaugh *et al.* argue against such a reductive kind of interpretation. For example, when requested to 'put the water on the carrot', Kanzi did not follow the request literally, but instead he put the carrot outside in the rain. So the outcome was the same as if he had poured water over the carrot. It is always possible to place exotic interpretations on individual episodes like this, but Savage-Rambaugh *et al.* state that in virtually all cases where Kanzi failed to interpret the request literally, he imposed an alternative non-literal meaning that made sense with respect to what we might infer the speaker was requesting. He certainly did not place completely irrelevant interpretations on requests. It is very tempting to say that Kanzi used what he understood of minds to assist him in placing intelligent interpretations on what was requested. This makes eminent sense if we were to suppose that it was a receptivity to other minds that allowed Kanzi to tackle the challenge of deciphering oral information issued by humans. Why would Kanzi even think to treat utterances as potentially informative in the first place if he were not attuned in some way to the possibility that another mind was trying to communicate with him?

EYE CONTACT AND COMMUNICATION

When a couple of humans are immersed in conversation with each other, they spend a large percentage of that time in a state of mutual gaze, looking into each other's eyes. This is especially notable in the person who is doing the listening. As a person switches from the role of speaker to that of listener, so there is a corresponding increase in looking into the eyes of the other (Argyle, 1978). If we stop and consider this for a moment, such behaviour seems rather strange. Why not look at the region of the mouth? Indeed, if we were hard of hearing, it would be essential to look at the mouth in order to figure out what words were being formed. Why is it that people with good hearing do not do the same? However good one's hearing is, there are many circumstances, e.g. a crowded room, where the speech is of impaired quality due to impinging background noise. Presumably the eyes hold an appeal because they offer a further clue to the meaning of the message that the speaker is trying to convey.

Eyes signal various things. They can tell us something about the attitude in which the message is conveyed. The speaker may declare in a serious tone that she has just seen your large Alsatian dog savaging a toy poodle, but her smiling eyes will betray that this is just a practical joke that she is playing. Meanwhile, the wild eyes displayed by the man in the car next to yours might suggest that he is suffering from a bout of road rage, and the dilated pupils of the eyes of your lover signal his deep affection for you. Yet the eyes convey not only something about the emotion experienced by the person speaking to you, but also something about the part of the world that has fallen under the spotlight of the speaker's attention. It is quite natural to shift our gaze to things in the world as we talk about them. Indeed, a skill one must acquire in playing the game 'I spy' is to avoid looking at the object one has in mind as one announces the first letter of its name. Likewise, in talking about a third party in a crowd of people, it can be very difficult to avoid tell-tale glances at that person as we gossip about his or her scandalous exploits.

It is tempting to say that we might be able to interpret people's eyes in a manner similar to the way in which we interpret their speech. For example, we might receive a clue as to what someone is thinking either by hearing them say 'teapot', or by tracing the direction of their gaze to the teapot that resides in the other corner of the room. Just as we can interpret referential speech, so we can interpret referential gaze. In other words, just as we interpret speech as being about something in the world, so we may treat gaze in the same way – speech has an 'aboutness', and so does gaze. Speech and gaze tell us something about the attentional focus of a person, a focus that we can share if we interpret the speech correctly, or look to the same place in space as another person. Tacitly, we would be acknowledging that the focus of my attention and yours is not the same by default, but that we have to take active steps to achieve a state of shared focus. This is to make statements of the obvious about the rudiments of communication, but what transpires is that a form of primitive communication can occur through gaze and mutual gaze. You stand to learn something about me, what I am thinking and also about the world by observing the direction of my gaze.

Butterworth and Jarrett (1991) discovered that being able to read the direction of gaze is an extremely precocious ability of human infants. They demonstrated this by having the mother and baby sit facing each other as shown in Figure 2.3. The baby was propped up in a high chair so that he had ample opportunity to make eye contact with his mother. Once eye contact was secured, the mother was under instruction to look to a predetermined point in the room, either to the baby's left or to his right. The researchers wanted to find out whether the baby would be able to track the mother's gaze and fixate on the same point in space, which is denoted by 'X' in Figure 2.3.

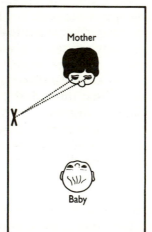

FIGURE 2.3 Mother and baby faced each other and acheived eye contact, whereupon the mother shifted her gaze to a predetermined point. Infants aged 18 months and above had no difficulty in fixating on the same location in space, which indicates a remarkable ability to calculate the geometry of another person's direction of gaze.

At 6 months of age, babies succeeded in tracking, so long as the mother's gaze was signalled by a rather gross turn of her head. If she just shifted her eyes whilst keeping her head still, then the baby did not react. At the age of about 12 months, babies would fixate on the space that was the object of the mother's gaze even when she just moved her eyes, and kept her head still. However, the babies would only do this if the target of the mother's gaze was actually within the child's immediate visual field. The 12-month-old baby failed to turn his head and locate a space behind him. This was some-thing that only a child of 18 months or older could achieve.

Apparently, by 18 months of age infants have a sophisticated capacity to identify what another person's gaze is about. At least implicitly, it seems that they are not taking shared attention for granted, but appreciate that experi-encing a common focus with another person is something one must work at. On the other side of the coin, the babies seem to grasp that the subjective focus of attention of two minds can differ. A capacity and inclination to trace another person's gaze seems to signal at least a primitive understanding of the existence of other minds. This understanding might also serve as the foundation for a broader communicative competence that is necessary as a catalyst for the birth of language. It suggests that, by 18 months of age, babies are receptive to having things singled out for them, whether by words or by the direction of gaze.

If bonobos and perhaps chimps are capable of understanding elementary forms of human linguistic communication, then presumably they would show sensitivity to the direction of another person's gaze. How could a chimp fathom the 'aboutness' of language if he could not even relate to the aboutness of gaze? Surely gaze direction is the more primitive capacity in which the chimp should show proficiency if he is to stand any chance of understanding language. Povinelli and Eddy (1996a) set out to find an answer to this question. The first thing we should note is that chimps read-ily make eye contact, and that they do so when feeling affectionate. Making eye contact with a chimp is a natural feature of friendship. In contrast, for many other animals, including certain primates, direct eye contact is regarded exclusively as a hostile and threatening act. At least, then, chimps have the basic qualification for being able to read the direction of another person's gaze.

Povinelli and Eddy (1996a) arranged their laboratory as shown in Figure 2.4. The room was divided in half by a transparent screen, and the chimp was ushered into her half of the chamber through a hatch and went to sit on a crate facing the experimenter who was waiting for her. The experi-menter faced the chimp directly until she made full eye contact. At this point, the experimenter shifted his gaze and fixated on a predetermined location above the chimp's head and to the left (or right). Meanwhile, the chimp was being videoed in order to determine whether she located the same point in space with her own gaze. Research assistants analysed the video tapes to detect where the chimp looked. In doing so they were unable to see where the experimenter had looked, owing to the strategic position-

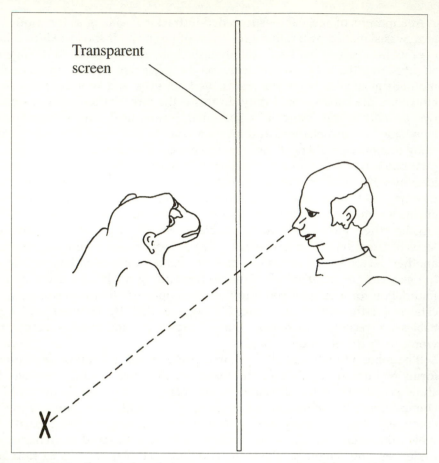

FIGURE 2.4 Like human infants, chimps were also able to calculate the target of another individual's gaze. In this case, the chimp willingly looked to the point in space behind her to locate the target of her trainer's gaze.

ing of the camera. The results of this intriguing study were extremely clear. The chimps were judged to be fixating on a point in space that happened to be the target of the experimenter's gaze. The chimps were using the experimenter's line of gaze as a reference to something in the world that was outside their immediate field of view. They showed a willingness to interpret a human's line of gaze as being about something that to which they were not currently privy.

In a second study, Povinelli and Eddy (1996a) introduced a modification to the screen positioned between the experimenter and the chimp. As shown in Figure 2.5, the area of the screen to the experimenter's right was covered in wallpaper to make it opaque. Having made eye contact with the chimp, the experimenter shifted his gaze according to the same line of regard as before. Obviously, when he was looking to the side that was opaque, the target of

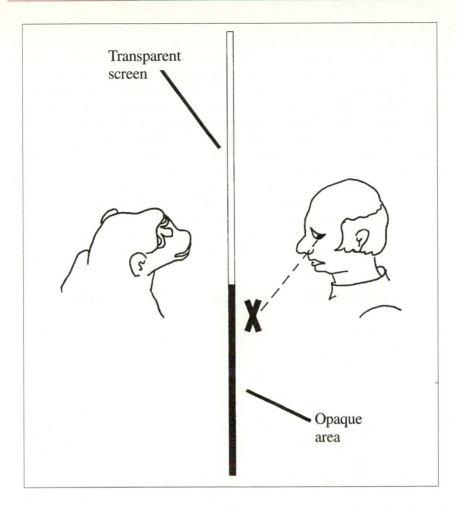

FIGURE 2.5 Chimps seemed to understand that an opaque screen is an obstacle to the line of gaze of another individual. They tried to fixate on the side of the screen that the trainer could see, and not beyond the screen, which the trainer could not see.

the experimenter's gaze was a point on the side of the screen facing him. Under a control condition, the experimenter held a forward gaze and reached out obliquely to deposit food at the same point on the screen.

If the chimps attended only to the experimenter's line of regard, they would scan to a point in space behind their own heads, as in the first study. Ironically, this is a place the experimenter was unable to see because the opaque screen was intercepting his line of sight. In fact, however, the chimps virtually never looked towards this point behind them, but instead leaned forward as if trying to see what was on the side of the screen facing the experimenter. They did this just as when the experimenter had deposited food on his side of the screen.

The astonishing finding reported by Povinelli and Eddy (1996a) shows that chimps have a remarkable level of insight into the meaning of gaze. Apparently they do not calculate the geometry in relation to the space that they themselves experience, but relate it specifically to the experimenter's space. They seem to take on board the fact that their own visual environment and that of the experimenter differ, and that the experimenter's gaze is to be interpreted within the visual space that he inhabits. It is very tempting to say that chimps are acutely aware that effort is required to bring about a shared visual world with another individual. They grasp that this is not something to be taken for granted, and may even assume that, by default, the object of another individual's attention is different from that of their own. In that context, it is understandable how language could become a more explicit and detailed tool of reference. Without understanding gaze as a form of reference to something in the world, it is hard to imagine how language could have developed into a vehicle of reference.

SECONDARY BENEFITS OF LINGUISTIC COMPETENCE

As with other characteristics, the evolution of intelligence owes a great deal to serendipity. The birth of one faculty then opens new horizons in other departments of expertise. It might be the case that language evolved as a medium of communication because this facilitated a meeting of minds. In other words, it might be that the advent of language was an adaptation to a social world in which *mind* was beginning to feature more and more prominently. Once language had emerged, however, it then existed as a cognitive tool that could be applied to new spheres of intelligent activity. For example, a written analogue could be created as an artefact that helps effectively to expand conscious space. All the elements of a problem can be considered together if they are written on a page (or a tablet of stone!), thus removing the risk of loss of attention to crucial pieces of the puzzle with which the individual is grappling.

Having the elements of the problem in writing is also bound to assist objectivity. The suggested solution remains there to be seen and cogitated upon by other individuals. The project under scrutiny could be how to construct a rigid shelter that is impervious to the vagaries of the weather, or it could be a list of tactics on how to defend the community against attack by marauders. It might even be a statement on how best to prepare various kinds of food.

When language is used deliberately as a tool in this way, it would not be surprising if it became further refined to suit this particular purpose. We could dispense with the niceties associated with verbal exchange, and strip the language down to the bare elements necessary for thinking and reasoning. Several thousand years later, the language in question might resemble algebra and other forms of abstract mathematics and formulae. This in turn would open up a plethora of possibilities that perhaps were actually manifest in history as the birth of the mechanical age and an advanced understanding of space and time. In other words, presumably the Renaissance period could not have occurred if it had not been for certain developments in mathematics and other aspects of language (defined broadly) that support advanced thinking and reasoning.

What I am speculating here (and it is a big speculation), is that culture and civilization are to a considerable extent by-products of language that arose initially in the social sphere. In other words, it might be that our technical, mathematical and logical intellect is supported by a capacity to use a refined form of language, a language that was originally a product of the social intellect. Expressed at its simplest, perhaps the logical intellect is subordinate to the social intellect. If so, this might explain why most people feel a good deal more comfortable when making intuitive (and highly sophisticated) judgements about their companions than they do when handling abstract mathematics. Yet, in a sense, much of abstract mathematics is something that can be handled by a dumb machine, whereas it is impossible to imagine how we would even begin to program a machine to display the kind of intuitive intelligence that would mimic a real mind. In summary, it might be that the essence and origin of human linguistic intelligence are to be found in the social rather than the technological sphere. Although the arrival of our ancestor *Homo habilis* seemed to herald a new technological intellect, what we understand less about is the social and communicative intelligence of this creature. For all we know, the latter may have appeared quite awesome in comparison with the rather elementary ability to use stones (and presumably sticks) as tools.

THE DAWNING OF LINGUISTIC COMPETENCE

According to Davidson (1991), the ability to use language developed about 40 000 years ago specifically in humans. In the context of the many millions of years of evolutionary adaption of life on earth, that is just a blink of the eye. Is it possible that a linguistic competence, or at least a receptivity to communication from other minds, predates this estimate? The evidence presented by Savage-Rumbaugh *et al.* (1993) does provide a strong clue to the effect that the capacity for receptivity to communication from other minds actually emerged several million years ago. To appreciate this argument, we need to consider the distinction between 'homology' and 'convergence'. Homology refers to similarities in characteristics between species owing to common descent. For example, the mammalian characteristic of feeding milk to young indicates that all mammals have a single ancestor in common. This certainly is not a case of convergence. That would be a case of different species evolving organs for feeding milk to their young in parallel but entirely independently of each other. Our defining mammalian characteristic of feeding milk to young is a legacy of our ancestry which is shared by all mammals.

Evolutionary convergence can occur, however. This may happen when the functional requirements of a characteristic provide individuals with a selective advantage, allowing the characteristic to evolve independently. For example, snails and tortoises both have shells. Obviously we can trace the descent of these species far enough back to identify a point where these creatures did have a common ancestor, whereupon we discover that this ancestor almost certainly did not have a shell. In that case, the two species evolved shells independently because of the advantage this conferred, and not because of common descent.

If apes and humans are united by a receptivity to communication from other minds, it is possible that this capacity has evolved independently in the various species concerned. However, it is much more likely that the sophisticated human receptivity to other minds was built upon a pre-existing competence handed down from our hairy ancestors. This competence has developed and blossomed in the lineage that led to the arrival of humans. Just as abilities have developed down the human line, so they are bound to have done so down the chimpanzee line. Although both species will be different from our common ancestor in some respects, none the less this ancestor is likely to have endowed both species with the kind of mind that is suited to interpreting information from other minds. It seems too much of a coincidence to suppose that both species have developed a specialized social intelligence independently, especially as both live in social groups, presumably like our common ancestor. As I mentioned previously, being receptive to other minds confers a very special advantage in that context. It is likely, then, although not definite, that what humans have in common with chimps and other apes, we probably also have in common with our mutual ancestor.

This ancestor, incidentally, was probably very much like a small bonobo, weighing about 30 kg. Like our common ancestor, the bonobo is adapted to living in woodland, and therefore has probably not developed the kind of specialisms that evolved in chimps and humans as they began to venture on to the savannah. The bonobo has developed into a slightly larger animal than our common ancestor, with the male weighing about 43 kg and the female weighing about 10 kg less. Interestingly, when the bonobo stands upright on its feet, it shows a remarkable resemblance to the prehuman known as Australopithecine. The common chimp is a larger animal than the bonobo, with the male weighing up to 70 kg. Both bonobos and chimps have a life span of about 60 years. The young of both species are weaned at about 4 years of age and remain heavily dependent on their mother until they are about 5 years old. They reach adolescence at about 7 years and begin reproduction at about 13 years of age. Bonobos, chimps and humans have over 98 per cent of their genetic pool in common, and are as similar to each other as species as dogs are to foxes. It is possible that, in an extreme emergency, a human could survive with a blood transfusion from a chimp.

We can see from Figure 2.2 that the human lineage diverged from the chimp and bonobo pathway about 8 million years ago. It is tempting to say that a receptivity to other minds, including communication from other minds, existed at least this long ago. Eight million years seems a very long time relative to the periods we normally think about, but in terms of evolutionary history it is fairly brief. This relatively short period of time, then, is probably a conservative estimate. The sensitivity to other minds in our ancestor could actually have prevailed for a very long time before the human and chimp lines diverged. How far back can we trace the capacity for sensitivity to mind? To find the answer to this question, we need to look at other aspects of understanding mind, which are the province of the next chapter.

3

THE DAWNING OF AN UNDERSTANDING OF MINDS IN APES

We humans pride ourselves on having a level of self-insight that enables us to place ourselves in a universe that possesses the qualities of time and space. We understand about the uniqueness of ourselves as individuals who differ from other inhabitants of the planet. We have a notion of life and death, and of past and future. We understand ourselves as sentient, conscious and self-conscious beings. What about chimps? How could we even begin to investigate what the chimp understands about itself as an organism? Does the chimp possess a self-concept?

MIRROR SELF-RECOGNITION

The first time your cat sees itself in the mirror, it will probably assume an aggressive posture, with arched back, fluffed out fur and bared teeth. It will spit and engage in the posturing behaviours typically provoked when encountering the cat owned by the neighbour. Eventually, your cat will come to ignore its own reflection, treating it neither as another cat nor as a reflected image of itself. The cat will come to treat the reflection as a meaningless image. If you hand a mirror to a chimp, initially it will behave as though confronted by another chimp. Having said that, it will act slightly differently from a cat in that it will repeatedly look behind the mirror. After a short while, however, the chimp will begin to show a pattern of behaviour that is entirely unlike anything we would ever see in a cat, dog or even a monkey (see Figure 2.2). The chimp will use the mirror as a tool for exploring parts of its body that it would not normally be able to see. For example, it will fixate intently on its nostrils and finger them while it does so (see Gallup, 1970).

We can intervene with a small test capable of offering a further insight into what the chimp understands of its reflected image. Suppose we have a capsule of red dye concealed in the palm of our hand. Suppose we then stroke the chimp's head in a friendly and affectionate gesture that, unknown to the chimp, is a ploy to deposit a stain of bright red ink on its forehead. Suppose we then hand a mirror to the chimp who already has some experience of looking into mirrors. On seeing its reflected image, it will characteristically react by reaching directly to its forehead in the region of the stain. It seems that the chimp has a body schema that incorporates zones which are not always in view but that can be seen with the aid of a mirror. The red dye will present a puzzle to the chimp, because this would not form a part of its self-image. The chimp's surprised reaction on seeing the red stain is thus evidence of a pre-existing conception of itself.

If we present exactly the same test to a monkey, the resulting behaviour we observe is quite different. No amount of experience with mirrors helps the monkey to touch its own head in this context. The contrast between the intelligent behaviour of the chimp and the apparent lack of insight of the monkey gives the strong impression that the conception of a body schema is species-specific. In particular, it seems that chimps have this while monkeys do not.

We need to dwell briefly on how to interpret the insightful behaviour of the chimp. We can assume that seeing oneself in a mirror is an experience not entirely natural to a chimp, although some opportunities for self-reflection do present themselves in its natural habitat, as for example when it peers into a pool of water. Despite the fact that mirrors are manufactured human products, it is possible that chimps are able to interpret their own images by holding a preconception of their self. This self-conception will remain incomplete until the chimp has an opportunity to see parts of itself that were previously out of view. In other words, success in self-recognition might be a sign not only that chimps can build a conception of themselves when presented with the relevant visual evidence, but also that they have a pre-existing self-concept capable of accommodating the new data.

Presumably, monkeys as well as chimps can see themselves in a mirror. The difference between the two species is that 'self' seems to hold a special significance for chimps but not for monkeys. Chimps but not monkeys appear to hold a concept that *self* is *me*. How should we define 'me'? At the very least, me is not you. I am me and you are you. Perhaps mirror self-recognition in chimps is a sign of an ability to differentiate between oneself and other individuals. Here, 'oneself' becomes an object of one's own conscious attention, meaning that self and others are individuated. This remarkable capacity might signal the dawning of consciousness about self as a sentient and thinking organism with a unique subjective experience, one that differs from other individuals. Hence, being able to recognize oneself in a mirror might be an important manifestation of a primitive and rudimentary conception of mind.

TRACING THE EVOLUTION OF A CONCEPTION OF MIND

The mirror self-recognition test has been carried out on many species of primates (see Povinelli, 1993, for a review). By documenting which species do and which do not show evidence of mirror self-recognition, we can begin to build up a picture of approximately when the most primitive ingredients that make up a conception of mind evolved. As before, we shall assume a homology in the event of cousin species showing success in self-recognition. In other words, for example, given that both chimps and humans are capable of mirror self-recognition, we shall assume that the ancestor common to both these species also had this ability. This permits us to say that a primitive self-consciousness evolved at least 8 million years ago, since this is when chimps and humans parted in their evolutionary development (see Figure 2.2).

Furthermore, we are able to place a limit on how far back we can trace the advent of self-consciousness. Monkeys branched off from apes nearly 30 million years ago. Monkeys seem to lack self-consciousness, and therefore it is likely that the ancestor common to monkeys and apes also lacked this capacity. Consequently, it would appear that self-consciousness evolved within the last 30 million years. We can be even more specific than this. Orang-utans display self-recognition, but gibbons do not do so. Using the same logic, it seems that the ancestor common to orang-utans, gorillas, humans, chimps and bonobos had self-consciousness. However, gibbons do not evince self consciousness and fail to show any sign of recognizing themselves in a mirror. They succeed in perceiving the image, but persist in reacting to it as though it were another individual. In that case, we can place the birth of self-consciousness between about 15 and 20 million years ago (see Figure 2.2).

There is one small problem with this otherwise neat account. By a process of deduction, we can infer that if orang-utans are capable of self-recognition, then gorillas should be capable of it as well. These two species were united by a common ancestor approximately 15 million years ago, an animal which we have already credited with self-consciousness. However, gorillas show little aptitude for self-recognition. How can we explain this anomaly? One possibility is that self-consciousness evolved *after* humans and chimps had branched off from gorillas, which would mean that the development of this self-insight took place about 8 million years ago in our own line of ancestry. If that were the case, we would have to explain self-consciousness in orang-utans by proposing that the capacity evolved spontaneously and coincidentally. This would be an instance of evolutionary convergence, where the functional advantages of having self-consciousness promoted its development in two populations independently of one another.

Another possibility is that gorillas 'lost' the faculty of self-consciousness. This is the explanation preferred by Povinelli (1993) on the grounds that there is evidence suggesting that some gorillas might, after all, be capable of self- recognition. Patterson (1984) submitted her gorilla Koko to an intensive programme of training in an artificial language that she had devised. Her interest was actually in apes' ability to communicate with language, but coincidentally she also tested Koko for mirror self-recognition, in which Koko succeeded. Povinelli suggests that the unusually stimulating social environment in which Koko was reared may have allowed her to resurrect a capacity for self-consciousness that lies dormant in most members of her species.

This explanation might seem convincing in one respect, but it does beg the awkward question of why gorillas should have lost such a valuable faculty as self-reflection. Povinelli's (1993) explanation is as follows. He notes that the rate of maturation seems to have accelerated in gorillas relative to that in chimps. It might be that chimp development has become less hurried in comparison with that of their ancestor, but it is equally possible that gorillas have become precocious. Gorillas are mobile at an earlier age than chimps, and there are also other features of early maturity. Povinelli suggests that a faster progression to maturity in gorillas was presumably advantageous in their particular habitat. For example, perhaps gorillas found themselves travelling further afield to forage for food, giving them more of a nomadic habit. If so, it would certainly be an advantage for the young to be independently mobile from an earlier age. However, the acceleration of development might actually have involved a developmental short cut in some respects. It might be that such a sophisticated faculty as self-consciousness matures over a protracted developmental period. Any speeding up of development might have interfered with this process, thus denying the gorilla the opportunity to acquire self-consciousness, unlike its ancestor species. Gorillas are perhaps endowed with the potential to achieve self-consciousness, but this remains latent due to the emergence of new developmental processes that inadvertently interfere with it. If the naturally swift development could be arrested, then perhaps the gorilla's potential for self-consciousness would be realized. Perhaps this is precisely what happened with Patterson's (1984) laboratory-reared gorilla.

REPORTS OF INSIGHTFUL BEHAVIOUR

A mystic might try to convince you of the supernatural by reporting episodes involving apparitions silently making their way through the dead of night, or acts of psychokinesis and mental telepathy. You would be persuaded to suspend disbelief if the person trying to convert you seemed particularly sincere, and your usual rational approach to things would be set on one side. The evidence presented to you would probably consist of a succession of stories, and in the context it would be bad form to challenge the veracity of these, since to do so would be to question the integrity of an esteemed person. You would thus be denied the opportunity to examine the evidence before you. The form of presentation in this respect will be an art in itself, and at least as important as the content of what is reported. It is more an exercise in the techniques of persuasion than a rational, objective scrutiny of evidence, explanations and counter-explanations.

Against this background, it is not surprising that people who subscribe to the accumulation of scientific knowledge have tended to shy away from anecdotal evidence that testifies to insightful behaviour in animals. However, our wariness of the presentational baggage that usually accompanies anecdotal reports threatens to blind us to an important source of information. If we were able to adopt a more objective attitude toward verbal reports of animal behaviour, then we might learn a great deal about how they think. As the old saying goes, it would not be wise to throw out the baby with the bath water. Whiten and Byrne (1988) pioneered the revival of anecdote as a category of scientific evidence in their survey of scientists who worked with apes. Their purpose was to document cases of apes behaving in a way which suggests that they have sensitivity to the minds of those around them. They focused on instances of what appeared to be insightful deception, which has to be distinguished from deceptive acts that are either genetically determined or learned.

Consider the remarkable behaviour of a species of bird that feigns a broken wing when its nest is under attack by a predator. As the predator approaches the nest, the bird limps about elaborately in the near vicinity. The predator responds to this spectacle as to an easy kill and promptly pursues the bird. The bird limps away and the predator gives chase. When both are a reassuring distance from the nest, the bird flies away to safety, and her chicks live for another day! The bird's behaviour is highly automated, being triggered purely by stimuli. This can be demonstrated by eliciting the behaviour in captivity with the presentation of the essentials of the predator stimuli. This need not necessarily involve an actual predator, but only the salient stimuli associated with the marauding animal. Feigning a broken wing is not deception in the sense that we understand it, but rather it is an unthinking and automated response that is executed without any final goal or outcome in mind.

There is no reason to think that learned deception is any more insightful. Suppose a fox being pursued by hounds heads for cover in a hollow tree, and suppose that within the fox's territory there are two hollow trees, but the fox reliably heads for one in particular each time the hunt takes place. This particular hollow tree has a special quality, since within it there is a burrow that leads the fox out to safety, while the hounds continue snarling at the tree as if the fox were still inside. If the fox had gone to the other tree, which has no burrow inside, then it would be doomed. Superficially, it might be tempting to say that the fox has the insight that the dogs believe (falsely) that the fox is inside the hollow tree, and the existence of the burrow within the tree permits the fox to slip away to freedom while the hounds are preoccupied with a misapprehension. However, an alternative possibility is that the fox is without insight, but by chance happens to have chosen to hide in this tree previously and survived as a direct consequence. Because the previous behaviour engendered a successful outcome, it is repeated in future. In other words, the fox who happens to survive will probably have done so by hitting upon behaviour that is to its own advantage, and it comes as no surprise that the life-saving behaviour is repeated in future. However, the fox could do all that without any conception of how it worked.

Insightful deception is different. It is carried out in the absence of specialized genetic programming and without specific learning. It would require the calculation of the consequences of one's behaviour, especially how that behaviour would be interpreted by another individual. It would therefore require a conception of the future and a conception of other minds as observers and interpreters of the behaviour in question. If apes have any sort of conception of mind, surely this would be apparent as an ability to deceive insightfully. The trouble we face is that it is virtually impossible to investigate acts of insightful deception in the laboratory. How do we request or encourage an ape to engage in deception? How could we ask the ape to deceive, and in any case what would be the ape's incentive to do this in a laboratory context? I shall say more about laboratory studies later, but first consider how tempting it is instead to examine spontaneous instances of apparently insightful deception in a non-laboratory context. Situations arise during ordinary interactions when an act of deception or concealment would be hugely advantageous to the individual. The uniqueness of the situation might help to persuade us that the act is insightfully deceptive rather than a mindless learned habit. Whiten and Byrne (1988) set out to document this type of case.

One of the most compelling instances of apparent deception which they document is of a baboon being chased by a hostile male in the group. Although these kinds of skirmish are usually settled without much physical harm being done, it is none the less potentially dangerous for the animal that is being chased, not to mention humiliating to have to yield to another male. This particular baboon, however, appeared to have an ingenious insight. He suddenly stopped and adopted an alert attitude, whilst fixating on the horizon. This kind of behaviour is unmistakable in character, and is the typical response when a predator is approaching. In this case there was in fact no predator, and none of the other baboons had shown any sign of there being one until this moment. Baboons ignore the behaviour of one of their band who has apparently spotted a predator at their own peril. This orienting response had a dramatic effect on the pursuing dominant baboon. It arrested its chase and, like the other baboons in the band, it switched to preparing for a predatory attack.

There was nothing creative or insightful about the predator-alarm response of the pursued baboon. However, its particular application could have been intelligent. It is possible that the baboon was aware of the consequences that its predator-alarm behaviour would have for others in the band, including the dominant male who was in pursuit. If so, it is tempting to conclude that this baboon had sufficient insight at least into the other animal's behaviour to allow him to mislead the dominant male into channelling all his energy into responding to a fictitious predator. We might say that the dominant male was duped! However, even with this generous interpretation of the pursued baboon's action, there is no reason to credit him with anything more than a conception of the behaviour of the dominant male, and not a conception of his mind.

Whiten and Byrne (1988) have reported another case involving baboons. A male had a carcass which was a trophy of his hunting expedition, and he was settling down to devour this greedily by himself when a hungry female approached and began to groom him. Grooming in these animals has a soporific effect and serves as a major form of recreation and bonding between adults. Such was the effect of the grooming that the baboon fell under his female companion's spell, whereupon he lost interest in his prized meat. At this point, the female suddenly grabbed the meat and bolted! She then hid and proceeded to feast on the carcass herself. Again, a generous interpretation is that the thieving female had a conception of the male's behaviour. It is tempting to conclude that she had the insight that, if she groomed him, then he would relax his claim to the meat to a point where she could snatch it from him.

A further report presents the case of a chimp concealing facts from another member of the band. The dominance hierarchy of the chimp band carries implications for mating rites. Basically, mating is a privilege that male elders claim as a priority over junior members of the band. It seems that junior members may mate only with the blessing of the senior chimps. Whiten and Byrne document the case of a junior chimp making surreptitious advances to a female. In doing so he was taking a considerable risk, for if he were to be caught by a dominant male he would be severely punished. It is actually rather difficult for a chimp to make discrete advances to a female, because his attempts to impress her will involve an ostentatious display of his erection. This was precisely the behaviour that the junior chimp was engaged in when a dominant male appeared unexpectedly. The junior chimp promptly and very deliberately covered his erection with his hands.

This intriguing act of concealment is highly suggestive of sensitivity to other minds, not to mention insight. It is tempting to conclude that the chimp understood that although his erection existed, what mattered critically is whether or not a dominant member of the band *knew* that it existed. It seems that the chimp might have understood that it was possible to prevent the dominant male knowing by instituting an impediment to his line of sight (hands covering the erection). Presumably, the chimp would not be going to this trouble if it were not for his insight or anticipation of the dominant animal's negative and punitive reaction.

I began this section with a note of caution regarding the limitations of anecdotal reports. Anecdotes are a valuable source of information, and it would be foolish to ignore them. However, we should maintain a cautious attitude.

This is not to say that we should disregard anecdotes, but rather that we should not treat them as a definitive source of evidence. To begin with, there is a question mark over accuracy. Even though the anecdotes were all reported by trained scientists who are highly attuned to the principle of objectivity, because their reports were of events that took place outside the constraints of the laboratory, it is possible that the scientists 'embroidered' their descriptions slightly in a way that would favour a richer interpretation of the behaviour in question. In any case, even if the description were perfectly accurate, it remains a possibility that the behaviour was not actually insightful in the true sense, but that it was the result of prior experience and learning. Perhaps what the apes did was more the product of unthinking habit that had served them well in the past, rather than the result of creative scheming. None the less, if the anecdotal evidence was found to contribute to the overall picture emerging from laboratory studies, it would support the view that certain species of primate have at least some insight into mind.

DO APES UNDERSTAND INTENTION?

There are two major studies that address this issue directly. The first, by Premack and Woodruff (1978), was conducted in conjunction with their chimp Sarah. The researchers had noted Sarah's apparent enjoyment of commercial television, which she seemed to find very absorbing. It is difficult to imagine what anyone might derive from many of the programmes if they did not understand something of the psychology of the various characters. For example, why should a character become upset if his desires are thwarted, and what would he have to do in order to get out of this predicament? Apart from requiring an understanding of other people's emotion, this episode also presents an opportunity for demonstrating an understanding of intention, that the character intends to release himself from the predicament. As viewers, we might also contemplate what the character must do to achieve his goal.

Premack and Woodruff (1978) presented a selection of short videos to Sarah that showed a character facing a problem, and then presented Sarah with a series of cards, one of which showed an item relevant to what we might infer about the character's intention. The rest of the cards were distracter items. For example, a man was depicted trying to leave a room unsuccessfully. He was heaving at the door handle, but apparently the door was locked. Sarah was then shown three cards which all displayed items that had some relevance to the solution, but only one of them would satisfy the man's goal. In this particular example, she was shown three cards with keys on them (see Figure 3.1). One was broken in the middle, another was bent, and a third was intact.

Sarah had been trained in her distinguished career as a research participant to offer a response by holding up the card showing the solution to the television screen. Prior to this, the problems had been of a logical nature,

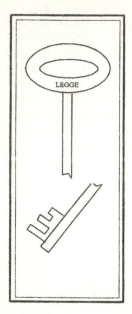 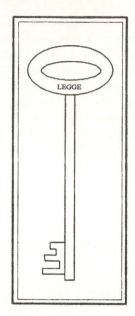 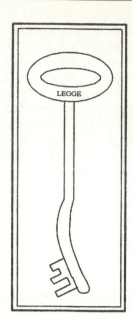

FIGURE 3.1 The chimp was presented with three cards, and had to choose one that was relevant to the video of a man heaving at a door that was locked. The chimp reliably chose the intact key in preference to the distracter keys.

but now Premack and Woodruff (1978) wished to assess her social intellect. Sarah reliably selected the card showing the intact key after watching the video. She was presented with a further three similar scenarios, and in each case she again chose the correct solution. Her correct judgements suggested that she was able to infer the actor's intention in the various sketches, although another possibility was that she did not consider the psychology of the actor but only the solution to the problem. Even so, she could not have identified the problem without assigning some kind of purpose to the actor's behaviour.

In any case, a further study suggested that Sarah was not just fixated on the solution to the problem, and that she was attuned to the psychology of the actor. She watched a man in a cage trying to reach through the bars to some bananas located outside the cage. There was a box in his way, with bricks on top of it, preventing him from getting the fruit. As before, Sarah was shown a set of pictures and invited to make a selection. In some of the trials she selected a picture that showed the man reaching the bananas successfully after having shifted the box to one side. However, a rather sinister finding was that under one particular condition Sarah reliably chose a photograph which showed the actor lying on the floor with the bricks from the top of the box scattered over him. Apparently, he was the victim of an accident. Sarah's behaviour seems slightly chilling when we reflect upon the identity of the two actors, both of whom were known to her. When she reliably chose a happy outcome, the actor was her trainer Keith, for whom

Sarah clearly had much affection. When she reliably chose the unpleasant outcome, the actor was her trainer Bill, with whom she did not get along! Evidently, she was not just oriented to solve the problem, but was also immersed in the psychology of the sketches that were acted out.

A further investigation of the chimp's understanding of intention was conducted by Povinelli *et al.* (1992). They designed a piece of apparatus in order to investigate the chimp's ability to exchange roles with another individual. If the chimp was successful in adopting another person's role, it would strongly suggest that it had assimilated and understood the intention of this individual to communicate something meaningful. The apparatus that they used is depicted in Figure 3.2.

The figure shows the apparatus as it would appear if we were looking down upon it from above. The two players sit on either side of the apparatus, one playing the role of informant and the other playing the role of operator. One of the players would be a human and the other a chimp. The chimps had already been trained to gesture imperatively by pointing, and to respond appropriately to the imperative pointing of another individual. In other words, they could point at an object to convey the meaning 'I want that!', and they would fetch an object when the trainer pointed to it. In this particular game, the two players were assigned randomly to one role

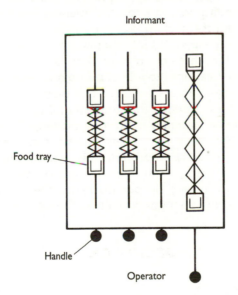

FIGURE 3.2 Plan view of the apparatus. One 'player' is situated at the top of the diagram (informant), while the other is situated at the bottom (operator). The informant can see which tray is bated, but the operator can only see the informant. For both players to obtain the food, the informant must indicate accurately which tray is baited and the operator must interpret this correctly by pulling the appropriate handle to extend the food trays within reaching distance of the players. Chimps appeared to understand the game, whereas monkeys did not.

or the other. Let us suppose that the chimp was playing the role of the operator, in which case he would be seated at the bottom of the figure. His task was to pull a handle if and only if the informant pointed to it. If the chimp did pull the handle, then he and the informant gained access to the food in the food tray. Pulling the handle brought food within reach on either side of the apparatus. Only one food tray was baited, but the chimp operator could not see which one it was, owing to the presence of a mini-screen erected on one side of each tray which blocked his view. On the other hand, the food was in full view of the informant. Hence, the two players had to co-operate in co-ordinating their respective roles to obtain the food prize.

After extensive practice, both chimps and monkeys learned to perform well in the roles to which they were assigned. That in itself is not especially interesting, since these are intelligent animals capable of learning complex behaviour. However, what was of more interest was whether the chimps could swap roles easily. Would their experience of receiving and acting upon messages from an informant allow them to play the role of informant themselves? If it did, this would suggest that the chimps had come to understand on a fairly deep level what it means to be an informant – that the informant's task is to communicate the whereabouts of the food in order to allow the operator to act appropriately. Hence we might say that the informant is intending to enlighten the operator regarding the whereabouts of the food, and if the chimps are to assume the role of informant, they surely must have grasped this intentional aspect of the informant's job.

The findings were that three out of four chimps tested by Povinelli *et al.* (1992) were easily able to adopt the role of informant following their experience as an operator. Their success indicated that they grasped the intentionality of the informant and applied that understanding to themselves when appropriate. In contrast, monkeys did not exchange roles very easily. Indeed, it was as though they were being trained from scratch when they were put in the position of the informant. It is possible, therefore, that the monkeys succeeded in acting as an operator only by trial-and-error learning, and in the absence of any deeper understanding. It seems that they were incapable of grasping the intentionality of the informant.

DECEPTION

Although chimps may have some primitive understanding of intentional communication, and although anecdotal evidence suggests that they have some grasp of deception, it would be reassuring if we had laboratory evidence for this. The pioneering research on this issue was conducted by Woodruff and Premack (1979), and was inspired by their earlier work in which their chimp Sarah showed a liking for one trainer in preference to another. Both trainers in that study were well intentioned, but that made no difference to Sarah in making up her own mind about who she did and did not like. In the new study, the researchers contrived the situation such that one trainer was scripted to be ostentatiously nice, while the other was overtly nasty. The nice trainer addressed the chimps in soft tones as though they were young children. He smiled, was attentive and stroked the chimps. The other trainer grunted irritably at the chimps and swiped at them when in close proximity. His eyes were concealed by sun-glasses, and a cloth covered the bottom part of his face so that he looked like a bandit.

After the four chimps had become acquainted with the foibles of the two trainers, the main part of the experiment commenced. The chimps took turns being housed in a small cage within the laboratory. A person entered the laboratory with a tasty morsel of food, which he deposited beneath one of two cups that were juxtaposed. He departed and then one of the two trainers arrived. Because the chimp was restrained by the cage, he was unable to gain access to the food. However, he now had the opportunity to obtain the food by informing the trainer where it was hidden. If the trainer was the 'nice' one, and the chimp gestured to the baited cup, the trainer promptly and reliably looked there, found the food, and then handed it to the chimp as a reward. If the chimp gestured to the empty cup, the trainer looked there, found nothing and then left without the chimp receiving anything. So in this case the chimp received a reward for giving an accurate and honest communication.

If the trainer was the 'nasty' one, then things were different. This trainer also looked under the cup indicated by the chimp but, unlike the nice trainer, on finding the food there he gleefully gobbled it up himself! On the other hand, if the chimp gestured to the empty container, the trainer looked there, found nothing, and then shuffled to the corner of the laboratory in despair. At this moment, the chimp was released from his cage and allowed to search under the remaining cup to claim the food for himself. Effectively, the chimp was being rewarded for communicating dishonestly. Would the chimps deceive the nasty trainer?

The answer is 'yes', but with qualifications. The four chimps who participated in the study did eventually differentiate between the two trainers in terms of the honesty of their gestures (Figure 3.3). However, none of the chimps discriminated systematically in fewer than 50 attempts. Initially, all chimps gestured honestly to both trainers. Then they began to show a general reluctance to do so, but still did not discriminate between the trainers. Finally, after at least 50 trials, the chimps did begin to gesture dishonestly specifically to the nasty trainer.

Because of the protracted period of learning required by the chimps to communicate dishonestly, it is difficult to conclude what this tells us about their understanding of mind. On the one hand, it might be that they understand the principle that dishonest communication has the power to mislead, with the consequence that the recipient will act under a misapprehension. If so, we would have to explain the lengthy learning phase by suggesting that the chimps did not readily grasp what the game was about. The difficulty in conducting experiments with chimps to assess their understanding

FIGURE 3.3 In order to win the hidden banana, chimps had to deceive the 'nasty' trainer by gesturing to the empty cup.

of mind is that researchers are always going to be hampered by not being able to explain the rules or aim of a game verbally. Were the 50 trials necessary to help the chimps to understand what the game was about? This is what we might expect from Boysen's (1993) study, described above, which suggests that chimps have a strong natural inclination to point to a baited container, not so much as an act of communication, but just as an imperative gesture. Perhaps the extensive training was necessary to help the chimps to overcome their natural inclination to gesture to the baited container. Alternatively, is it the case that chimps do not understand much about mind or deception, and therefore were only able to gesture in a way advantageous to themselves in a manner that was actually mindless? The chimps perhaps know nothing about mind, but simply act according to the behavioural rule that if they gesture to the baited cup in the presence of the nice trainer, then they get food, and if they gesture to the empty container in the presence of the nasty trainer, then again they get food. The findings are consistent with the chimps understanding something about dishonesty, and therefore mind, but the results are open to less interesting interpretations as well.

LINKING SEEING WITH KNOWING

Perhaps the most ingenious and convincing investigation of the chimp's conception of mind was conducted by Povinelli *et al.* (1990). The procedure had two parts, which was a special quality of the research, as will become apparent. In the first part, the chimp observed the trainer with a treat, which he deposited in a hiding place. The hiding places in the room were two upturned cups. A screen was erected between the chimp and the cups, so that although she could infer that the trainer had hidden the treasure, on account of his empty hands following its concealment, she could not tell which of the two cups housed the treasure. Subsequently, the screen was removed to reveal the two upturned cups and a second trainer arrived. Both trainers then pointed, one to cup A and the other to cup B. The chimp was then free to search under just one of the cups. The sensible strategy would be to search under the cup indicated by the trainer who did the concealing, since we can assume only he knew about the location of the treasure. Presumably the other trainer was just guessing, so it was possible that he could guess wrongly.

Initially, the chimps seemed to make an arbitrary choice. Eventually, however, they began to be more systematic, and tended to search in the place indicated by the person who did the concealing. After all, they were selectively rewarded for allowing themselves to be informed by this particular trainer. The problem we have at this point is the same one that arose from Woodruff and Premack's (1979) study. Why did the chimps take a long time to attend specifically to the gesture of the trainer who did the concealing? Is it because they learned mindlessly to pay attention to the person who handled the treat and was present throughout? If so, the chimps presumably had no deep understanding that this individual had *knowledge* of the whereabouts of the treasure. Yet it is not possible to engage a chimp in this kind of game without a lengthy training period. The drawback with research involving chimps is that we cannot instruct them with words as to what the task is about and what they are supposed to do. After all, the task is highly artificial.

The brilliant feature of this research is that it incorporated a second phase. In this, both trainers were present at the moment when the treasure was hidden, and a third person hid the bait. One of the trainers, who would later gesture, was a passive onlooker, while the other was standing beside him with a bucket over his head and therefore saw nothing (Figure 3.4). Finally, as in the first part of the procedure, the screen was removed to reveal the two upturned cups to the chimp, and the two trainers pointed. As before, the informed trainer, who had been a passive onlooker, pointed to the cup that actually housed the reward, while the guesser, who had previously sported a bucket as headgear, pointed to the empty cup.

Just suppose that the chimps had a genuine understanding that the person who watched the hiding knew the location of the treasure and was therefore qualified to announce its location accurately. Their experience in

 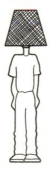

FIGURE 3.4 Chimps were more trusting of a message-gesture to indicate the location of food made by a trainer who had seen food being hidden than one who had not because he had a bucket over his head.

the first part of the procedure would have served to instruct the chimps to search in the place indicated by the informed person and to ignore the location indicated by the guesser. Hence the chimps should search correctly immediately; they had already benefited from the training necessary to figure out the peculiarities of this artificial game. So long as they had genuine understanding of the relationship between seeing and believing, they would be expected to search correctly in the place indicated by the trainer who saw where the treasure was hidden.

On the other hand, suppose the chimps came to discriminate between the two trainers in the first part of the procedure without any deep understanding of knowledge and ignorance. If so, presumably the chimps formed a mindless association between the trainer who was present throughout and gesturing to the place where the food was actually located. Without understanding why, perhaps the chimps just came to recognize that this was the individual who pointed to the place where the food was located. If that were the case, then in the second part of the procedure the chimps would revert to searching under the cups randomly, as was the case at the beginning of the first part of the procedure. This would happen because in the second part of the procedure both trainers were present throughout, including the time when the treasure was hidden.

The findings provided very strong support for the possibility that at least two of the four chimps who participated had a deep understanding of knowledge and ignorance. Two of the chimps were immediately able to discriminate between the two trainers, and allowed themselves to be informed exclusively by the informed trainer. A third chimp required a small amount of practice before she performed well, and the fourth required a lot more training. It seems that at least two of the chimps understood who had knowledge and who was ignorant, and did not just rely on gross cues such as who was present and who was absent.

RELATIONSHIP BETWEEN UNDERSTANDING KNOWLEDGE AND MIRROR SELF-RECOGNITION

It seems that an understanding of knowledge might be impossible in the absence of a capacity for mirror self-recognition. Two kinds of evidence testify to this, one on the level of inter-species differences and the other on the level of developmental differences. If a species does not evince mirror self-recognition, then it seems unable to understand anything about the concept of knowledge. For example, Povinelli *et al.* (1990) assessed the ability of monkeys to allow themselves to be informed specifically by a trainer who had witnessed the hiding of treasure, in preference to a trainer who also pointed but did not witness the hiding. No matter how much training the monkeys received, they were never able to discriminate between the two pointing trainers. Consequently, the question of whether the monkeys could transfer their good performance to the second part of the procedure never even arose. As I reported earlier, monkeys are highly intelligent animals in many respects, but show no sign of recognizing their own image as themselves in mirrors. Instead they persist in reacting to their own image in a hostile manner, as if it was an unfamiliar monkey.

With regard to human children, signs of mirror self-recognition are seldom shown prior to the age of 18 months. A typical 15-month-old child will search the area behind the mirror, as though expecting to see another infant there. If she has a conspicuous spot of rouge on her forehead, and it only becomes apparent to her when she sees herself in the mirror, she will look with interest and may even finger the mirror in the region of the bright red dye, but she will never use the mirror as a guide to touch her own forehead. In sharp contrast, a 24-month-old child is likely to reach promptly to her own head on seeing the peculiar blemish reflected in the mirror. Povinelli and DeBlois (1992) presented to children the task that Povinelli *et al.* (1990) had devised for chimps, i.e. two research assistants each pointed to a different upturned cup. The child had previously observed that one of the assistants had witnessed the hiding while the other had not, on account of the fact that she had a paper bag over her head. From about the age of 36 months and above, children began to allow themselves to be informed selectively by the assistant who had witnessed the hiding of the treasure. Prior to that age, children chose one cup or the other randomly. Povinelli (1993) suggests that it is a necessary developmental sequence for children to acquire an understanding of their own individual uniqueness and to develop a rudimentary self-concept (as shown by recognition of oneself in a mirror), before they are able to understand that knowledge varies between people.

Interestingly, a developmental trend similar to that in humans also emerged in chimps. Povinelli *et al.* (1993) report that not until about 6 to 8 years of age do chimps begin to recognize their own image in a mirror. As with children, it was only the chimps who had already acquired a conception of themselves who were able to discriminate between a trainer who knew the location of food and one who was ignorant of it. It thus seems that passing the mirror self-recognition test portends an understanding of self that captures the distinction between 'me' and 'others'. Unlike monkeys, perhaps apes and humans are able to appreciate the implications of recognition of one's own uniqueness. If I am unique in my mental life and subjective experiences, then that means that what I think, feel, want, know, hope, wish and intend is not necessarily shared with others. That is, mental life varies between people. Expressed in this way, the faculty of self-awareness allows you to begin to speculate about the mental state of other individuals. The finding that monkeys lack self-awareness makes sense of the finding that they show no notion of the existence of other minds. Being capable of self-awareness might be a necessary preliminary step in the long odyssey toward understanding other minds.

LIMITATIONS IN THE CHIMP'S CONCEPTION OF MIND

Chimps appear to have a remarkable understanding of mind, but it would be foolish to pretend that they match humans in this respect. Instead of being content with celebrating what chimps can do, Povinelli and Eddy (1996b) conducted a major research programme to explore the limit of the chimp's conception of mind. This built upon the success of the earlier work by Povinelli *et al.* (1990), which showed that chimps regard the communication (pointing gesture) from a trainer who saw the hiding of a treat as more reliable than that of one who did not see. It seems that Povinelli was troubled by a lingering doubt about how much his chimps' success in discriminating between two trainers was due to pure insight and how much it was due to the toil of learning to respond correctly according to a mindless strategy. For example, perhaps the chimps learned to trust the trainer whose face was visible throughout. In the study by Povinelli *et al.* (1990), the face of only one of the trainers was visible for the entire duration of the study. In the first part of the procedure the other trainer's face vanished when he left the room, whereas in the second part of the procedure, the same occurred when the trainer placed a bucket over his head.

In the new research, Povinelli and Eddy (1996b) used a different procedure which the researchers hoped would not engender a lengthy training phase. One component of the chimp's natural repertoire of behaviour is a begging gesture, in which the chimp assumes a distinctive posture and extends one hand with palm face-up. This is a request for food, and is something chimps do spontaneously without any prior training. When hungry, chimps routinely approach their trainers and beg for food. Povinelli and Eddy questioned whether chimps understand much about the psychology of begging. At the most basic level, there would not be much point in begging in front of someone who could not see you, but that would only occur to you if you understood the relationship between seeing and knowing.

Chimps were ushered into a testing chamber within the laboratory, where they obediently sat on a crate. In one control condition, a trainer was sitting in front of the chimp and had access to a food reward situated nearby. The chimp could not grab this herself because there was actually a transparent partition separating the chimp from the trainer. However, this screen had holes in it that allowed the chimp to extend her hand through in order to beg the trainer to give her the food. Chimps did this quite readily and spontaneously, and the trainer obliged by handing over the reward. Under another control condition, two trainers were present, one of whom held food while the other held a block of wood. The chimps easily discriminated between these two individuals by directing their begging specifically to the trainer who had the food.

Having established that chimps are comfortable in discriminating between a pair of trainers, according to which of them is in possession of food, Povinelli and Eddy (1996b) then investigated whether the chimps could discriminate according to who was in possession of the *knowledge* of food and who could see the chimp's gesturing. Food was placed on the table adjacent to the trainers. One of them was facing forward and therefore could see both the food and the chimp, while the other sat with his back to the chimp. Would the chimps beg specifically to the trainer who could see them? The answer was that they did, and no period of preliminary training was required to enable them to make the appropriate discrimination. Does this mean that chimps understand about the relationship between vision and knowledge?

To find out whether this is the case, Povinelli and Eddy (1996b) conducted a sequence of studies to establish more precisely what chimps understand about the eyes in particular as a window of information out into the world. Recall from the previous chapter that Povinelli and Eddy (1996a) demonstrated that chimps are at least able to calculate the target of another individual's line of sight. Moreover, they recognize that solid opaque objects serve as obstacles to the line of sight. Does it follow that chimps grasp that what people see imprints itself as knowledge on their minds? Put the other way round, would they understand that someone who has not perceived a critical fact must remain in a state of ignorance? The research of Povinelli *et al.* (1990) addressed itself to these kinds of issues but, as I mentioned previously, seeds of doubt had been sown in Povenelli's mind about exactly how rich the chimp's understanding of the relationship between seeing and knowing might be.

Povinelli and Eddy (1996b) continued their investigation by confronting chimps with two trainers, one wearing a blindfold over his eyes and another wearing a gag over his mouth. Unlike the findings in the previous procedure involving a trainer facing forward and one facing backward, the chimps did not show any discrimination at all between these trainers, one of whom could see while the other could not. In another test, one trainer covered his eyes with his hands, while another covered his ears. Again, the chimps did not discriminate between them. In yet another test, one trainer had a bucket over his head, while another held the bucket over his shoulder in such a way that his view was unimpeded. Finally, both trainers sat with their backs to the chimp, but one turned to look over his shoulder in the direction of the chimp. Again, the chimps did not discriminate between these two individuals. Figure 3.5 depicts some of the pairings of trainers. The findings of Povinelli and Eddy (1996b) are both vivid and striking. The spectacle of a chimp begging to a blindfolded person, when a sighted person is sitting right next to him, does seem very peculiar, and is revealing of the chimp's limitations in understanding the relationship between seeing and knowing.

Having said that, with repeated testing the chimps did begin to discriminate appropriately between the trainers. However, this was not based so much on who could or could not see, but on whose face was visible or invisible. The chimps first started to discriminate between a trainer with a bucket over his head versus one without, and one with his back turned but looking

FIGURE 3.5 Chimps found it easier to discriminate between a pair of trainers when one had his face in view while the other did not. They do not appear to attach significance to the eyes in particular when deciding who does and who does not know something.

over his shoulder versus one with his back turned but looking straight ahead. Their learning was not restricted to these particular manipulations, since they were able to discriminate between two trainers, one with a screen in front of his face, and the other with the screen over his shoulder. So long as the face of only one of the trainers was visible, even in this novel condition, the chimps made the appropriate discrimination in their begging gesture. They still had not grasped the importance of the eyes, though, and were content to beg to a trainer with his eyes closed just as readily as to one with his eyes open.

As a point of comparison, Povinelli and Eddy (1996b) adapted their procedure to allow young human children to participate. The children were confronted with two experimenters, both of whom had access to prized stickers. The children had to make a gesture to one or other of the experimenters in order to request a sticker. One experimenter had no impediment to his vision, while the other was unable to see because he was wearing a blindfold, or for some other reason as in the procedure involving chimps. Even 2-year-old children easily discriminated between the two experimenters, and preferentially directed their gestures toward the experimenter whose vision was unimpeded.

Evidently, chimps are limited in what they understand about the eyes as a perceptual window on the world, and are much more limited than very young humans. They do appear to have some primitive understanding of who knows and who does not know, but do not readily grasp the role of the eyes as transducers of information. Although it is striking that chimps lack the ability to discriminate between two people specifically according to their visual access, perhaps we should caution against being overly pessimistic. We take it for granted that we understand the eye's role in acquiring visual information. However, suppose a higher form of intelligence, such as an alien with advanced intellect, were to test humans on their understanding of seeing and knowing. Suppose that two 'trainers' of our human participants wore spectacles, and that one of them was wearing ordinary sunglasses, while the other was wearing glasses with special lenses that allowed him to see the ultraviolet part of the spectrum. In front of these two trainers was a reward, but only ultraviolet light radiated from it, and it was therefore only visible to the trainer with ultraviolet spectacles. Now we, as participants, might eventually deduce that only the participant with ultraviolet spectacles has privileged visual information, but this would not be obvious initially. The alien researcher might conclude that humans have a limited understanding of the relationship between seeing and knowing. For example, most humans lack any explicit understanding that normal vision does not extend into the ultraviolet part of the spectrum of light (although obviously a trained physicist would understand this). Hence the alien might conclude that there is a severe limitation in the human conception of mind, especially with respect to the relationship between seeing and knowing. The point I am trying to make is that understanding the link between seeing and knowing is not absolute but relative. We understand more about this than chimps, but I would not like to conclude that we have this understanding whereas chimps do not.

The second point I would like to make is that we should not overlook the finding that chimps succeeded in learning to discriminate between trainers on a sensible basis, even if not strictly according to the cue of who could and who could not see. We are assuming that there is a selective advantage in the Darwinian sense to understanding the link between seeing and knowing; any individual who was born with this knowledge would have a selective advantage over those without it. It goes without saying that in a group of individuals who lacked this knowledge, an advantage would be gained by one who was capable of learning about the link. We might say, then, that there would probably be an evolutionary progression as follows: (1) knowing nothing about the link between seeing and knowing and not being able to learn anything about the link – monkeys seem to be in this category; (2) being born without full knowledge of the seeing-knowing link, but having the capacity to learn about the link – chimps seem to be in this category; and (3) being born with considerable knowledge of the seeing-knowing link, or at least with an aptitude to learn about it easily – humans seem to be in this category. Viewed in this way, the chimp's receptivity to learning something about the link between seeing and knowing indicates that its conception of mind is of an impressive quality.

Chimps have a well-developed conception of mind compared with monkeys, but when compared with humans their deficiencies become apparent. Chimps are receptive to other minds and have an aptitude for learning about them. This is evident in several respects. First, they show a capacity for rudimentary comprehension of human language (at least this is true of the bonobo). Second, they have a rudimentary self-concept that allows them to distinguish themselves from other individuals. Third, they are capable of learning how to make deceptive gestures selectively to a person who would cheat them out of a reward. Fourth, they understand (or are capable of understanding) much about knowledge along with the link between seeing and knowing. This capacity is most apparent with respect to understanding the target of another individual's line of sight, in conjunction with understanding that opaque obstacles represent a barrier to what is seen. Their understanding also allows them to discriminate in a rather gross manner between two people, one of whom has experienced informational access to a fact while the other has not. Despite all this, chimps are no match for humans. They do, however, possess the necessary credentials for having a degree of political sophistication. They seem to have a sensitivity to others that includes some understanding of their psychological states that is bound to help them to function effectively in a complex social organization that requires some understanding of self in relation to others. The successful chimp has to be a politician. Finally, then, let us return to considering the chimp (or bonobo) as a social creature living skilfully in harmony with others.

CHIMPANZEE SOCIETY

Understanding minds permits sophisticated social co-ordination, which in turn gives rise to society. To gain a feel for how chimps use their social intellect, we shall examine the social behaviour of chimps within their naturally created societies. For a more detailed account of this, see de Waal (1995).

Chimps patrol their territory and the area beyond it in exclusively male bands. They hunt monkeys and other mammals, and then return to their home base to share their spoils with the females. Their hunting band works efficiently owing to the trust that develops from members having close bonds with one another. This enables each member to work co-operatively and selflessly. The band will be structured in a power hierarchy, where junior members defer to the authority of elders. If a band of chimps encounters another band of unfamiliar chimps from a totally different community, mortal combat is likely to ensue. In consequence, females greatly outnumber males, and inevitably sexual relationships tend to be polygamous. Chimps are unquestionably tribal and territorial creatures, and are entirely intolerant of males from another community. However, males are willing to accommodate females from alien communities. It is only the females who migrate between communities, and even this is not particularly common. Male chimps are dominant, and will subdue females with brutal violence on occasion. They make use of stones and sticks as primitive weapons and tools. For example, they use stones as hammers to crack nuts, and they use sticks to draw termites from their nests.

Bonobos have quite a different temperament and character. They lack the aggression of chimps and inhabit a matriarchal society. The females seem to enjoy highest status, even though they are of smaller stature than the males. A male will remain strongly bonded to his mother until she dies, and the status he enjoys will be determined largely by the importance his mother assumes within the community. Bonobos are not great meat eaters and hunting is not a major activity. This could explain their more placid temperament, compared with chimps who perhaps need to be aggressive in order to be effective as hunters. The strongest bonds to be found in bonobo society exist between adult females.

Both chimps and bonobos display emotions by means of intricate facial expressions. They exhibit a repertoire of emotional contortions unlike that of any other animal, apart from humans of course. Both creatures also show a considerable capacity for play as juveniles. de Waal (1995) has reported the common game of blindman's buff, in which a bonobo will cover its eyes with its hand and then blunder about bumping into objects and other members of the band just for fun.

With regard to politics and persuasion, bonobos are quite different to chimps. Chimps often attempt to influence others by throwing their weight around in a display of brute force. In contrast, the more placid bonobos seem to achieve the same outcome by trading sexual favours as a form of diplomatic currency. For example, on stumbling across a supply of food, bonobos promptly indulge in frantic copulation before feasting. According to de Waal (1995), this ritual helps to consolidate a communal attitude of caring and sharing; it helps to ward off individualistic greed, which could rear itself in principle when the band is confronted with a wealth of nourishment.

Sexual activity also features prominently in reconciliations. If a pair of bonobos have quarrelled, they will then typically make up subsequently with the aid of sexually stimulating actions. Two females will rub their genital regions together, while two males might take turns in mutual scrotal rubbing. Indeed, bonobos compare only with humans in their indulgence in sexual activity for purely recreational as opposed to reproductive purposes. Also like humans, they often copulate face to face. In contrast, other primates, including chimps, mate in the manner of dogs. The significance that sex has assumed in bonobos is apparent from the oestrus cycle. Females are sexually receptive and therefore attractive to males almost continuously, whereas chimp females are receptive to males for only about 6 days of each month.

Both chimps and bonobos create complex social structures within their societies that are based on bonds of affection and respect. Chimps maintain their social order to a large extent through aggression and submission. In contrast, bonobos appease and charm each other with sexual favours. The social structure of both species has a complexity that demands a social intellect to ensure that individuals get along together in a way that is mutually advantageous and avoids exploitation. Presumably those with greater social wisdom are destined to have a profitable life in terms of status, reproductive rites and priority in feeding. The intriguing social intellect of our ape ancestry has endowed us with a legacy that we have exploited with dividends. We are now ready to take a detailed look at the human conception of mind in order to examine how it develops and what happens when it goes wrong.

4

BACKGROUND OF AUTISM

INTRODUCTION

Apart from the fact that autism is a disorder that deserves special attention and concern, the study of autism is particularly relevant to investigations into the development of a conception of mind. A claim made within the last couple of decades is that autism practically amounts to either a deficient or a deviant theory of mind. It is very difficult to specify what a conception of mind is in all its complexity and richness, particularly since it is a faculty that we unreflectingly take for granted. By analogy, it is almost impossible to specify precisely how we generate and process spoken language. If we were able to specify this, then we might be able to program a computer to comprehend speech, but this technological achievement is a long way off. Generating and processing language is something we do expertly without knowing how. Similarly, we have a remarkable talent for understanding other minds, yet we are ignorant of the exact nature of the necessary processes. One way to try to understand what it means to have a human conception of mind is to explore what happens when development goes wrong to a point where such a conception either fails to develop at all, or develops abnormally. We thus potentially stand to gain insight into the development of a conception of mind by studying the unfortunate case of autism.

HISTORY

Autism was first identified as a disorder in its own right in the mid-twentieth century by two physicians working independently and in ignorance of one another. They were Leo Kanner, working in the USA, and Hans Asperger, working in Austria. Because of the relatively recent discovery, it does not necessarily follow that autism is a modern disorder, like AIDS. It just means that prior to Kanner's and Asperger's landmark papers, people afflicted with autism were assigned a different diagnostic label. Those who were severely autistic, to a point where they showed little speech or aware-ness of other people, may have simply been labelled as 'imbeciles'. People with autism who were more intellectually able, and perhaps even gifted in some domains, may have been labelled as 'idiot savants', or diagnosed as suffering from childhood schizophrenia.

In fact, childhood schizophrenia is no longer recognized as a clinical cate-gory, and an individual must be aged 18 years or older to be diagnosed as having schizophrenia. Schizophrenia is a mood disorder in which, in classic cases, the individual hears voices that are perceived as forming a part of reality. Hence the individual loses the ability to distinguish between reality and the product of the imagination. When coupled with paranoia, the voices assume a more sinister character, telling the individual that others are conspiring against him or her. These characteristics are quite distinct from the defining features of autism. Like people with schizophrenia, peo-ple with autism are socially isolated, but that isolation is of a different order and occurs for different reasons.

Autism is usually detected from the age of about 4 years or older. This does not necessarily mean that autism is typically acquired at 4 years of age. Rather, it is a syndrome that affects behaviours and abilities that first make their appearance at about this age. By analogy, an individual might have abnormalities in his or her reproductive organs that have negative conse-quences for the progression toward the adolescent hormonal balance that is characteristic of puberty. In turn, this may hamper the development of pubescent characteristics. Although the individual may have had this unfor-tunate condition since birth, it would only be manifest outwardly from a certain stage in development and thereafter. In the case of young children, we see a burgeoning of social awareness at the age of about 4 years, and autism that has remained latent until then might inflict serious constraints on that vital period of development.

So the picture we have is that children who are diagnosed as having autism usually receive this diagnosis at the age of 4 years or older. If they are older, this almost certainly does not mean that they have acquired autism at an older age. Rather, it would be a question of applying a new label to existing patterns of behaviour. Hence, children do not 'acquire' autism, and neither does the autism progress in those who are identified as being affected by the disorder. A child diagnosed as having mild autism will not develop severe autism. On the contrary, there is much adaptation and compensation from other domains of development that allow the individ-ual to cope with the autism to some extent. Having said that, there is no known cure for autism, although programmes of special education can be dramatically successful in the developmental advances that can be achieved with hard work and much patience.

In some respects, the development of autism resembles that of Down's syndrome. As with autism, children with Down's syndrome have the condi-tion from birth, and there is no cure at present, although adaptation and development can and do occur. A less marked similarity concerns learning difficulties, which are a characteristic of Down's syndrome and are also common in autism. Approximately two-thirds of children with autism have an IQ score in the range that identifies them as having learning difficulties (70 or less). Around 40 per cent of children with autism have an IQ of 50 or less. However, some people with autism can have a normal or even above-average IQ. The percentage is hard to calculate, because the autism becomes more difficult to diagnose, or escapes diagnosis altogether, with increasing intelligence. It is likely that between 5 and 30 per cent of children with autism have a normal IQ or even a score that is better than average. It is impossible to determine whether autism necessarily impairs IQ. Although some people with autism have an above-average IQ, it is possible that their IQ would have been even higher had they not been afflicted with autism. It might be the case, however, that there is such a thing as 'pure autism', a condition that cruelly inflicts social debilitation on the individual but otherwise leaves him or her unaffected.

There is an important medical sense in which Down's syndrome and autism are very different. Down's syndrome is classified according to a chromosomal abnormality. Due to an error in the production of the egg by the mother, there will be two chromosomes at site 21, when in fact there should be only one contributed by the mother. Hence, when the mother's chromosomal contribution is combined with that of the father there will be three chromosomes at site 21 rather than two. Strictly speaking, Down's syndrome is diagnosed on the basis of detection of that chromosomal abnormality. If it so happened that the afflicted individual miraculously showed none of the characteristics of Down's syndrome, he or she would still receive that medical classification. If the individual did not manifest any of the learning difficulties or any of the physical features of Down's syndrome, this would make no difference to the diagnosis. Autism is completely different. The diagnosis depends on the presence of characteristic behaviours in accordance with a specific social, affective and cognitive profile. An individual who matches the profile is autistic by definition, and one who does not match it is not. This effectively amounts to an admission that we do not know the cause of autism, and neither do we know much, if anything, about its physiological basis. Indeed, it might be that there are multiple causes and it is possible that there is no one-to-one physiological correlate. We shall explore these issues later. However, at this point, what is coming into focus is the image of autism as a syndrome that is defined and maybe understood in terms of behaviour and whatever affective or cognitive factors underlie it. We shall now detail the behavioural manifestations of autism.

STORIES

In order to gain some impression of what it means to say that an individual is autistic, we shall begin by looking at fictional stories, and also one that is reputedly factual. Two examples of autism spring to mind in the recent history of cinema. One is Rain Man, in which Dustin Hoffman portrays a socially debilitated individual who has an aptitude for obscure probability calculations that allows him to win a fortune at gambling. The character Hoffman plays apparently has little or no social insight, and as a direct consequence is bereft of friends. He is absurdly naïve and therefore at the mercy of an unscrupulous and Machiavellian brother who exploits him extensively. The autistic character is also highly literal in his interpretation, as though he does not conceive of any meaning that lies behind the literal words of the message that are uttered. These peculiarities are portrayed in the film, which provides a fair insight into what it means to be autistic. Another, rather more remote portrayal of autism, this time perhaps unintentional, is to be found in the character of Mr Spock, the famous Scientific Officer in Star Trek. Mr Spock is supposedly a Vulcan, which excuses his autistic tendencies, but if he were human, then he might just be diagnosed as suffering from Asperger's syndrome, i.e. mild autism which would typically occur in the absence of conspicuous secondary impairments.

In a sense, Mr Spock epitomizes the paradox of autism. On the one hand, he has remarkable logical capacities. Indeed, his talent for logic is portrayed rather romantically as benefiting from being free of the emotional and intuitive baggage that we normally regard as the essential human qualities. On the other hand, Mr Spock is apparently mystified by emotional connectedness and bonding between people. Whilst he seems to have a primitive conception of loyalty, it does not extend to emotional warmth and caring. Note that Mr Spock is not a particularly shy individual. It is not the case that autism is just the extreme of a continuum of introversion. Some people can be socially isolated owing to extreme introversion, but such 'hermits' may have a perfectly good intuition about people. Using Spock as an example, people with autism can be far from introverted, yet still be unable to form any sense of connection with another person.

The final story is that of the Wild Boy of Aveyron. In France, toward the end of the eighteenth century, a feral child was captured. The boy, named Viktor, was aged about 12 years at the time. He caught the attention of intellectuals because one topic they enjoyed debating around the dinner table was whether the savage was noble or a beast. Does civilization tame our otherwise wild nature, or alternatively are we good and peaceful creatures in our natural state who can become perverted by society? The capture of Viktor seemed to promise some answers to these ancient questions. The eminent physician E.M. Itard tackled the challenge of offering Viktor patronage, and set about the arduous task of educating him. However, it eventually became apparent that Viktor's education was a virtually impossible goal.

His manner and exploits suggest that he was autistic, according to Frith (1989). He was described as being unable to form attachments with anyone. He did seem to show some preference for his caretaker, but this was largely instrumental, rather than being based on a developing bond of affection or loyalty. He would show interest in his caretaker when food or some other treat was on offer, but only then. Indeed, it was almost impossible to gain

Viktor's attention. If a plate were smashed right next to him, then he might not even flinch. On the other hand, if he heard or saw something that would satisfy his immediate needs or wants, then he immediately tried to grasp it. For example, he was partial to walnuts, and if he heard the distinctive sound of a nut being cracked open behind him, then he promptly turned round and snatched it from the hand of whoever was holding it. He behaved in this manner whether the person holding the nut was well known to him, or whether it was someone he had never seen before. At dinner, in the company of cultured guests who were observant of etiquette, this situation made no difference to Viktor. He entered the room, made directly for the riches of food organized elegantly on the table, and stuffed his mouth and then his pockets with anything within reaching distance. The astounded guests observed the spectacle with horror.

After a couple of years of education and enculturation, Viktor's mentor, E. M. Itard, escorted the boy to the house of a prominent socialite for a dinner party. As usual, Viktor seemed to be oblivious to the presence of other people. He gobbled down the food, and then stood up and left before the other guests had barely begun to eat. Shortly afterwards, the guests watched aghast as he ran across the lawn naked and scrambled up a tree. Apparently his clothes served no useful purpose to him and merely impeded his free movements, so he dispensed with them!

In periods when Viktor was not so lively, he would huddle in a corner of the room and rock back and forth, sometimes for long periods of time. He appeared to be devoid of an inner mental life and to lack imagination, and had nothing to occupy him apart from the largely impulsive or reactive behaviour that he exhibited during his lively moments. His gaze also seemed to suggest an absence of mental activity. When we interact with a normal person, we can often sense the 'cogs turning' in their mind, which are betrayed by tell-tale shifts in gaze, from one object or person to another. Apparently these clues were absent from Viktor's gaze, which gave the impression of a blank expression and a blank mind.

Viktor did not learn to speak, but he did make vocalizations. These were often rather shrill animal-like noises. His posture was equally ungainly and inelegant. He seldom actually walked anywhere but scampered or ran, as if whatever had caught his eye had to be reacted to or dealt with instantly. According to Frith (1989), all of these mannerisms and traits contribute to a portrait of Viktor as an archetypically autistic boy. So in answer to the question, 'what is autism like?', the case of Viktor serves as a useful illustration. Having said that, the portrayal of this boy does appear something of a caricature compared to typical cases of autism. That might be because he just happened to be a rather colourful example of this syndrome, or it might be that the story-telling of his exploits was embellished with some artistic licence.

An obvious question that arises is whether isolation from other people during his formative years led to Viktor's apparent autism. According to Frith (1989), it is much more likely that it was his autism that led his family to desert him. It is possible that they cast him into the wild as it dawned on them that he was substantially abnormal. If that were the case, then it is likely that he was not living in the wild from an early age. Indeed, it is difficult to imagine how any child could live under those harsh conditions, let alone a psychologically handicapped one. Apart from this, Viktor did not suddenly appear out of the blue. In fact he was known to the village people, who used to leave food out for him. However, they had only seen him around for 2 years prior to his capture. The circumstantial evidence suggests, then, that he was probably abandoned at about 10 years of age, 2 years prior to his capture. It seems correct to use the term 'capture' here, since Viktor shunned human contact, and only ventured near the village in order to obtain food during the winter. In this case, social isolation seems not so much a cause of his autism as a consequence of it.

DEFINING AUTISM

The Autistic Society provides a highly informative leaflet, which captures the essence of autistic behaviours (Figure 4.1). Some of the characteristics of autism that are portrayed in this leaflet are as follows. The child has difficulty with social relationships, and he or she will show little or no interest in participating in group activities or playing with other children. Although some normal children who are shy require prompting and encouragement to play with other children, they soon become immersed in the activity and appear to abandon their inhibitions. In contrast, children with autism are not so much shy, but rather seem to derive no satisfaction from being a part of social events. When in the context of a social event, the child's abnormal gaze prevents him from becoming involved in the activities. When another person looks at the child and addresses him, he will not reciprocate with a mutual gaze, but might look in another direction as though utterly uninterested. In social situations, just as in other circumstances, children with autism can be prone to bursts of laughing, giggling or tantrums that appear to be totally unconnected with anything that is going on.

The lack of interest in social events shown by autistic children is compounded by impairment of verbal and non-verbal communication. Some severely autistic children, especially the younger ones, do not speak at all. They may communicate non-verbally purely for instrumental purposes, e.g. grasping an adult's hand as though it were an inanimate object that is to be set in motion to carry out a task that will satisfy the child. The child might take the adult's hand to the drawer that contains chocolates and place it on the handle, as though that would be sufficient to prime the routine of the adult opening the drawer and handing the chocolate to the child. Those who do speak sometimes engage in inappropriate echolalia, which is to repeat in a parrot-like manner an utterance they have just heard, whether the utterance was directed at them or just something they overheard. This tendency for echolalia gives the impression that they are confused about the use of per-

Autism is...

a perplexing life long mental disability affecting more than 115,000 people in Britain today. Isolated in a world of their own, people with autism need help to fit in. The first step towards progress is recognition of the condition.

These pin people illustrate *some* ways in which autism is displayed.

Displays indifference

Joins in only if adult insists and assists

One-sided interaction

Indicates needs by using an adult's hand

Does not play with other children

Talks incessantly about only one topic

ARE YOU GOING? *AREYOU GOING?*

Echolalic – copies words like parrot

- Difficulty with social relationships
- Difficulty with verbal communication
- Difficulty with non-verbal communication
- Difficulty in the development of play and imagination
- Resistance to change in routine

Bizarre behaviour

Inappropriate laughing or giggling

Handles or spins objects

FAMILIAR ROUTE   DIFFERENT ROUTE

No eye contact

Variety is not the spice of life

Lack of creative, pretend play

But some can do some things very well, very quickly but *not* tasks involving social understanding

Early diagnosis is essential if people with autism are to achieve full potential. It is only when their disability is understood that they can be helped to maximise skills and minimise problems.

For more information contact:

THE NATIONAL AUTISTIC SOCIETY 276 Willesden Lane London NW2 5RB Telephone 0181-451 1114 Reg. Charity no. 269425

Graphic design based on illustrations used by Prof. J. Rendle-Short, Australia and National Society for Autistic Children, USA.

FIGURE 4.1 Leaflet issued by the Autistic Society, summarizing some of the behaviours characteristic of autism. Reproduced with kind permission of The National Autistic Society, London, UK.

sonal pronouns. They sometimes call themselves 'you' and another person 'I'. More verbal children with autism characteristically talk insistently about a single topic for a protracted period, no matter what cues emanate from the other person suggesting that they cannot tolerate much more.

When offered toys, a normal child will readily incorporate them into part of a more general drama that he or she creates from imagination. This is the hallmark of pretend play. A child with autism does not do this. He or she will merely organize the toys in straight lines, or arrange them in stacks of towers, or spin them. More generally, the lack of imagination is apparent in their resistance to a change of routine, or variety in activities.

On the other hand, some children with autism seem to be gifted in certain activities. Famous examples are the drawings of Stephen Wiltshire and Nadia. Both of these young autistic artists capture tremendous realism and detail in their line drawings. The drawings are not just remarkable because they seem awesome by the standards of the average adult, but because they are entirely unlike the drawings of normal children. The drawings made by normal children are highly characteristic, and depict not so much the scene as it appears, in the manner of a photograph, but more what the child knows of the scene. For example, if drawing a car from a side view, they might attach wheels to the roof as well as to the base of the car in order to ensure that all four wheels appear in the scene. In fact, only the two wheels facing the child would be in view from the child's perspective. In general, normal children seldom adhere to the principles of scale and perspective in their drawings. In the drawings by Nadia and Stephen, the perspective and viewer-specific details are present in abundance. It is as though they see the world as a camera does, in that their knowledge of what they are seeing does not contaminate how they construe it – unlike the situation in normal children.

Other people with autism can develop numerical obsessions which enable them to make obscure calculations of the day of the week of any particular date during the last century. Similarly, some individuals develop an obsession with train or bus timetables and are able to announce details of times, routes, destinations, and so on, when this information is requested. Other people with autism can show remarkable musical talent, with an astonishing capacity to remember tunes in detail after a single hearing, and the ability to repeat these on an instrument.

DIAGNOSIS: KANNER, ASPERGER AND THE TRIAD OF IMPAIRMENTS

Kanner described two cardinal features with respect to autism. These are autistic aloneness and the obsessive insistence on sameness. By autistic aloneness, he meant that it is impossible for the child with autism to experience a meeting of minds. He did not mean that children with autism are merely extremely shy and withdrawn. As I mentioned previously, an irony of autism is that it is possible for the individual to be in the presence of a throng of social activity, yet to have no sense of the human contact that non-afflicted people enjoy. Kanner went on to assert that people with autism are severely impaired in their ability to experience affective contact with others. They have a poverty of facial expression and a failure to focus gaze on a particular object, which suggests that they are attentionally vacant. This impression is strengthened by the further observation that people with autism appear to be highly impulsive and stimulus-driven. Their actions do not seem to be the result of carefully formulated plans, but rather people with autism appear to be compelled to react to whatever stimulus bombards them. None the less, Kanner acknowledged that people with autism can show signs of a good logical aptitude. In summary, children with autism can appear to have considerable intelligence, paradoxically coupled with a profound lack of common sense.

The diagnosis of autism is undertaken by a psychiatrist, who makes a professional judgement based on an interview with the child and its parents, together with psychological tests that can be administered. The psychiatrist's wisdom stems from clinical experience, coupled with the guidelines detailed in check-lists for diagnostic criteria. The most widely accepted check-list is provided by the American Psychiatric Association and, at the time of writing, many existing diagnoses of autism will be based on the version entitled DSM III or IIIR. Items on this check-list include, for example, 'Pervasive lack of responsiveness to other people', which is intended to capture the state of autistic aloneness. The list also draws attention to impairment of language and communication with 'Gross deficits in language development' and 'If speech is present, peculiar speech patterns such as immediate and delayed echolalia and pronoun reversal'. With regard to insistence on sameness, the check-list probes this with 'Bizarre responses to various aspects of the environment (e.g. resistance to change)...'. To differentiate between autism and other disorders such as schizophrenia, the check-list insists that there should be an 'Absence of delusions, hallucinations, loosening of associations and incoherence'.

Further items include '...inability to be consoled when upset...', '...lack of appropriate fear reactions...' and 'abnormalities of speech, such as question-like melody or monotone robotic-like voice'. The psychiatrist is also guided to be on the alert for an inability to form friendships with other children, an absence of pretend play, and a lack of imitation of adults.

A common misconception of autism is that it amounts to a severe aloofness. Consequently, worried parents may sometimes think that their rather reserved child might be autistic. However, in the vast majority of cases where parents fear that their toddler is not relating to people in the appropriate way, it usually turns out that the child is not autistic. It might be the case that the child has learning difficulties, but not necessarily. On the other hand, many of the children who do eventually receive a diagnosis of autism are referred for clinical assessment in the first instance because their language development is unusually slow, or conspicuously abnormal. Some children with autism do not speak much before the age of 4 or 5 years. However, it does not follow that a child who has seriously delayed language development is autistic. Indeed, only a minority of such children do receive that diagnosis eventually. Some of them might instead be diagnosed as having a hearing difficulty, while others might have a different kind of developmental disorder. There is an asymmetry here, in that whilst delay or peculiarities in language development certainly do not necessarily imply autism, a child who is diagnosed autistic will almost certainly show problems with language development.

In a ground-breaking article, Wing and Gould (1979) characterize autism as consisting of a triad of impairments in the domains of socialization, communication and imagination. They conducted a survey of all the children living in Camberwell, south London, who were below the age of 15 years. In total, the survey included 35 000 children. In the initial phase, the aim was to identify from official records any child who had severe learning difficulties, social impairment, delayed or abnormal development in communication or an insistence on following routines or a tendency toward repetitive behaviour. There were 132 children who fell into one or more of these categories. The children were then subdivided into those who were socially impaired (74 children) and those who were not socially impaired (58 children). Of the socially impaired children, 17 individuals had the classic symptoms of autism. The 74 socially impaired children showed the triad of impairments listed above. This led Wing and Gould to characterize autism as a syndrome that involves a constellation of impairments. It seems that there is an underlying factor that unifies the triad, such that if there is an autistic impairment in socialization, then inevitably there will be related impairments in communication and imagination. The children who had learning difficulties but otherwise were not characterized by any one domain of the autistic triad tended not to be impaired in the other domains of the triad either.

It seems that autism occurs at an incidence of approximately one or two per 1000 live births. In Wing and Gould's (1979) study, if a very strict criterion of classic autism is adopted, then the prevalence is about one per 2000 live births. On the other hand, if the criterion is based simply on the triad of impairments, then the figure is closer to one per 500 live births. Approximately similar figures were obtained by Lotter (1966), who surveyed all children aged between 8 and 10 years in the county of Middlesex with postal questionnaires addressed to teachers, and by scouring medical archives. A total of 35 children conformed to Kanner's description, giving a ratio of approximately one per 2000 live births.

Curiously, autism is related to the sex of the child. Boys outnumber girls by a ratio of approximately 4 or 5:1. Certainly the ratio is of this order among the higher ability people, usually those labelled as having Asperger's syndrome or mild autism. In the more seriously affected population, boys still outnumber girls, but by a ratio of 2:1.

THE CAUSE OF AUTISM

In fact the cause of autism is unknown, but research has thrown up some clues. It is extremely likely that there is no single cause, just as paralysis can be caused by a bang on the head, by a virus, by a genetic defect, or by other traumas and accidents. What matters, probably, is the site of the damage, not how that damage came about. We should also try to rule out certain possible causes, the most obvious of which is parental style.

Several decades ago, a common view was that autism resulted from 'refrigerator parenting'. This is an interpersonal style that is aloof and lacking in warmth or affection. The myth was fuelled by Kanner and Eisenberg (1956), who reported that of a sample of 23 children with Asperger's syndrome, 11 children had fathers who appeared to be socially impaired and lacking in imagination, with a consequent restricted range of esoteric if not intellectually stimulating interests. A typical example is compiling a scrapbook on the various shapes and sizes of electricity pylons. It seemed hardly surprising that any child who experienced the bizarre domestic regime that must have prevailed with such parents should, as a direct consequence, acquire peculiar values and patterns of behaviour.

However, there are at least two lines of evidence that argue against parenting as the causal factor. The first is that autism seems to strike indiscriminately to a substantial extent. It has no respect for boundaries of social class or family environment. It can affect a child who has extremely warm and loving parents, and who has siblings without any trace of autism. At the very least, then, parenting cannot be the sole cause. In any case, another way of interpreting the results of Kanner and Eisenberg's (1956) study is to conclude that autism is heritable, and clues to autistic tendencies are likely to be present in the parents of children with autism. Even if the parent does not have full-blown autism, some autistic mannerisms might be present.

The genetic evidence has been reviewed by Piven and Folstein (1994). The issue of interest is the rate of concordance between siblings and twins. In other words, given that one child in the family has autism, what is the probability that his twin brother or sibling will also have it? The answer is that if they are ordinary siblings or fraternal (non-identical) twins, then the rate of concordance is slightly less than 3 per cent. Although the figure is very small, it is in fact about 50 to 100 times greater than would occur if the children were not related to one another.

Ordinary siblings share 50 per cent of their genetic constitution with each other. Identical twins, on the other hand, share 100 per cent of their genetic constitution. Several studies have investigated the rate of concordance for autism in these individuals, and the figures that they yield range between 30 per cent and 80 per cent. The figures probably vary so widely because they all involve such small samples. Autism is rare, and so are identical twins, and the prospects of finding autism in a member of an identical twin pair are therefore very remote. Consequently, an additional twin pair either with or without concordance in autism can radically shift the percentage of concordance. The least we can do is to draw two conclusions. First, it seems most likely that there can be a genetic component to autism. It would be difficult to explain the relatively high rate of concordance in identical twins relative to ordinary siblings if that were not the case. Second, there must be an environmental component. If the factor were exclusively genetic, then there would be 100 per cent concordance for identical twins. Hence, conducting a survey with identical twins not only suggests a genetic component, but also confirms the role of environmental factors. Note that when I say 'environmental', I am not necessarily alluding to the social or emotional environment of the family. Environmental factors could include the diet, exposure to toxins, the trauma of birth, or a host of other factors that convert a genetic risk into an autistic reality.

The genetic component of autism is illuminated to an extent by studies of concordance not of autism but of the associated language impairments and learning difficulties. In the case of identical twins, if one has autism, then sadly it is almost a certainty that if the other does not, he or she will have a more general intellectual impairment. There is also an elevated risk of intellectual impairment in the ordinary siblings of a child with autism. The figure seems to be of the order of 10 per cent, according to Piven and Folstein (1994). These authors also report a survey conducted on the parents of children with autism, providing a more detailed analysis than the earlier one conducted by Kanner and Eisenberg (1956). They conclude that approximately 30 per cent of parents who have children with autism show at least some autistic mannerisms, e.g. deficiency in turn-taking during conversation, such as speaking for too long or too short a period, or having difficulty with the timing of turns and interjections, with the consequence that they frequently speak at the same time as their conversational partner. Such parents were also prone to misinterpreting or not even noticing implied meanings of their conversational partner's utterance. In contrast, parents of children with Down's syndrome, who served as controls, showed no such difficulties compared with ordinary members of the population.

A further way of exploring the heritability of autism would be to conduct a survey on the child of a parent who has autism. However, in practice this is impossible, since there is only one known instance of a person with autism having a child. This rarity seems to arise because autism produces severe social isolation, and the prospect of the unfortunate individual finding a partner, or having any interest in doing so, is exceedingly remote.

Until now, we have considered the genetic factor as having a fairly direct causal relationship with autism. However, there is at least one clearly established indirect causal link between genes and autism. This is the case of phenylketonuria (PKU), a condition caused by a single pair of defective genes, one transmitted from each parent. A child who had one defective but one intact gene would be a carrier of the disorder rather than a sufferer. The children of parents who are both carriers have a 25 per cent risk of inheriting the disorder and a 50 per cent risk of themselves becoming carriers. Possession of such a pair of defective genes means that the intestine fails to synthesize an enzyme that is essential for breaking down a certain amino acid (phenylalanine) in the diet. This amino acid then enters the blood-stream in its unaltered state and acts as a neurotoxin, which means that it destroys brain tissue. The problem can be rectified almost completely by feeding the child on a diet free of phenylalanine, but this would depend on diagnosing the condition at an early stage.

Children with PKU who go undiagnosed and therefore receive an ordinary diet from their parents are destined to suffer from learning difficulties, sometimes severe ones. They are also at very considerable risk of being diagnosed as autistic. Consequently, it seems likely that the damage caused by the neurotoxin phenylalanine tends to affect a site in the brain that, among other things, gives rise to autism. Here we have a simple genetic cause of autism that is mediated by an environmental factor (diet).

Another genetic risk seems to be associated with fragile X syndrome. This is a condition that affects boys, but can be carried by girls. It seems that defective genes are carried on the X chromosome, and the Y chromosome, being smaller, has no corresponding gene that could compensate. Consequently boys, who by definition have an XY complement (girls are XX), acquire fragile X if they inherit this kind of faulty X chromosome. Fragile X syndrome is the second most common genetic cause of learning difficulties (the first being Down's syndrome). Apart from suffering from learning difficulties, those who are afflicted with the condition tend to have a prominent jaw and large ears. It seems that there might be a small risk of autism in such individuals, which might be approximately of the order of 10 per cent, according to Piven and Folstein (1994). However, the risk is certainly not as great or as clear-cut as with PKU.

The evidence arising from genetic studies contributes substantially to a picture of autism that stems from an abnormality in the structure of the brain. It remains a possibility that this unknown abnormality does not inevitably create a condition of autism, but only does so when present in conjunction with certain environmental contingencies. Some of these contingencies may even exist in the social environment, but if so they are likely to play a very small role. Certainly, it would be cruel and unfair to blame the parents, who already have a great deal to contend with in caring for a child with autism, without having to carry the extra burden of guilt that they would experience if blamed for the disorder. It is also possible that autism could be caused by a virus or by an accident, e.g. from complications that can arise during birth. There is no single cause, then, although the evidence does converge in implicating a physical abnormality of the brain. The next obvious question to ask is where that abnormality is located.

THE SITE OF AUTISM WITHIN THE BRAIN

Nobody knows what part of the brain causes autism when it is damaged. Certainly the autistic brain differs from the normal brain, but as yet it has been impossible to pinpoint a focal area. We shall confine the discussion briefly to three possible sources of abnormality. The first is the lack of a division of mental labour distributed between the two hemispheres of the brain. In the normal brain there are differences between the hemispheres both in anatomical terms and according to functional criteria. Perhaps the most obvious difference is related to language. In the vast majority of the population, the language-processing centres are located predominantly in the left hemisphere, especially in people who are right-handed. In such individuals the right hand is controlled by the left hemisphere, owing to the crossing over of nerve fibres between brain and body. In autism, it seems that this hemispheric specialization with regard to language may not be so prominent. This is evident from studies which have monitored the electrical activity of the brain, and found that there is more of a symmetry in autism than we might expect in clinically normal people. In one sense, this finding is not surprising. Given that we know language and communication are impaired in autism, implying that the left hemisphere would not be as active in this respect as in normal people, it is to be expected that this would be reflected in measurements of brain activity.

Another area that is implicated, although in the absence of hard evidence, is that of the frontal lobes. Non-autistic adults who suffer an injury to certain parts of the frontal lobe that does not necessarily involve the site of primary language production can be left with specific impairments in social interaction. Without becoming extroverted, they can appear to lose their inhibitions, with the result that they engage in antisocial behaviour in public that might normally be reserved for the confines of privacy. It is as though they act on impulses as and when a need arises. Such individuals are also known to lose the capacity for tact and discretion. In addition, they have a tendency to interpret statements over-literally and appear to experience attentional inflexibility. They lose interest in other people, and show no desire to participate in social interaction or to have the company of other people. In these cases, afflicted individuals are said to be suffering from frontal syndrome. They certainly would not be diagnosed as autistic, but some of the symptoms have an uncanny resemblance to those found in people diagnosed as having mild autism or Asperger's syndrome. This has led researchers such as Baron-Cohen and Ring (1994) to engage in elaborate speculation on how abnormality in certain regions of the frontal lobe might be involved in autism. However, to date this hypothesis has received no support from anatomical evidence.

On the other hand, there is a fair amount of evidence to implicate the cerebellum. This is a structure located at the rear and beneath the brain, which nestles between the occipital lobe and the brain stem. On first consideration, it seems a rather unlikely structure to feature in autism. Until recently, its function was thought to be in regulating the rhythm of movement, along with its rate, force and accuracy. Even on that level, however, there could be a superficial connection with autism. One of the behavioural manifestations of autism that sometimes occurs is an awkwardness of gait, together with lack of fine control of speech sounds. These peculiarities could certainly arise from abnormalities in the cerebellum. What is very much more controversial is whether the cerebellum has a role in imagination, social behaviour and general understanding of mind. According to Schmahmann (1994), this could well be the case. He speculates that just as the cerebellum regulates the execution of behaviour, so it also regulates the speed, flexibility and appropriateness of cognitive processes. He bases his speculation on anatomical evidence showing the existence of neuronal pathways that allow information to be received from and transmitted to areas of the cerebral cortex that are the seat of thinking and planning. Meanwhile, several studies have reported abnormalities in the anatomy of the cerebellum that seem to be specific to autism (e.g. Courchesne *et al.*, 1988; Bauman and Kemper, 1994). To date, then, the best evidence seems to implicate the cerebellum as the physiological substrate involved in autism. However, it remains a possibility that abnormalities in this structure are a consequence rather than a cause of autism. It might still be the case that an abnormality resides further upstream, so to speak, which has a knock-on effect with regard to the development of the cerebellum.

The physiological basis is certainly unlike that of paralysis. The paralysis an individual suffers, perhaps due to stroke or injury, can be detected at the physiological level in a living brain with the aid of a positron emission tomography (PET) scan. The patient takes a minute amount of radioactively labelled sugar, which can then be detected through bone and flesh as a computer-generated image. The computer highlights different concentrations of the sugar by means of different colour codes. Areas of the brain which remain dark suggest that there is focal damage in that region. When these kinds of imaging study have been conducted on people with autism, no 'hole' in the brain can be detected (Horwitz and Rumsey, 1994). Whatever the physiological basis of autism, then, it is subtle and not focalized.

CONCLUSIONS

The purpose of this chapter was to offer a picture of the various facets of autism that serve as a vital backdrop for the investigation of specific cognitive and affective deficiencies that pinpoint impairments in the development of a conception of mind. To date, we have a description of the behavioural manifestations of autism, which strongly appear to implicate a lack of understanding of mind, but we have not yet defined precisely what form the lack of understanding of mind takes, and how it relates to the various manifestations of autism. Is there a single factor that could unify the symptoms of autism under a single cognitive umbrella? That is the question we shall face in the next chapter.

5

THEORY OF MIND HYPOTHESIS OF AUTISM

INTRODUCTION

We require a practical definition of 'conception of mind', that would have validity in unifying the components of the triad of impairments identified by Wing and Gould (1979). Perhaps what we need is a test of the child's understanding that people hold beliefs. Reality is not transparent to the mind. Instead, the mind constructs a mental model of reality that is assembled from information obtained via the sensory organs, from prior knowledge and from a process of inference. In common parlance, we say that people hold simple factual beliefs (as distinct from attitudes or religious beliefs). It is these beliefs that substantially determine how people will behave.

For example, if it is Smith's habit to attend church on Sunday, then to determine his behaviour it is not so much the day of the week that is significant but what day of the week Smith believes it to be. It so happens that usually the actual day of the week and the day Smith believes it to be are one and the same – unless he is suffering from a delusional disorder. This is demonstrated by the following. Suppose a mischievous acquaintance decided to play a joke on Smith by slipping a sleeping drug into his bedtime cocoa on Saturday evening, and the effect of the drug was to extend his period of sleep by 24 hours, so that Smith would wake not on Sunday but Monday. Because Smith, like the rest of us, is oblivious to the passage of time while asleep, he assumes it is Sunday when he wakes. What will he do next – go to work or go to church? Because it is Monday, he should be going to work, but that is not the relevant point. What matters is that he believes it is Sunday, and therefore he will go to church.

If you did not understand that minds hold beliefs, then you would probably be inclined to treat people as machines rather than as organisms that are striving to make sense of the world. You would not be oriented towards trying to help them to understand what is out there in the world or what is the meaning that lies behind the literal words of another person's utterance. Evidently, the individual would experience serious difficulty in relating to others and communicating with them, which accounts for the first two elements of the triad of impairments in autism. What about the final element, namely impairments in imaginative activities? In fact it would be possible, in principle, to have some capacity for imagination without being able to deploy it for considering the content of other people's minds. However, if one lacked a capacity for imagination to conceive of the hypothetical, then it would be impossible to acknowledge the existence of beliefs. Beliefs cannot be observed directly, so to understand their existence requires a leap of the imagination. A capacity for imagination, therefore, is necessary but not sufficient for understanding about the existence of beliefs. It would not be surprising if a lack of imagination coincided with a lack of understanding about beliefs, but the link between the two is perhaps not inevitable. In short, to claim that a lack of conception of mind in autism reduces to a failure to understand about belief makes eminent sense within the context of the triad of impairments introduced by Wing and Gould (1979).

All we need now is a test to probe the child's understanding of the existence of beliefs. If an individual can acknowledge beliefs, then perhaps he or she should be credited with having a theory of mind (Dennett, 1978). However, it would not do to ask the child to make a judgement about a person's true belief. Suppose Smith put his watch in his bedside drawer, and we asked a child who had observed the scene to judge where Smith thinks his watch is. If the child answered 'in his bedside drawer', we could not be entirely sure that the child was reporting Smith's belief: perhaps he or she was just reporting the true location of the watch. The child may simply interpret the question, 'Where does Smith think his watch is?' as 'Where is Smith's watch?'. We require a better test, one which shows that the child understands the difference between beliefs and reality. As mental models of reality, beliefs can actually be false. Therefore, a test of understanding false belief would suit our purpose admirably. Suppose while Smith was asleep, his wife moved his watch to the bathroom cabinet. Then the answer to the questions 'Where is Smith's watch?' and 'Where does he think his watch is?' should be different, namely 'bathroom' and 'bedside drawer', respectively. If a child were able to discriminate between belief and reality, a distinction that a test of false belief allows us to detect, then perhaps we should credit the child with a theory of mind (Dennett, 1978). If a child lacked a theory of mind, then perhaps he or she would fail to acknowledge false belief. Consequently, failing to acknowledge false belief could (although not necessarily) be a symptom that the child lacks a theory of mind.

UNDERSTANDING ABOUT FALSE BELIEF

Investigations into the development of understanding of false belief in normal development were pioneered in seminal work by Wimmer and Perner

(1983). They devised the unexpected transfer test, which involved telling children a story enacted with small dolls, which is depicted in cartoon form in Figure 5.1. The story was about a boy called Maxi, who had a bar of chocolate. The scene was Maxi's kitchen and, not being a greedy boy, he decided to save some of his chocolate to eat later, so he deposited it in the green drawer (Scene 1). He then left the room to play outside. In his absence, his mother appeared and started to make a cake. In doing so, she needed some of Maxi's chocolate to decorate the cake, so she took it out of the green drawer, used some, and then returned what was left to a different drawer with a blue exterior (Scene 2). Subsequently, Maxi returned and wanted to finish off his chocolate. Observing child participants were asked where Maxi would look for his chocolate.

Wimmer and Perner (1983) observed a sharp developmental trend, which is shown in Figure 5.2. The majority of children aged 4 and 5 years

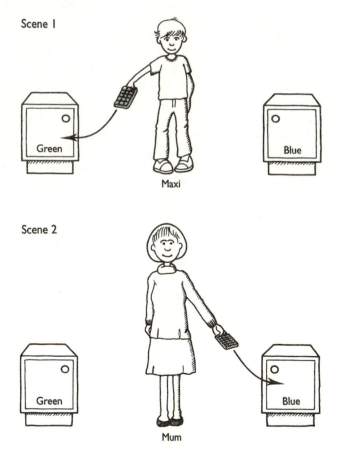

FIGURE 5.1 Unexpected transfer test of false belief. Maxi puts his chocolate in the green drawer and then leaves. His mother transfers the chocolate to the blue drawer in Maxi's absence. Observing children judge where Maxi will look for his chocolate when he returns.

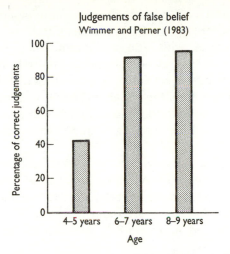

FIGURE 5.2 Children's ability to acknowledge Maxi's false belief in the unexpected transfer test. Note the sharp improvement in correct judgements between 5 and 6 years of age.

judged wrongly that Maxi would look in the blue drawer where it was at present. They were judging as though they had been asked 'Where is Maxi's chocolate?' rather than 'Where does Maxi think his chocolate is?'. In stark contrast, nearly all the children aged 6 and 7 years took into account the falseness of Maxi's belief, and judged that he would search in the place where he last saw his chocolate.

This research has at least two methodological virtues. The first is that the presentation of a memory question allowed the researchers to argue that the children's difficulty was specific to their lack of understanding of belief and not due to more general difficulties in comprehending or remembering the vital elements of the story. At the end of the story, the children were asked, 'Do you remember where Maxi put the chocolate in the beginning?'. Eighty per cent of the children who had wrongly judged that Maxi would search in the place where his mother had left the chocolate (in the blue drawer) none the less correctly recalled that in the beginning he had put the chocolate in the green drawer. Their memory for the sequence of events was good, but apparently they were unable to use that knowledge to impute a false belief to Maxi.

The other strength of the research is that the children were not asked to comprehend or define mental state terms. On the face of things, one might suppose that an investigation into what children understand about mind and belief would involve asking them profound philosophical questions that would mystify even adults. Yet as Wimmer and Perner (1983) demonstrated, it is possible to make an inference about what the child understands of beliefs and mind by asking a harmless question about where Maxi will look for his chocolate. Children's difficulty, then, is due to their lack of understanding of mind itself, and not due to misunderstanding the obscure vocabulary that philosophers use to discuss the mind.

What about children with autism? Would they have difficulty in acknowledging false belief? Indeed, dare we begin to think that autism ultimately reduces to a failure to acknowledge false belief? If that is how autism should be characterized, then the social and emotional impairments typical of that disorder would be secondary to a cognitive impairment. This would amount to an enormous breakthrough with regard to how we should construe autism.

The seminal study was conducted by Baron-Cohen *et al.* (1985). They retained the vital elements of Wimmer and Perner's (1983) unexpected transfer story, but introduced modifications to make it shorter and simpler, and more appropriate in content for older children. Their story was about two dolls called Sally and Ann, and it is depicted pictorially in Figure 5.3.

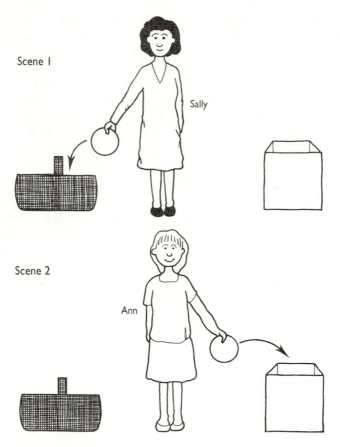

FIGURE 5.3 Adaption of the unexpected transfer test for children with autism. Sally puts her ball in the basket and then leaves. Ann moves the ball to the box in Sally's absence. Observing children judge where Sally will look for her ball when she returns

Sally had a basket and Ann had a box. Sally put her marble in the basket, and then departed (Scene 1). In her absence, Ann transferred the marble to the box (Scene 2). Sally was about to return for her marble, and observing participants had to judge where she would search.

The results are shown in Figure 5.4, which indicates how striking the poor performance of the children with autism was specifically when they were answering the belief question. Unlike the clinically normal children aged 4½ years that they tested, the great majority of children with autism judged wrongly that Sally would look in the place where her marble was at present, as if they had been asked 'Where is Sally's marble?'. In other words, they made the error that is characteristic of clinically normal young children – yet the mean age of the children with autism was 12 years. Their serious difficulty with the task could not be explained by a general failure to comprehend the story, since they had no difficulty in recalling that the marble was originally in the basket.

Perhaps the children with autism had difficulty in judging Sally's belief not specifically because of their autism, but because of their more general learning difficulties. In particular, it would not be surprising if they had difficulty with this verbally based task if their verbal mental age was less than 4 years. We would not expect a clinically normal child below that age to succeed in acknowledging Sally's false belief. In fact, the mean verbal age of the children with autism was about 5½ years, and if we look at the data only from the children with a verbal mental age above 4 years, we still find little or no sign of an ability to acknowledge false belief.

If the difficulty experienced by children with autism was due to their general learning difficulties, then we would expect to find that other children with learning difficulties but without autism would struggle to acknowledge Sally's false belief. For example, we might expect children

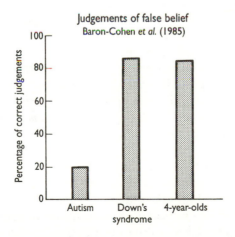

FIGURE 5.4 Children's ability to acknowledge Sally's false belief in the unexpected transfer test. Note the relatively poor performance of the children with autism.

with Down's syndrome to fail in this task. Fortunately, Baron-Cohen *et al.*
(1985) included a control group of children with Down's syndrome in their
study. The great majority of these children succeeded in acknowledging
Sally's false belief without difficulty, despite being slightly younger on average than the children with autism, and despite having a slightly lower verbal mental age. Hence it did seem that the difficulty experienced by
children with autism was specific to acknowledging false belief, which in
turn stemmed from their autism and not from their more general learning
difficulties.

CRITICISMS OF THE SEMINAL STUDY

Although in many respects the study by Baron-Cohen *et al.* (1985) is very
rigorous with regard to the controls that were employed, there are two
fairly obvious impediments to a straightforward conclusion that children
with autism have a specific difficulty in acknowledging false belief. The first
relates to the fact that children with autism have difficulty engaging in
imaginative activities and make-believe. de Gelder (1987) pointed out that
the children with autism may have experienced difficulty in acknowledging
false belief not because they had an impaired conception of mind, but
because their autism prevented them from becoming immersed in a story
that required them to suspend disbelief. If de Gelder is correct, then the
findings of Baron-Cohen *et al.* tell us no more than we already know,
namely that children with autism have difficulty engaging in make-believe.
The second impediment to a straightforward interpretation of the results,
which is linked to the first, is that, since Sally is merely a doll, she has no
mind and therefore the question concerning the content of her beliefs does
not arise.

Leslie and Frith (1988) overcame these methodological problems by
incorporating the unexpected transfer test of false belief into a real-life interaction. The child participant was in the company of both researchers, and
all three co-operated in depositing a penny underneath an upturned cup.
Subsequently, Frith departed, whereupon Leslie and the child conspired to
transfer the penny to an adjacent upturned cup. Frith then returned and
the child participant was asked to predict where this researcher would look
for it. As was found by Baron-Cohen *et al.* (1985), the great majority of children with autism who participated predicted wrongly that Frith would
search under the cup that they knew it was currently hidden beneath.
Hence their difficulty in acknowledging false belief was not confined to a
procedure that involved mindless dolls.

Leslie and Frith (1988) included a control group of children with learning
difficulties who belonged to a different category to those tested by Baron-
Cohen *et al.* (1985). Whereas the latter authors had demonstrated that children with Down's syndrome were able to acknowledge false belief, Leslie

and Frith assessed whether children with specific language impairments, but without autism, would succeed in acknowledging false belief. In many respects, children with a specific language impairment are a better match for children with autism. As noted in the previous chapter, autism is frequently most conspicuous as a language and communicative disorder. None the less, the children with specific language impairment but without autism, who were matched with the autistic sample in chronological and verbal age, generally succeeded in acknowledging false belief. Again, the evidence was converging on the possibility that serious developmental delay in acknowledging false belief is specific to autism.

Although Leslie and Frith (1988) succeeded in re-creating the unexpected transfer test within a real-life interaction, the difficulty children with autism seem to experience with false belief would appear even more striking if they failed a variety of different tests of false belief. Perner *et al.* (1987) came to the rescue with the 'deceptive box' task (see Figure 5.5). The child participant is shown a familiar box, such as a 'Smarties' tube. He or she is asked to guess what is inside, and quite sensibly will usually reply 'Smarties' or 'sweets'. The experimenter then opens the lid to reveal that, surprisingly, there is only a pencil inside. After the child has acknowledged this, the experimenter returns the pencil to the tube and closes the lid to restore it to its initial state. Finally, the child participant is asked to anticipate what another child, who has yet to look inside the tube, will think it contains, or will say it contains. Perner *et al.* presented this simple test to clinically normal children aged 3 to 5 years. Their results were similar to those of Wimmer and Perner (1983), in that the older half of the sample tended correctly to anticipate that the next child would mistakenly think the tube contained Smarties. In sharp contrast, the younger children typically judged that the next child would think that

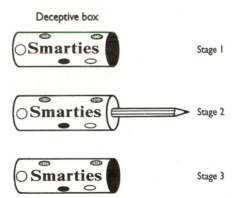

FIGURE 5.5 The deceptive box task has three main stages. In the first stage, the child sees the box for the first time and guesses its content. In Stage 2 the unexpected content is revealed and then returned to the box. Finally, the child is asked to make a judgement of belief – either own prior belief, or another person's past, present or future.

the tube contained a pencil. Once again, the younger children responded as though they had been asked 'What is inside the box?' instead of 'What will Johnny think is inside the box?'

This task lends itself to an investigation of children's ability to acknowledge their own prior false belief. Instead of asking the child participant to judge what another person will think is inside the Smarties tube, we could ask her to judge what she herself thought was inside the tube when she first saw it and before we opened the lid. This is precisely the modification that Gopnik and Astington (1988) introduced, and they found that children aged 3 years had at least as much difficulty acknowledging their own prior false belief as they did in anticipating another person's future false belief. Those who made errors answered the question as if it had been 'What was inside?', rather than 'What did you think was inside?'. Moreover, the children who experienced difficulty in acknowledging their own prior false belief tended to be the very same children who failed to anticipate another person's false belief.

Despite the sharp age trend that the researchers observed, it was not just a case of the younger members of the sample failing all the questions, while the older children passed them all. If that were the case, then the correlation in performance between the two kinds of judgement of belief might just be coincidental to the more general improvement in both tasks with increasing age. However, Gopnik and Astington (1988) were able to apply sophisticated statistical analyses which showed that the relationship between performance on the two tests of false belief was maintained independently of their mutual relationship with chronological age. Gopnik and Astington concluded that there is a single cognitive deficit in the young children that explains their poor performance across a variety of tests of false belief. They asserted that at approximately 4 years of age, clinically normal children benefit from a radical conceptual shift in their thought that equips them with a representational theory of mind. This theory of mind is a theory of all minds, including their own. Children who did not understand that minds hold beliefs, would also fail to grasp that their own minds hold beliefs, and therefore would not conceive that they could ever entertain a misapprehension about anything.

Working on the hunch that children with autism do not experience the conceptual shift that is an essential feature of normal development, Perner *et al.* (1989) proceeded to present the deceptive box test to children with autism. What they found concurred entirely with the results reported in the previous studies on autism (Baron-Cohen *et al.*, 1985; Leslie and Frith, 1988). The great majority of the children wrongly judged that another person would think that the tube contained a pencil. They also failed to acknowledge their own prior false belief. They answered as though they had been asked 'What is inside the tube?' in both cases. Like clinically normal young children, then, the children with autism did not appear to understand that minds hold beliefs, whether it was their own mind in question or that of another individual.

Clinically normal young children have another related difficulty – in acknowledging the difference between appearance and reality. Flavell *et al.* (1983) showed clinically normal children a sponge that was disguised with paint to look like an authentic rock. The researchers showed the object to the children and asked them what it was. The children were fooled by the fake, and answered 'rock'. They were then allowed to finger the object, whereupon they learned that its true identity was a sponge. Finally, they were asked what it was really and what it looked like. A common pattern of error in the children aged 3 years was to answer that the object was really a rock and that it looked like a rock. In contrast, older children correctly answered that it looked like a rock but was really a sponge. Gopnik and Astington (1988) found that children who had difficulty in acknowledging their own prior false beliefs, and false belief in others, also tended to experience difficulty in acknowledging the difference between appearance and reality. Gopnik and Astington suggested that, in order to understand about misleading appearances, the child must grasp that the mind constructs models of reality – models that can be erroneous. In other words, only minds can be seduced by surface appearances, when the underlying reality is different. Understanding the difference between appearance and reality is tantamount to understanding the existence of mind, so it is not surprising that children who fail to acknowledge false belief also fail to acknowledge the difference between appearance and reality. What about children with autism? Baron-Cohen (1991a) showed his participants the fake rock and they behaved in much the same way as the clinically normal children aged 3 years tested by Flavell *et al.* (1983), that is, they failed to differentiate between appearance and reality.

Altogether, then, the picture is emerging even more sharply to suggest that children with autism have a specific difficulty acknowledging false belief that perhaps is the essence, in cognitive terms, of their disorder. If children with autism do have a specific difficulty in acknowledging that the mind holds beliefs, then we can proceed to make various predictions about what tasks they will or will not be able to perform successfully. The relevant evidence will be discussed in the next section.

IMPAIRMENT OF COMMUNICATION

Autism is often conspicuous as a linguistic and communicative impairment. In particular, children with autism appear to be substantially lacking in common sense when they interpret other people's requests, to the extent that they interpret speech too literally – sometimes to the point of absurdity. For example, if asked 'Can you pass the salt?', a child with autism might characteristically reply 'Yes', as though the utterance had been a request for information rather than action. Anybody with an ounce of common sense would realize that the speaker already assumes that one has the physical ability to pass the salt, and therefore his request must be an invitation to act by handing over the salt. Can we make a precise link between failure to understand false belief and excessively literal interpretations of speech, which are the hallmark of autism?

Josephine Isaacs and I set out to address precisely that question (Mitchell and Isaacs, 1994). We 'borrowed' a procedure that we had created previously to assess the development of interpretation of utterances in clinically normal children (Robinson and Mitchell, 1992). Since it seemed that the difficulty experienced by children with autism was not to do with general story comprehension, but specifically with understanding the mentalistic features, we presented a scenario to them in story form. The story is depicted as a cartoon in Figure 5.6, although we enacted the version presented to the children with small dolls. In this, 'Mum' has two bags that contain balls of wool. She puts one of these in the drawer and the other in the cupboard, and then leaves to go into another room. In her absence, John

FIGURE 5.6 In Scene 1, Mum puts one bag in the drawer and the other in the cupboard. In Scene 2, John swaps the bags round without Mum's knowledge. Finally, Mum requests one of the bags by location (the bag in the drawer). It is appropriate to interpret this non-literally to mean that she wants the bag in the cupboard.

arrives, gets the bags out in order to play with them, and then puts them back when he has finished. The important thing is that he gets the bags mixed up and swaps them round. Later, Mum was still in the adjacent room and had begun to knit a jumper. She needed one of the bags of wool in order to finish this task, and it was very important that she got the correct bag, or her jumper would look silly. She called through to John, 'I need one of the bags of wool. It's the bag in the drawer.' Observing child participants were invited to get Mum the bag she really wanted.

Of course, the bag that Mum wants is not the one in the drawer, as she says, but the one in the cupboard. We can make this simple inference on recognizing that Mum had formulated a mental model of the bags' locations that corresponded to the places where she had left them. In her mental model, the bag that is in the drawer is, in present reality, in the cupboard, owing to the fact that John swapped the bags round. If we take Mum's request to refer to her mental model, and then relate that to the present scene, we find that the bag she wants is in the cupboard. This seems like rather a complex process for interpreting Mum's request non-literally, yet in practice it is something we find easy to do with barely a second thought. Indeed, it is so simple that even most children aged 4 and 5 years correctly reach to the cupboard (Robinson and Mitchell, 1992). The good performance of these children appeared even more striking when compared with their judgements in a control condition. This involved a story that was almost identical except that, when John had finished playing with the bags, he returned them to exactly the same places as Mum had put them. Subsequently, Mum made the same request, and observing child participants were asked to interpret this by a question worded in precisely the same way. This time, the children correctly interpreted literally by reaching to the drawer. Hence, whether or not children interpreted non-literally, depended upon whether the speaker of the utterance was in possession of an outdated belief. This task thus offers a precise link between failing to understand false belief and interpreting speech too literally.

We wasted no time in presenting the same task to children with autism (Mitchell and Isaacs, 1994). Predictably, they interpreted Mum's request literally whether she had a true belief (John returned the bags to the places where Mum had left them) or a false one (John swapped the bags round). This was despite the fact that the children with autism had a verbal mental age above 4 years. In contrast, as we had found previously, many clinically normal children of that age succeeded in interpreting the request non-literally, specifically when it was appropriate to do so. In a further study, we found that the majority of children with Down's syndrome, who were matched for chronological and verbal age to the children with autism, also succeeded in interpreting non-literally, specifically when this was appropriate (Mitchell *et al.*, 1996c).

In the follow-up study, we also asked a vital control question, namely 'Which is the bag Mum put in the drawer?'. To answer correctly in either version of the story requires no understanding of the mind. All the child has to recall is that the bag that was originally in the drawer is currently in the cupboard when John has swapped the bags round. The children with autism easily discriminated between the two versions of the story when answering that question. They answered correctly that the bag Mum had put in the drawer was now in the cupboard specifically when John had swapped the bags round. When John returned them to the same places where Mum had left them, the children answered correctly that the bag Mum had put in the drawer was still in the drawer. In this respect, the good performance of the children with autism was indistinguishable from that of the clinically normal children aged 5 years and the matched children with Down's syndrome; their difficulty was specific to a condition that required a non-literal interpretation from a speaker who held a false belief. In summary, these studies show how a failure to conceive of mind could be directly connected with a tendency to interpret speech over-literally.

Autistic impairments linked with a deficient theory of mind are evident not only in the interpretation of speech, but also in speech production. Children with autism give the impression of being naïvely honest, which might be because they are unable to grasp the significance of telling a lie. Lies can lead the victim of the message to believe something that is false. Hence, an understanding that lies can serve to conceal the truth from another person might only be possible if one understood that people hold beliefs that can either be true or false. Perhaps children with autism seldom tell lies because they do not understand the special significance of lies with respect to false belief. Sodian and Frith (1992) conducted a systematic investigation into the ability of children with autism to tell lies to a nasty thief who wanted to steal a treat from them. The treat was deposited in one of two miniature treasure chests. A character then entered the scene in the persona of the nasty thief, who explicitly demanded the treat and interrogated the child participant as to its whereabouts. The children with autism had the opportunity to tell lies by saying that the treat was in the empty box, but instead they seemed to be compelled to report its true location, thus surrendering the treat to the thief.

It might have been that the children felt reluctant to resist the thief's demand. However, that possibility was eliminated with a control condition, in which children could prevent the thief from obtaining the treat not by telling lies but by locking the baited treasure chest. The children with autism had no difficulty in succeeding in this task, which led the authors to conclude that the children with autism were able to sabotage the thief's efforts, but were unable to effect the same outcome by means of lies. It seemed that the children with autism wanted to thwart the thief's attempt to obtain the treat, but were helpless to use a lie to that end. In contrast, clinically normal children aged 4 and 5 years succeeded in telling lies in the required strategic manner. Altogether, we can see how a deficient theory of mind could lead to impaired verbal communication in autism, both in comprehension and in production of speech.

Children with autism show communicative impairments in the non-verbal as well as the verbal domain. Can we shed any further light on this peculiarity from the knowledge that they are lacking a conception of mind? Baron-Cohen (1989a) distinguished between pointing gestures that are imperative and those that are declarative. Suppose you asked a child what kind of sweets she wanted from the counter of a confectioners' shop and the child pointed. The pointing in this case is imperative, where the child expresses her wants by pointing. Now suppose that you are walking in the street when the child suddenly points across the road, where your eyes fall upon the spectacle of a colourfully attired clown. That pointing would be a declarative gesture, which serves to focus joint attention on an interesting experience.

The imperative gesture could be purely instrumental, functioning to deliver something of desire to the individual. On a drinks dispenser, you point to a button to select your desired drink and extend your finger so that it connects with the button, and then you receive the drink. Arguably, pointing imperatively requires no more understanding of mind than does pressing a button on a drinks dispenser. Both are just instrumental actions. In contrast, pointing declaratively serves no instrumental purpose. It is done merely to inform another individual, whom one might suppose would remain ignorant of the spectacle if one did not redirect their attention. Surely, however, one would only begin to think in that way if one grasped that people have minds that are actively striving to formulate a model of what exists out there in the world – a model which could become obsolete and inaccurate if it were denied access to the appropriate information. Baron-Cohen (1989a) thus predicted that children with autism would show understanding of imperative pointing but not declarative pointing.

To determine whether this was the case, Baron-Cohen (1989a) sat in front of his participants and made two kinds of pointing gesture and observed how the participants reacted. One category of gesture involved pointing to various objects that were distributed around the room. Children with autism reacted to these imperative gestures appropriately by fetching the target object and handing it over to Baron-Cohen. Another kind of gesture involved wandering over to the window and pointing to something out there that the child could not see from where he was sitting. Children with autism made no reaction to these declarative gestures, but assumed a blank expression. In contrast, matched children with Downs syndrome and clinically normal children above the age of 4 years reacted appropriately by joining Baron-Cohen at the window and looking at whatever he was pointing to. Presumably, these children were eager to discover something new – something that they did not yet know. In contrast, perhaps the children with autism had no conception of their own ignorance, in which case they would not appreciate the need to go and seek out new information.

What about the production of gestures? Phillips *et al.* (1995) investigated the manner in which young children with autism (aged about 4 years) use gestures to make requests. Children were led into a room which was populated with a variety of toys that are known to be appealing to children with autism. Once a child began to show a preference for playing with one toy in particular, the experimenter took it from the child and placed it out of reach on a high shelf. How would the child go about trying to retrieve the object? They could make an imperative gesture to the experimenter, or they could behave as though the experimenter were absent and drag a chair over to stand on it in order to reach the high shelf.

The children with autism tended to rely upon two kinds of strategy. One was to ignore the presence of the experimenter and to drag a chair over. The other was to try to drag the experimenter over to the shelf with force, as though the experimenter were a heavy physical object that had to be shifted. When behaving in this manner the children with autism seldom made eye contact with the experimenter, which contributed to the impression that the experimenter was being treated as an inanimate object. In contrast, clinically normal children of a similar intellectual level (aged about 2 years) and children with learning difficulties, who were matched to the autistic sample with regard to intellectual level, behaved differently. They seldom dragged over the chair, but instead either dragged the experimenter over or more gently tugged at the experimenter whilst looking back and forth between the experimenter's eyes and the toy on the shelf. The authors concluded that the non-autistic children behaved as though the experimenter was a perceiving subject, whilst the children with autism were inclined to treat the experimenter largely as a non-sentient object, along with other inanimate objects. So even when children with autism gesture imperatively and instrumentally, there is evidence to suggest that they do not grasp the significance of another person's attentional focus.

We can see, therefore, that children with autism have difficulty with both verbal and non-verbal aspects of communication, in a way that seems to be linked specifically with their lack of understanding of mind. The 'theory of mind hypothesis of autism' not only states that children with autism have difficulty in acknowledging false belief, but it also sheds light on their communication impairments. It specifies the precise circumstances under which children with autism will struggle to interpret communications appropriately and to make communication themselves. We begin to see how the conspicuous communicative impairments in autism could fall under the umbrella of 'deficient conception of mind'.

IMPAIRMENT OF EMOTIONAL RELATEDNESS

Another conspicuous feature of autism is impairment of emotional relatedness with other people. Children with autism display an emotional indifference to others, and typically treat people they are very familiar with no differently from the way in which they treat complete strangers. Is it conceivable that this peculiarity in their emotional response is also secondary to a cognitive deficiency in failing to understand about beliefs? Baron-Cohen (1991b) set out to investigate this possibility. He told children a story about a character called Jane, and the observing child participants had to judge how she felt – happy or sad – in a variety of situations. In one sketch, Jane had cut herself. Here, children with autism correctly judged that she felt sad. In another sketch, she was having a birthday party, and children with autism correctly judged that she felt happy. From these judgements, it appeared that the children knew a good deal about emotion. Indeed, they judged just as well as clinically normal children aged 5 years and children with Down's syndrome.

The children with autism showed a good understanding of other people's emotions in another respect. They were informed that Jane liked Rice Krispies, and judged correctly that when she was given this kind of cereal in the story, it made her happy. On the other hand, they judged correctly that she felt unhappy when she was given cornflakes instead. However, the children experienced serious difficulty in judging whether Jane was sad or happy when they had to take on board her belief. Baron-Cohen (1991b) removed Jane (i.e. the doll) from the scene and swapped the contents of the Rice Krispies box with those of the cornflakes box. He asked the children how Jane would feel when offered the Rice Krispies box (which now contained cornflakes), and those with autism wrongly judged that she would be sad, while those with Down's syndrome and the clinically normal children aged 5 years correctly judged that she would be happy. He went on to ask the children how Jane would feel when offered the cornflakes box, and the pattern of results mirrored that yielded by the Rice Krispies condition, i.e. those with autism wrongly judged that she would feel happy, while the children with Down's syndrome and the clinically normal children correctly judged that she would feel sad.

These findings suggest that children with autism can make accurate judgements about how certain situations give rise to certain emotions, and they also seem to understand that if one has a desire that is not fulfilled, then that can lead to sadness. Evidently they are not fundamentally impaired in their understanding of emotions. On the other hand, they make incorrect diagnoses of emotion if such judgements depend upon making accurate inferences about false belief. Once again, then, a conspicuous peculiarity of autism, such as failing to understand emotion, can be explained by failure to understand about belief.

FURTHER DIFFICULTIES IN UNDERSTANDING ABOUT MIND

A symptom which indicates that children with autism do not understand about beliefs is that they fail a test of false belief. However, we assume from this that children with autism do not understand anything about any beliefs – including true ones. The fact that we present them with a test of false belief does not mean that we assume their impairment is confined to a lack of understanding about false beliefs. It is just that an effective way to reveal difficulty in understanding about belief is to present a test of false belief. If children with autism have a difficulty that extends beyond the specific case of false belief, as we suppose, then they should make tell-tale errors in other tasks that require understanding of beliefs and thoughts.

One quality of thoughts is that they lack a physical existence, and therefore do not have a persistent and enduring character (Wellman, 1990). Consequently, the thoughts of one individual are not available to be scrutinized by another individual, that is, thoughts are private rather than public. Do children with autism understand that thoughts possess this quality? To find the answer to this question, Baron-Cohen (1989b) told children with autism a story about a couple of characters called Sam and Kate, both of whom were hungry. For this reason, Sam's mother gave him a cookie. For the same reason, Kate was thinking about a cookie. Baron-Cohen asked the children who could eat the cookie, who could save it until tomorrow, and who could give it to a friend to eat. Clinically normal children aged 5 years and children with Down's syndrome correctly answered that only Sam could do these various things with the cookie. In contrast, the children with autism, who matched the children with Down's syndrome in their general verbal abilities, answered indiscriminately. They were just as likely to answer that Kate could eat the cookie as they were to answer that Sam could eat it. It was as though the children with autism could not comprehend what it meant when we say that someone is 'thinking about' something. Once again, the children with autism did not appear to understand that the mind thinks and holds beliefs.

Baron-Cohen (1989b) proceeded to ask children directly about the functions of the brain. He asked them where the brain was located and, as a point of comparison, he asked them where the heart was located. He also asked about the functions of these organs. The results are shown in Figure 5.7. The children with autism correctly judged the location of the brain and heart, as did children with Down's syndrome and clinically normal

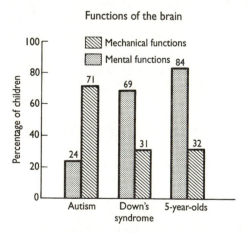

FIGURE 5.7 Children's judgements of the functions in the brain. The children with autism acknowledged mechanical functions even more than the other participants. In contrast, they tended not to acknowledge mental functions.

children aged 5 years. They also correctly judged that the heart is involved in the circulation of blood at least as well as the other two groups. However, when it came to judging the functions of the brain, their answers were quite unlike those of the other two groups of children. On the one hand, the children with autism correctly judged that the brain helps one to speak, to see and to walk. Curiously, the children with Down's syndrome and the clinically normal 5-year-olds tended not to mention the brain's role in these activities. Instead, they said that it is one's legs that make one walk, one's eyes that make one see and one's mouth that makes one talk. On the other hand, the children with autism very seldom judged that the brain makes one think, whereas the other two groups of children correctly acknowledged the brain's role in thought. In short, the children with autism tended to acknowledge the brain's role in mechanical activities but not in mental activities. The children with Down's syndrome and the clinically normal 5-year-olds showed exactly the opposite tendency.

Seemingly, children with autism are not completely unaware of the existence of the brain and all its functions. Indeed, they even appear to be especially well informed about its involvement in some mechanistic processes. However, they seem to be oblivious to the brain's mental activities. In the light of this intriguing study, it is hardly surprising that children with autism tend to relate to others as though they were machines rather than people.

CONCLUSIONS

The 'theory of mind hypothesis' of autism seems to be highly convincing and powerful. It is convincing in the sense that difficulty in acknowledging false belief seems to be peculiar to autism in those aged above about 4 or 5 years. It is a difficulty that remains robust across a wide variety of different methods of investigation. It certainly is not confined to a story method of testing, and is just as striking when the child is involved directly in a real-life interaction. The hypothesis is powerful in the sense that pinpointing a specific cognitive deficiency explains a wide range of behaviours that are characteristic of and specific to autism. Much if not all of autism is characterized by the triad of impairments, and this triad can be explained by reference to an underlying impairment of acknowledgement of the mind as an organ that formulates beliefs. We can see in a precise way how a failure to understand beliefs would confine the child to excessively literal interpretations of speech. In addition, we can see how a failure to relate to people emotionally could also be explained as an inability to comprehend their belief states. It seems that the difficulties experienced by children with autism in understanding emotion might be largely confined to those cases where they also have to infer belief. Given how appealing the theory of mind hypothesis appears, it might come as a very big surprise, therefore, to discover that a substantial amount of anomalous evidence is accumulating to undermine it. This is something we shall investigate in the next chapter.

6

BEYOND THE THEORY OF MIND HYPOTHESIS OF AUTISM

INTRODUCTION

It would be an outstanding breakthrough if we established that autism reduces to an impaired theory of mind in the child as diagnosed by failure to acknowledge false belief. It would engender a radically new insight into autism and would stand as a triumph for the cognitive approach to psychology in general and to clinical disorders in particular. Autism would be seen primarily as a cognitive impairment, with affective, communicative and social impairments existing secondary to that. If we wished to plan a way of treating the disorder (a cognitive impairment) rather than the symptoms (affective, communicative and social impairments), we ought to proceed down the cognitive route. If we wished to improve methods of diagnoses, again we should be thinking in terms of cognitive tests. That would be the case if we had water-tight evidence in support of the theory of mind hypothesis of autism. However, it turns out that this appealing hypothesis has a variety of serious drawbacks, which we shall examine in this chapter.

SUCCESS IN ACKNOWLEDGING FALSE BELIEF

Since the seminal study by Baron-Cohen *et al.* (1985), researchers from many different institutions all over the world have replicated and extended the basic findings (see Happe, 1994, for a review). Although these studies usually confirm that the majority of autistic children studied fail to acknowledge false belief, there is nearly always a minority of children with autism who reliably succeed. How can we account for these anomalous findings? It seems that there are at least three ways in which we could approach this discrepancy. At one extreme we could dismiss the anomalous data by saying that people who succeed in acknowledging false belief are not autistic after all and have been wrongly diagnosed. At the other extreme, we could say that the theory of mind hypothesis seemed like a good idea at the time, but actually it has turned out to be completely wrong. In between those two poles we could say that there is some truth in the claim that autism involves an impairment in understanding mind, and that a test of false belief can be diagnostic of that, but with qualifications. Perhaps we would have to admit that autism does not reduce to a lack of a conception of mind, that a lack of a conception of mind is not the primary element of the disorder, that autism entails a great deal more than impairment in understanding mind, and that ultimately a test of false belief is not really very useful after all with respect to autism.

The problem with pronouncing that anyone who acknowledges false belief cannot be autistic is that it would make the theory of mind hypothesis a circular one. We would be restricted to saying that anyone over 5 years of age who reliably fails to acknowledge false belief is autistic – because they fail to acknowledge false belief. And anyone who succeeds in acknowledging false belief is not autistic – because they succeed. Hence, by definition, those who fail to acknowledge false belief are autistic. The sign that an individual is autistic is one and the same as the evidence that is used to support this as the appropriate method of diagnosis. This blinkered approach would actually be absurd, and the theory of mind hypothesis would become a hindrance rather than a help. Autism is currently diagnosed when the child exhibits a constellation of behaviours that conform to an autistic profile. That is the starting point from which we wished to identify a unifying underlying cognitive factor. As it happens, there is a lack of correspondence between failure to acknowledge false belief and showing the classic signs of autism. Being autistic does not necessarily mean that the individual will fail to acknowledge false belief.

SECOND-ORDER BELIEF ATTRIBUTION

Baron-Cohen (1989c) stepped in to salvage the theory of mind hypothesis by presenting his autistic participants with a test of second-order belief attribution. Once again, Perner and his colleagues had pioneered a suitable test which they had used to assess the development of understanding mind in clinically normal children (Perner and Wimmer, 1985). The purpose of the test is to determine whether children understand that people hold beliefs not just about reality but also about other people's beliefs. As usual, the scenario is presented as a story enacted with small dolls (shown schematically in Figure 6.1). The story consisted of the following four episodes.

- Episode 1. Mary and John saw the ice-cream van in the park.
- Episode 2. Mary went home for some money, and meanwhile John saw the ice-cream van move to the church.
- Episode 3. Mary unexpectedly sees the ice-cream van at the church, so her belief about the van's location remains true.

Episode 1   Episode 2

John   Mary   John

Episode 3   Episode 4

Mary   John

FIGURE 6.1 Attribution of second-order beliefs. In Episode 1, John and Mary see the ice-cream van in the park. Mary leaves, then John sees the ice-cream van move to the church (Episode 2). Later, unknown to John, Mary also sees the van by the church (Episode 3). Finally, children judge where John thinks Mary thinks the ice-cream van is. Correct answer = 'park', incorrect answer = 'church'.

■ Episode 4. John sets out to look for Mary whom, he is told, has gone for an ice-cream.

Participants are asked where John finally thinks Mary has gone (park or church). The correct answer is the park.

In essence, participants make a judgement not about where John thinks the ice-cream van is, but about where John thinks that Mary believes it is. In this case, John (wrongly) thinks that Mary holds a false belief, whereas in fact she holds a true belief. Children aged about 7 years and older tended to give the correct answer, showing that they could acknowledge John's false belief about Mary's belief.

Baron-Cohen (1989c) proceeded to present a version of this task, along with a simple test of false belief, to a group of children and adolescents with autism. He confirmed that some members of his sample could succeed in acknowledging false belief in its simple form, as presented in the standard version of the task. However, these individuals failed to make a second-order belief attribution. They judged wrongly that John thought Mary was at the church. Baron-Cohen concluded that, although people with autism might find a means of giving a correct judgement in a simple test of false belief, this does not mean that such individuals have now acquired a fully fledged theory of mind. They still have autism and they still have an impaired theory of mind. Their autism is obvious from their behavioural profile, and their impaired theory of mind is obvious from their failure in second-order belief attribution.

Perhaps we can shift the goalposts, then, to suggest that being autistic at the very least means that one will fail to make second-order belief attributions. This modified account will not work either. Bowler (1992) presented a test of second-order belief attribution to a sample of adults with autism who generally had good intellectual abilities. Many of these people succeeded in the task, yet they still exhibited an autistic profile. Hence, being able to acknowledge beliefs and even second-order beliefs does not prevent the individual from being autistic. Evidently, having autism and having difficulty in acknowledging beliefs does not amount to one and the same thing.

FURTHER PROBLEMS WITH THE THEORY OF MIND HYPOTHESIS

The difficulties that the theory of mind hypothesis presents do not end there. A weaker version of the hypothesis could have been salvaged by saying that there is a strong likelihood of children with autism, especially younger children, showing a developmental delay in being able to acknowledge beliefs and other phenomena related to mind. Perhaps we could retract the claim that autism amounts to a lack of ability to acknowledge beliefs, and instead argue for a specific developmental delay in this ability. That is, we would no longer be claiming that impaired communication and socialization stem from a failure to acknowledge beliefs. We would, however, maintain that failing to acknowledge belief beyond the age of 4 or 5 years is peculiar to autism. Yet even this reformulation of the theory of mind hypothesis will not work.

Two studies have revealed that there are populations without autism who have difficulty in acknowledging false belief. Peterson and Siegal (1995) presented one such task to a group of adolescents who had been born deaf. Despite their severe hearing impairment, these individuals had normal non-verbal intelligence. The authors presented them with a test of false belief that was specially adapted for deaf people and was explained with sign language. Surprisingly, the great majority of the participants failed a simple test of false belief. According to Peterson and Siegal, being denied a rich linguistic environment prevented their participants from grasping the linguistic subtleties of the task, thus hindering them from responding correctly. These hearing impaired adolescents were people who failed to acknowledge false belief but who certainly did not show any of the classic characteristics of autism.

Another study that demonstrates difficulty in acknowledging false belief in a sample without autism was reported by Hobson (1995). He tested a group of participants in middle childhood who had been born blind. These children had normal intelligence. However, despite this and their advanced age, they failed simple tests of false belief that were adapted for children with visual impairment. Hobson reports that children with congenital visual impairment do tend to show some of the behaviour patterns of autism, especially with regard to the social behaviour of relating to other people, but the children he tested certainly would not be diagnosed autistic. Once again, then, it seems that there is a non-autistic population that is characterized by having difficulty in acknowledging false belief. In short, failing to acknowledge false belief does not appear to be specific to autism, and those with autism do not necessarily have difficulty in acknowledging false belief.

Even so, it still looked impressive for the theory of mind hypothesis that difficulty in acknowledging false belief did not extend to a control group with learning difficulties, that is, children with Down's syndrome. However, a study by Zelazo *et al.* (1996) identified difficulty in acknowledging false belief in both self and others, plus difficulty in acknowledging the distinction between appearance and reality in a sample of adults with Down's syndrome. People with Down's syndrome are not all alike with regard to their intellectual impairments, but rather they display a wide range of different abilities. Those tested by Baron-Cohen *et al.* (1985) seem to have been high functioning children with Down's syndrome, whereas those tested by Zelazo *et al.* (1996) tended to be more severely impaired. Although the participants were adults, their mental age was only 5 years. These individuals had great difficulty in acknowledging false belief or appearance as distinct from reality, and performed much worse on the tasks than a sample of clinically normal children aged 5 years. So here we have yet another non-autistic population in which acknowledging false belief poses a serious difficulty. Together, these findings substantially undermine a strong version of the theory of mind hypothesis which states that impairment of conception of mind virtually means that the individual is autistic.

EXECUTIVE DYSFUNCTION IN AUTISM

It remains tempting to conclude that an impaired conception of mind is the core deficiency in autism. It still seems to be the cognitive factor that unites the majority of people with autism. At least that appeared to be the case until the executive dysfunction hypothesis was proposed. Although people with autism are socially impaired and have communication difficulties, there is another defining feature that seems to have been downplayed by advocates of the theory of mind movement. This is the observation that people with autism insist on sameness, and can become upset if a trivial change is made to routine. Furthermore, people with autism tend to have a very narrow range of interests, and appear content just to arrange items into lines repetitively. It is very difficult to imagine how these characteristics could be related to an impaired theory of mind. Rather, it seems more likely that children with autism have a specific attentional problem.

To a substantial extent, we are the masters of our own conscious or attentional focus. We can switch attention to one domain, such as the solving of a mathematical puzzle, and suppress attention to stimuli which are irrelevant to that problem, such as the hubbub of a party that is taking place around us. The party might pose something of a distraction but, to a large extent, most of us are sufficiently self-disciplined in our attentional focus to be able to shut out noise. However, if we so chose, we could instantly switch our attention to a conversation taking place in the near vicinity, for example if we heard our own name mentioned. Effectively, we have a capacity to control our own attentional focus, and this is known as the executive function. If we suffered from an executive dysfunction, then that could be manifested as a tendency to be distracted very easily by irrelevant stimuli. We might also find that we had an excessive tendency to persist in our current attentional focus.

Executive dysfunction is noticeable in certain unfortunate individuals who suffer damage to the frontal area of their brain as a result of either accident or illness. Such people can show a narrowing of attentional focus and persistence in repetitive activities, which at times can seem to be to the exclusion of paying attention to other people. A couple of tasks reveal the attentional problem that these individuals suffer, namely The Tower of Hanoi and the Wisconsin Card Sort.

Tower of Hanoi

The participant is presented with a board that has three vertical pegs. Three loops are arranged in descending order of diameter over the left-hand peg, as shown in Figure 6.2, Stage 1. The aim of the task is to transfer those loops one by one to the right-hand peg, as shown in Stage 8. However, the transfer is restricted by the rule that one must never put a large-diameter loop on top of a small-diameter one. It is therefore necessary to proceed through the various stages shown in Figure 6.2 in order to achieve the desired outcome. Evidently, the task requires a great deal of planning prior to action, and it is planning that benefits from temporarily shutting out the knowledge that the loops must end up on the right-hand peg. The trouble with that knowledge is that it might cause one to shift the loops directly from the left peg to the right one. People with damage to certain parts of their frontal brain area seem especially impaired in the ability to plan several stages ahead, and are more inclined to act impulsively by wrongly attempting to transfer the loops directly from the left to the right peg.

Wisconsin Card Sort

Suppose I have a pack of cards, in which each card has an image printed on it that can vary across two dimensions. One is the geometric shape and the other is the number on its face (see Figure 6.3). Suppose I draw cards from the pack one at a time, and your task is to place each of them into one of two trays. Each time a circle is drawn, it is to be placed in Tray 1 and each time a square is drawn from the pack, it is to be placed in Tray 2. I do not tell you this in so many words, but just inform you on each occasion whether you placed the card correctly or incorrectly. You would very rapidly work out that shape is the criterion for sorting, and so do people with damage to the frontal part of their brain, so there is no mystery so far.

Suppose I then switch the sorting principle, so that shape is no longer relevant, and number becomes the dimension of interest, as shown in the bottom part of Figure 6.3. Now, all the even numbers should go into Tray 1 and all the odd numbers should go into Tray 2. I do not announce that the sorting principle is changed, but it will be obvious to you that it has because

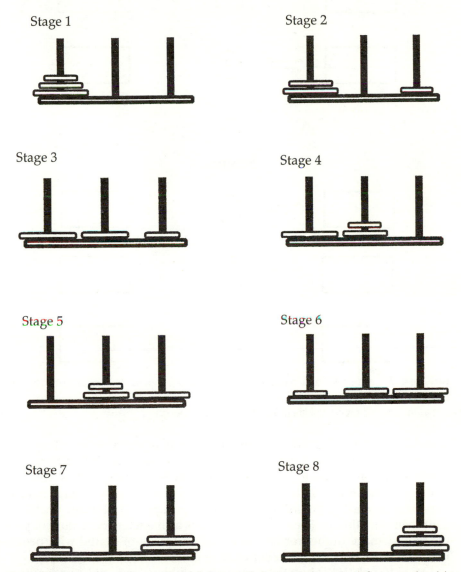

Stage 1 Stage 2 Stage 3 Stage 4 Stage 5 Stage 6 Stage 7 Stage 8

FIGURE 6.2 Tower of Hanoi. The task is to shift the loops from the left peg to the right one. A large diameter loop must never be placed on top of one with smaller diameter, and only one loop at a time can be moved.

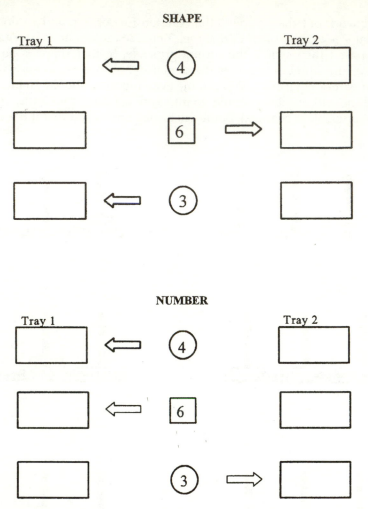

FIGURE 6.3 Card sort. Participants sort cards into two boxes. In the initial phase they can infer from feedback that the sorting principal is based on shape (circles vs. squares), but in the second phase it shifts to number (even vs. odd).

sometimes you will be told that you are incorrect to put a circle in Tray 1 (as when it shows an odd number). Again, you would have little difficulty in shifting your attention to a different criterion for sorting, unless you had damage to the frontal area of your brain. People with such damage tend to persevere in sorting according to the first principle, and seem unable to shift their attention to a new criterion. This is a characteristic feature of people with damage to the frontal brain area, and it is not shared with people in whom there is damage to other parts of the brain.

Ozonoff *et al.* (1991) questioned whether children and adults with autism had executive dysfunction, like people without autism who had damage to frontal brain areas. If they did, this would explain why people with autism have such a narrowing of attentional focus, why they rigidly persevere in repetitive behaviours, and why they insist on sameness. Note that these peculiarities seem at the very least to be peripheral to an impairment of their theory of mind. Ozonoff *et al.* proceeded to present the Tower of Hanoi and Wisconsin Card Sort tasks to people with autism who tended to have intelligence levels that extended well into the normal range. They also presented a variety of tests in order to probe the extent of impairment of their theory of mind, including tests of simple false belief, but also tests of second-order belief attribution.

The findings reported by Ozonoff *et al.* (1991) are both striking and problematic for the theory of mind hypothesis of autism. As we have come to expect, many of the participants with autism passed a simple test of false belief, and some even passed the test of second-order belief attribution. However, the two tests that are diagnostic of executive dysfunction (the Tower of Hanoi and Wisconsin Card Sort) posed problems for all of the participants with autism. They tended to act impulsively, and seemed to be unable to shift their attentional focus from one principle to another. In the Card Sort, they persevered in sorting by shape even when it was obvious that the principle had become obsolete. In the Tower of Hanoi, they seemed unable to plan several moves in advance, and simply attempted to shift the loops directly from the left peg to the right one. Hence impairment of theory of mind did not appear to be the common denominator in cognitive terms, but executive dysfunction did.

It is intriguing that people with frontal brain damage but without autism display social unresponsiveness and insensitivity, quite apart from their executive dysfunction. Their problem is not so extreme that they should be diagnosed as autistic, but it is tempting to conclude that they show some autism-like behaviours. Is it possible, then, that a pervasive executive dysfunction in autism is actually responsible for an impaired theory of mind? To explore this possibility, we need to specify how an executive dysfunction could give the impression that the individual has a deficient theory of mind. This challenge was tackled audaciously by Russell *et al.* (1991), who devised something they called the Windows task, in which participants are presented with two closed boxes, one of which is baited with a chocolate reward. The participants have to try to win the chocolate, but do so not by pointing to the baited box, but by pointing to the empty one. In a preliminary phase of the procedure, participants are unaware which box is baited, since both boxes are closed and have opaque sides. This phase presents an opportunity to learn the principle that if by chance one points to a box that turns out to be baited, then the chocolate is promptly collected by the other person playing the game. On the other hand, if by chance one points to the box that turns out to be empty, then the experimenter proceeds to open the other box, removes the chocolate and hands it directly to you. Effectively, you are rewarded for pointing to the empty box, but in this preliminary phase you are helpless to do so reliably because you do not actually know which is the empty box at the time of pointing.

In a second phase of the procedure, windows are opened in the boxes, revealing which of them is empty and which is baited. Apart from that, the task is exactly the same as before, in the sense that to obtain the chocolate, one must point to the visibly empty box and resist pointing to the box that is seen to contain chocolate, as illustrated in Figure 6.4. Russell *et al.* presented this task to children with autism and to clinically normal children aged between 3 and 5 years. The children with autism and the normal children aged 3 years behaved in much the same way, and both groups performed differently from the normal children aged 5 years. The children with autism and the 3-year-olds seemed unable to resist pointing to the baited box in the second phase when they could see the chocolate. They did this time after time, thus repeatedly denying themselves the chocolate treat. In sharp contrast, the children aged 5 years had little difficulty in pointing to the empty box, and thereby won the chocolate time after time.

The difficulty experienced by the children with autism can be characterized as an imperative gesture that means 'I want that chocolate'. It is perhaps not so much a request for the assistance of another person as just a natural reaction to a desirable object. Ironically, in this case the natural pointing to the chocolate frustrated the children's wish to acquire it. The children with autism simply could not help responding impulsively, yet from an adult perspective it would seem to take so little to pause and take a more deliberate, planned and thoughtful approach to the problem, which would have resulted in winning the chocolate. In other words, success in this task required an intact executive function, which the children with autism, and the clinically normal children aged 3 years, appeared to lack.

So how does this help to shed light on impaired theory of mind in autism? The Windows task could be construed as a test of the ability to deceive. In pointing to the empty box, the children arguably are telling lies with their gesture about the location of the chocolate. The other person playing the game acts on the gesture, does not find the chocolate in the location indicated, and the chocolate remains in the other location for the child participant to collect. Just as anecdotal reports indicate that children

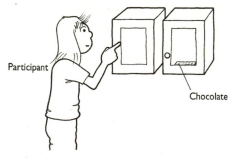

FIGURE 6.4 Windows task. To obtain the chocolate, the participant must inhibit an impulsive tendency to point to the box where it is located. Instead, she should point to the empty box.

with autism have difficulty in telling lies, so they seemed helpless in the Windows task to do anything other than point to the place where the chocolate really was. However, it is quite another matter to conclude that children with autism are naïvely honest because they do not understand the significance of lies with regard to another person's belief state. On the contrary, the results of Russell *et al.* suggest that understanding belief was not the issue, but just fixation on the place where the chocolate was really located. To help clarify the matter further, Hughes and Russell (1993) presented a version of the Windows task to children with autism which did not involve another person searching in the location to which the child gestured. Quite simply, the child received the chocolate if he pointed to the empty place, but not if he pointed to the baited box; deception was not an issue here. Yet children with autism made precisely the same error of persistently pointing to the baited box. In short, an executive dysfunction could give the impression in this case that children with autism had an impaired theory of mind, but concluding that an impaired theory of mind accounts for children's difficulty with the Windows task would constitute the wrong level of explanation.

Why make so much fuss about the results of an isolated task? Even if an executive dysfunction explains the difficulty children with autism experience in the Windows task, and even if their naïve honesty stems from executive dysfunction, surely this does not detract from the findings that many children with autism struggle to acknowledge false belief. However, according to Russell *et al.* (1991), executive dysfunction is certainly the appropriate level of explanation for this. Consider the unexpected transfer test, featuring Maxi and his bar of chocolate. Just as children with autism gesture impulsively to the baited box in the Windows task, so they do precisely the same when asked where Maxi will look for his chocolate. It is not so much that they fail to take into account Maxi's false belief, but rather that they react impulsively to the place where the chocolate is located. Likewise, when performing the deceptive box task, children with autism would just blurt out what is currently inside the box (a pencil) when asked what they used to think or what someone else thinks (Smarties). Their executive dysfunction would lead them to act impulsively on their environment. When performing on a test of second-order belief attribution, people with autism who could pass a simple test of false belief would tend to revert to acting impulsively once again in the face of the added complexity of the story.

The executive dysfunction hypothesis thus begins to assume very substantial credibility as a general explanation for the spectrum of autistic behaviours. It no longer seems appropriate to say that the essence of autism is a deficient theory of mind, but rather it is an executive dysfunction that explains their inability to acknowledge mind plus a whole variety of other autistic phenomena. However, the executive dysfunction hypothesis then begins to run into difficulties as a contender for the primary cognitive explanation of autism.

PROBLEMS WITH THE EXECUTIVE DYSFUNCTION HYPOTHESIS

The obvious problem is that people with damage to the frontal region of the brain who show the classic signs of executive dysfunction are not autistic. Although they exhibit a very mild social impairment, this is nothing like the scale of disorder that would require a diagnosis of autism. Hence executive dysfunction and autism cannot be one and the same thing. Moreover, executive dysfunction does not inevitably result in the individual having difficulty in acknowledging beliefs in particular or the existence of mind in general. There is no evidence to suggest that people with frontal brain damage have a specifically impaired theory of mind.

In defence of the executive dysfunction hypothesis, it is tempting to say that it is not executive dysfunction per se that is responsible for a manifestly impaired theory of mind, but being inflicted with an executive dysfunction during the formative years when clinically normal people are becoming acquainted with their psychological environment. That is, perhaps a cocktail of executive dysfunction plus immaturity equals autism. However, that hypothesis does not work either, as explained below.

Welsh *et al.* (1990) tested children with PKU (see Chapter 4) on a battery of executive dysfunction tasks. As detailed in Chapter 4, children with PKU have a genetic abnormality that leads to a certain amino acid remaining unmetabolized when it enters the bloodstream. In this state it is toxic to the nervous system, and causes brain damage. This can be avoided by feeding affected children a diet free of the amino acid phenylalanine. Children in whom this disorder goes undetected until it is too late are at risk not only from brain damage in general, but also from developing autism in particular. Welsh *et al.* presented the executive dysfunction tasks specifically to children with PKU who had been diagnosed at an early stage and reared on a special diet free of phenylalanine. These children had intelligence levels well within the normal range, and certainly were not autistic, which is testament to their parents' rigorous observation of dietary requirements. None the less, the children showed impairment of executive function tasks. Here therefore was a cocktail of executive dysfunction plus development, but without autism as the consequence. Evidently executive dysfunction and impaired conception of mind are not one and the same thing, even in a developmental context. Executive dysfunction appears to coincide with impaired theory of mind in autism, but it does not amount to the same thing.

There is one more reason for disbelieving that executive dysfunction and impaired conception of mind amount to the same thing, and this is perhaps the most compelling reason of all. It relates to the findings of the false photo task, devised originally by Zaitchik (1990) for clinically normal children. The task acquires its name from the fact that it was designed to resemble a false belief task, except that no theory of mind would be required for success. Zaitchik positioned a doll on a mat and then helped the child participant to take a photograph of the scene with her instantaneous camera. The photographic cardboard issued from the front of the camera but remained temporarily blank while the chemicals processed the image. Meanwhile, Zaitchik conspicuously moved the doll from the rug to the box as the child watched. Finally, the child participant was asked where the doll would be in the photo – on the rug or on the box. The child had to respond to the question before the image began to emerge. The task is illustrated in Figure 6.5.

Zaitchik (1990) saw this task as being similar to the unexpected transfer test of false belief, in the sense that the child participant had to acknowledge how the scene had been represented, and in doing so had to suppress her knowledge of how the scene actually appeared at the present time. On this occasion, however, the representation in question was in a photograph rather than in a mind. Zaitchik found that clinically normal children aged about 3 years tended to judge wrongly that the doll would be sitting on the box in the photo, just as they wrongly judged that Maxi would look for his chocolate where it currently was rather than where he had last seen it. Effectively, the children were responding as though they had been asked not 'where is the doll in the photo?' but 'where is the doll right now?'. In sharp contrast, older children correctly anticipated that, in the photo, the doll would be on the mat, just as they anticipated that Maxi would look for his chocolate in the place where he last saw it.

This is a very interesting finding because it suggests that the difficulty young children experience in making these kinds of judgements is not confined to belief, so it seems odd to conclude that the child has an undeveloped theory of mind. In one sense the child does have a demonstrably undeveloped theory of mind, but his or her problem is much more general. On the other hand, the young child's incorrect judgements in the false photo task are precisely what we might predict from the executive dysfunction hypothesis, which states that young children act impulsively by blurting out the current location of the doll. That is, just as children impulsively indicate the place where the chocolate is currently located when asked about Maxi's false belief, so they indicate the place where the doll is currently located in the photo task. The false photo task thus stands as a clear

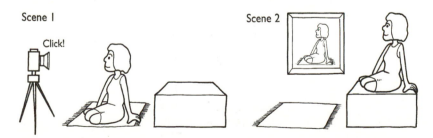

Scene 1   Scene 2

Click!

FIGURE 6.5 False photo. In Scene 1, a photo is taken of the doll sitting on the mat. In Scene 2, the doll is moved to the box, and children have to anticipate where the doll will be sitting in the developing photo.

demonstration of how executive dysfunction could lead to errors in tasks that require suppression of impulsiveness, whether or not belief is at issue. Again, being able to acknowledge false belief appears to be secondary to overcoming an executive dysfunction.

The prediction made about autism by the executive dysfunction hypothesis is clear. Just as we would expect many children with autism to fail to acknowledge false belief, so they should also fail to acknowledge the content of an outdated photograph. In both instances, we would expect them to report current reality wrongly. Two independent studies were carried out to test children on the false photo test (Leekam and Perner, 1991; Leslie and Thaiss, 1992). The results were entirely consistent across the studies, and completely counter to what we might have expected from the executive dysfunction hypothesis. Nearly all of the children with autism gave a correct judgement on the false photo task by stating that, in the photograph, the doll will be on the mat. On the other hand, the majority of the children with autism failed to acknowledge false belief. Meanwhile, clinically normal children aged 3 years had as much if not more difficulty with the false photo task as they did with acknowledging false belief. The striking pattern of the data (from Leslie and Thaiss, 1992) is shown in Figure 6.6.

Since we can assume that the demands on executive function were about the same across the false photo and false belief tasks, we cannot explain the autistic contrast in performance between tasks by reference to executive dysfunction. Indeed, the false photo task positively demonstrated that the executive demand of the false belief task is something children with autism can handle, even if they do have a finer executive dysfunction that can be identified by the Tower of Hanoi task and the Wisconsin Card Sort task. It appears that we have no choice but to conclude that the difficulty children with autism experience in acknowledging false belief is not due to executive

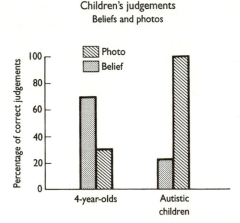

FIGURE 6.6 Children with autism give correct judgements in the false photo test but incorrect judgements in the false belief test. In striking contrast, 4-year-olds find the belief test easier than the photo test.

dysfunction. Rather, it might after all be the case that children with autism have a primary and irreducible difficulty in acknowledging the mind along with its contents. Children with autism can be described as having two kinds of cognitive deficiency. One kind makes it hard for them to acknowledge false belief, and causes them to have an impaired conception of mind in a way that contributes to (but does not entirely account for) their autistic behaviours. The other kind is an impaired executive function which accounts for their narrowing of interests and insistence on sameness.

At this point, we have said about as much as we can about the cognitive aspects of autism with respect to deficient theory of mind. Is there any further mystery in autism that needs to be unravelled? We have assumed that social and emotional impairments in autism stand secondary to cognitive impairments, but it is worth taking a second look at this claim.

ANOTHER LOOK AT SOCIAL AND AFFECTIVE IMPAIRMENTS

Some authorities subscribe to the view that even in normal development, an understanding of false belief and therefore a true understanding of mind is not acquired until about 4 years of age (see, for example, Perner, 1991). Normal children below that age are not autistic, but none the less they are claimed to have no more insight into mind than children with autism (Frith, 1989). Consequently, if a child had autism from birth, it would not be possible to detect this with regard to impaired understanding of mind until the child was aged 4 years or over. It follows that if an inability to relate to others socially and affectively in autism stems from a cognitive impairment of understanding mind (Baron-Cohen, 1991a), then these social and affective abnormalities would not be in evidence until the age of 4 years either. That follows because we are confined here to considering only those social and affective behaviours which stem from an understanding of mind that under normal circumstances develops at the age of 4 years. Advocates of the theory of mind hypothesis are committed to denying that there are social and affective impairments in autism that do not stem from an impaired understanding of mind.

This allows us to put the theory of mind hypothesis to the test as follows. Suppose we document social and affective behaviours in normal development that are characteristic of babyhood. These behaviours cannot depend on the child having an understanding of mind if such understanding develops at 4 years of age. Therefore, these social and affective behaviours should be intact in autism. If they are also impaired in autism, then the theory of mind hypothesis cannot provide a general explanation of the constellation of social and affective impairments. In that case, autism could not amount to a cognitive deficit in the form of an impaired understanding of mind.

Klin *et al.* (1992) conducted a survey of parents with autistic children using the Vineland Adaptive Behaviour Scales. This is a standard questionnaire that asks about basic affective and social behaviour. A striking and consistent finding was that the parents who participated in the survey reported that their children with autism did not and had never anticipated being picked up. When a mother approaches her normal toddler with arms outstretched, the child will characteristically greet this spectacle with arms extended in anticipation of the mother holding him or her beneath the arms. Children with autism do not do this. Instead, they remain stiff and unresponsive. Here is a behaviour that predates an ability to acknowledge false belief in normal development by at least 2 years. Therefore it cannot be a behaviour that depends on the kind of understanding of mind that requires an insight into beliefs.

In contrast to the children with autism, those with Down's syndrome and other developmental disorders showed no specific impairment in this or other forms of basic social and affective contact. Klin *et al.* (1992) were also careful to check that it was not general impairment of movement that was responsible for the failure to anticipate being picked up in autism. The researchers established by independent tests that the children had no difficulty in voluntarily raising their arms. Apparently they simply did not appreciate that it was appropriate to do so when the parent approached them. It seems, then, that children with autism have a basic affective and social impairment that is even more primitive than their cognitive impairment in understanding mind.

A specific impairment in perceiving emotion was investigated by Hobson *et al.* (1989). They reasoned that in humans, perhaps more so than in other animals, emotional states are characteristically manifested as a facial expression, and we easily interpret these facial expressions as externalizations of emotional states. Hobson *et al.* suggest that we virtually perceive the emotion itself, rather than just a contorted face. They further suggest that this aptitude for perceiving emotion is impaired in autism, in accordance with Kanner's original account of autism. These researchers showed a series of photographs of faces wearing various expressions of ecstasy and agony, and were asked to describe the emotion displayed in each of them. People with autism consistently named the emotions wrongly, compared to people with learning difficulties matched with regard to their intellectual profile. The people with autism had the requisite vocabulary of emotional terms, but failed to use it properly. They also showed a related difficulty in naming the emotion expressed in tone of voice, again in comparison with matched control participants without autism.

In another study, Hobson *et al.* (1988) found a further peculiarity in the autistic perception of faces. Participants had to categorize faces by matching them to a target. Either they had to group together all the faces that showed the same emotional expression, using the target as the point of reference, or they had to group together examples of the same face but showing various emotional expressions. The participants with autism showed some impairment in performance of this task relative to people without autism, but an intriguing finding emerged when the faces were presented upside-down. Clinically normal people can easily misinterpret the emotions in faces presented upside-down. For example, a smiling mouth can be mistaken for a sad mouth when the face is inverted. The schematic faces shown in Figure 6.7 give an impression of this phenomenon. It was no surprise to find that the non-autistic participants deteriorated in their categorization of faces when these were presented upside-down. However, the participants with autism showed very much less deterioration in their categorization of faces under this unusual condition of presentation.

Hobson *et al.* (1988) suggest that clinically normal people do not perceive faces as a geometrical pattern, consisting of a set of elements, but as an emotional whole. They claim that people cannot help but see a face as an expression of emotion. When a face is presented in an unusual orientation (e.g. upside-down), this interferes with our natural tendency to read emotion into a face, and leads to a considerable breakdown in our judgements about it. In autism, however, these authors maintain that emotion is not automatically read into faces, and that faces are just seen as a collection of meaningless shapes. Because there is no irresistible tendency to read emotion into faces in autism, this process cannot interfere with judgements of faces. In autism, so these authors claim, people just categorize faces as though they were any other pattern, and therefore performance deteriorates little when the stimuli are presented upside-down. Ironically, then, the relatively good performance

FIGURE 6.7 People generally find it easier to recognize faces presented the right way up rather than upside down. In contrast, children with autism are almost as effective in recognizing faces upside down as the right way up.

in categorizing faces upside-down in autism appears to be a sign of impairment of perception of emotion in faces.

It seems that autism is typified not only by impaired perception of emotion but also by impaired expression of emotion. Mundy *et al.* (1993) noted the usual suppression of shared attention, communication and pretence in autism, but not the complete absence of these activities. What remained, however, was of a conspicuously 'autistic' nature. When a clinically normal child is involved in symbolic pretend play, excitement and glee emanate from him or her. Similarly, the child is characteristically animated when showing another person something (joint attention) or conversing with another person. On the rare occasions when children with autism engaged in these activities, they were more robotic. For them, there was no external sign that sharing experiences, talking and pretending were pleasurable, and they differed not only from clinically normal children but also from children with learning difficulties who formed the control sample. These findings are highly consistent with the impression to be gained from interacting with a child with autism. It is not just that symbolic and social behaviours are suppressed but that when these behaviours do occur, they are of an entirely different character to those in clinically normal children. The theory of mind hypothesis might succeed to an extent in accounting for the suppression or absence of these behaviours from a cognitive perspective, but it is not clear how the hypothesis accounts for the accompanying emotional profile. In this respect it is easy to understand how Kanner (1943) depicted autism primarily as an affective disorder.

IMPAIRED CONCEPTION OF MIND IN OTHER PSYCHOLOGICAL DISORDERS

At least superficially, two distinct clinical populations (apart from people with autism) appear to show abnormalities in their understanding of mind. These are psychopaths and people with schizophrenia. We shall consider schizophrenia shortly. Psychopaths are capable of extreme acts of violence without showing remorse, guilt or empathy for the victim. Piaget suggested a link between cognitive and moral development many decades ago. Although he was not attuned to the theory of mind hypothesis as it is currently formulated, his thinking was broadly sympathetic to this hypothesis. Essentially, he argued that if one does not possess the cognitive capacity to adopt another individual's perspective, then one cannot empathize with that person. If one cannot empathize, then one stands little chance of sympathizing. Hence, if one lacked a conception of mind, one would have an underdeveloped sense of morality, especially with regard to the feelings of other people, and that is precisely what appears to be the case in psychopathy. Does that mean that psychopaths have an impaired conception of mind in common with people with autism?

An alternative possibility is that psychopaths have more of a pure impairment with regard to morality. However much they might be able to adopt another individual's perspective, they might remain emotionally cold with regard to that person's plight, perhaps because they do not grasp that some laws and conventions have not just arisen from tradition but exist to preserve basic human rights. If psychopaths do not understand this, they might not see any difference between violating rules that protect people and violating rules that protect conventions. Rules that protect conventions can be suspended on the decree of an individual authorized to pronounce on the matter. For example, in the classroom there might be a rule that children are to remain silent. However, the teacher is empowered to suspend that rule and to allow the children to talk freely. On the other hand, rules that serve to protect people are fundamental, and cannot be suspended by the word of an authority figure. For example, if the teacher announced that today it is acceptable to throw stones at little Johnny, it would still remain wrong to commit the act. It would be morally incorrect.

Blair (1995) set out to investigate the ability to draw the moral-conventional distinction in psychopaths. He presented them with brief scenarios in which an authority figure announced that a rule was suspended, with two kinds of scenario in question. In the first kind, the rule merely served a convention, whereas in the second kind it served to protect basic human rights. Participants then judged whether the behaviour was acceptable after an authority figure had pronounced its suspension. The psychopaths who he interviewed were 10 residents at a secure hospital who had committed acts of extreme violence against others; they had all been found guilty of murder. Members of a control group were resident at the same institution but were not psychopathic. The non-psychopaths judged appropriately that an authority figure is empowered to suspend a conventional rule, and judged that it would be acceptable to carry out a deed if the rule forbidding it were withdrawn. They also judged correctly that an authority figure was not empowered to suspend a rule forbidding an antisocial act that would harm or endanger another person. In contrast, the psychopaths judged in the same way in both kinds of scenario, whether moral or conventional. When asked to justify their judgements, the non-psychopaths frequently made reference to the victim's welfare, but the psychopaths seldom did so.

On the face of things, it is tempting to speculate that psychopaths have an impaired understanding of other people's minds, because it is hard to imagine how they could conduct antisocial acts against other people if they did have some notion of how it would feel to be the victim. However, Blair (1995) also tested a sample of people with autism, and these participants had little difficulty in drawing the moral-conventional distinction. They judged correctly that an antisocial act would not become acceptable on its suspension by an authority figure. If people with autism have an impaired understanding of mind, then this finding suggests that being able to make the moral-conventional distinction does not depend on insight into mind. Rather, it is possible that the issue is a purely moral one. In short, psychopaths seem to have a problem primarily with morality and not with understanding other minds. It might be that they understand something about other people's feelings, but simply do not consider that those feelings are to be respected.

Intuitively, people with schizophrenia are also candidates for an impaired understanding of mind. People with this disorder appear to lose the ability to think coherently about the world around them, not just the physical world but also the psychological environment. The latter is perhaps most notable in the case of people with paranoid delusions. The classic signs are a bizarre and extreme set of beliefs that others are plotting against one. When such delusions are unfounded, then it is accurate to say that the individual has lost the capacity to make accurate inferences about the thoughts of other people. It is not that they deny the existence of others' thoughts – on the contrary! Rather, they appear to have become unable to diagnose those thoughts sensibly.

This led Frith and Corcoran (1996) to postulate that people with paranoid schizophrenia would show impairment in making correct judgements of false belief. They recruited a sample of patients with paranoid schizophrenia, together with another group of participants, also with paranoid schizophrenia, but who were in a state of remission at the time of testing. They presented an unexpected transfer test of false belief based loosely on Wimmer and Perner's (1983) story about Maxi and his chocolate. In this test John had left five cigarettes in his packet, but in his absence Janet took one of them. Participants were then asked how many cigarettes John thought he had left. Frith and Corcoran also presented a test of second-order belief attribution, based loosely on that of Perner and Wimmer (1985). The results showed that while the participants with paranoid schizophrenia succeeded in making correct judgements about belief (both first- and second-order) on the majority of occasions, they were significantly less likely to succeed than the control participants. This was not due to general failure to comprehend the stories, because the authors were able to show a specific problem in answering belief attribution questions, and this contrasted with success in answering general story comprehension questions. Although this research is in the early stages, it appears that schizophrenia might give rise to impairment of the ability to diagnose beliefs in other people. If that is so, then schizophrenia is quite unlike autism for at least two reasons. First, people with schizophrenia are not oblivious to minds, whereas some claim that people with autism are. Rather, the problem lies in the diagnosis of belief in schizophrenia. Second, people with schizophrenia have had the ability to diagnose beliefs accurately, but this is a capacity that is impaired with the onset of symptoms. This is suggested by the finding that people who have a record of schizophrenia begin to make accurate judgements of belief once their symptoms wane. Presumably the ability to make accurate judgements of belief fluctuates with the presence of paranoid symptoms.

CONCLUSIONS

Although there is compelling evidence to suggest that many children and adults with autism have an impaired ability to acknowledge false belief, it is not appropriate to conclude that autism amounts to an impaired theory of mind. Some populations also show impairment in acknowledging false belief. Moreover, people with autism have characteristic autistic behaviours that cannot be accounted for by an impaired theory of mind. For example, they seem to have an executive dysfunction. However, neither is it the case that executive dysfunction accounts for impaired theory of mind. Furthermore, people with autism appear to have an affective impairment that cannot be accounted for by impaired theory of mind, although it does seem to be the case that people with autism tend to have a mildly or severely impaired understanding of mind. The theory of mind hypothesis of autism has thus offered a powerful new insight into this enigmatic disorder.

7

THE NORMAL DEVELOPMENT OF AN UNDERSTANDING OF MIND

INTRODUCTION

I shall begin with a summary of what has already been presented in the last two chapters with regard to normal development. Wimmer and Perner (1983) devised an unexpected transfer test of false belief. Maxi put his chocolate in the green drawer in his kitchen and then departed. In his absence, the chocolate was moved to a blue drawer. Observing participants had to predict where he would look for his chocolate on his return. Nearly all those aged 6 years successfully took into account Maxi's false belief by correctly anticipating his futile search in the green drawer, where he had left the chocolate. In contrast, many children aged 4 and 5 years failed to acknowledge Maxi's false belief and judged that he would look in the blue drawer where the chocolate was currently located. Wimmer and Perner remarked upon the sharp developmental trend by suggesting that the older children had benefited from a radical conceptual shift in their thinking that allowed them to take into account another person's false belief. They suggested that the younger children had a cognitive void where other people's simple factual beliefs are concerned.

Perner *et al.* (1987) devised a deceptive box test of false belief, with the most famous example involving a Smarties tube that actually contained a pencil. Children had to judge what another person who had never seen that particular tube before would think it contained. Most children above the age of 4 years correctly anticipated another person's false belief by judging that they would think it contained Smarties. In contrast, 3-year-old children simply reported current reality by judging that another person would think that the tube contained a pencil. Meanwhile, Flavell *et al.* (1983) found that most children aged 3 years appeared to be unable to acknowledge the distinction between the way an object looks and what it really is. In the classic example, children were shown an object that convincingly resembled a rock, but then its true identity as a sponge became obvious when the child was allowed to feel the object. Finally, children were asked what it looked like and what it really was. Most of those aged 3 years gave the same response to both questions, usually 'sponge' and 'sponge'. Older children, in contrast, successfully judged that although the object really was a sponge, it looked like a rock.

Children seemed to have another difficulty with appearance-reality in a domain that was more obviously and intuitively relevant to understanding mind. Harris and Gross (1988) demonstrated that, just as young children appeared to be unable to acknowledge that a sponge can look like a rock, so they seemed unable to acknowledge that someone who was smiling could actually feel unhappy. That is, young children appeared to be unable to acknowledge the distinction between real and apparent emotion. They seemed unable to appreciate that the way in which an emotion is experienced and how it is expressed could differ. The children did not seem to grasp the distinctive existence of mind that resides behind the surface behaviour.

Gopnik and Astington (1988) found another way in which young children experienced difficulty in acknowledging false belief. Children were presented with a Smarties tube and asked what they thought was inside it. When they had replied 'Smarties', the experimenter opened the tube to reveal an unexpected pencil, then returned it to the tube, closed the lid, and then asked the child what he or she had thought was inside originally. Most of those over 4 years of age correctly responded 'Smarties', and thereby acknowledged their own initial false belief. In contrast, most of those below 4 years of age simply reported current reality. Moreover, Gopnik and Astington found that the children who failed in one of the tasks tended to fail in the others as well. That is, children who failed to anticipate another person's false belief tended not to report their own prior false belief and tended not to recognize a distinction between appearance and reality.

It became fashionable to claim that children experience a radical conceptual shift in their thinking at the age of about 4 years. There was a substantial consensus with the view put forward by Wimmer and Perner (1983), except that the age of acquisition of a theory of mind was pushed down by about 1 year. The prevailing view was that those who succeeded in acknowledging false belief had the cognitive credentials of an adult. The adult differs only in the ability to make more accurate diagnoses of belief, but is not better equipped to acknowledge the difference between belief and reality. The popular view continued that children who failed to acknowledge false belief, usually those aged 3 years and under, lacked a theory of mind. That is, absence of a correct judgement was taken to be a sign of absence of the requisite underlying cognitive competence.

The studies described so far were conducted in four different countries, namely Austria, the UK, Canada and the USA. Is it possible that the age of success in acknowledging false belief and related abilities is not something natural to human development, but rather something peculiar to child-rearing in Western civilization? To find out whether this might be the case, Avis and Harris (1991) trekked through the rain forest in the Cameroon. Their expedition brought them to the Baka tribe of pygmies who lived a traditional hunter-gather life. These people were largely uncontaminated by Western culture, and so were ideal for the purpose of investigating whether the sudden onset of success in acknowledging false belief at about 4 years of age is peculiar to Western civilization.

Avis and Harris (1991) devised a test of false belief that was appropriate for young members of the Baka community. It was an unexpected transfer test that was incorporated into a real-life interaction. An adolescent boy who, unknown to the child participant, was actually working in collaboration with the experimenter, was cooking mango in a pot over the fire inside his hut. While the fruit was cooking, the boy left the scene ostensibly to join his friends for a smoke outside. In his absence, the experimenter conspired with the observing child participant to move the mango from the cooking pot to a bowl in another part of the hut. Subsequently, the adolescent boy was about to return and the child participant was asked where the adolescent thought his mango was located. Most of those estimated to be aged around 5 years and over correctly judged that the adolescent would look for his mango in the cooking pot; they acknowledged his false belief. In addition, they correctly judged that he would feel happy before he opened his cooking pot. In contrast, younger children judged that the adolescent would look for his mango in the bowl, were it currently was. When they judged in this way, the experimenter insisted that the adolescent would look in his cooking pot, and were then asked how the adolescent would feel when he did so. The young children wrongly judged that he would feel sad, as though they were assuming the duped adolescent had a true belief.

The study by Avis and Harris (1991) in the Cameroon jungle yielded compelling evidence in support of the view that it is natural to human development for a competence in acknowledging false belief to emerge at approximately 4 years of age. It was starting to become apparent that children the world over progress through a radical conceptual shift at around the age of 4 years which serves to implant a theory of mind in their cognition that equips them with a theory of mind.

HAVE CHILDREN BEEN UNDERESTIMATED?

We do not have any positive evidence to suggest that 3-year-old children lack a theory of mind. Rather, all we know is that there is a lack of positive evidence that they can acknowledge false belief. It might well be that 3-year-old children fail to acknowledge false belief because they are bereft of a theory of mind, but another possibility is that they simply misunderstand the test question asked by the experimenter. Such young children who are novices at interacting with unfamiliar adults are bound to be prone to misunderstand what is being asked of them. An obvious candidate for miscomprehension surrounds the time reference in the test question, which would be critical to how the child answers. For example, in the deceptive box task, perhaps 3-year-olds wrongly think that the experimenter is asking what another person will think is inside after he or she has opened the lid and taken a look (and seen the pencil in there). This possible source of difficulty was identified by Lewis and Osborne (1990), who clarified the test question by simply rephrasing it as 'What will she think before she opens the lid?'. With this modification, many more children aged 3 years succeeded in acknowledging another person's false belief compared with those who were asked with the more vague wording used by Perner *et al.* (1987). Furthermore, Lewis and Osborne found that 3-year-old children stood a better chance of acknowledging their own prior false belief if asked what they had thought was inside before they opened the lid and peeped inside. Although Gopnik and Astington had taken precautions to be clear about the point in time to which they were referring in their task, Lewis and Osborne made even more precise reference to the time they meant by mentioning that it was before they had opened the lid.

Siegal and Beattie (1991) made a similar point with regard to the unexpected transfer task. When Maxi is returning for his chocolate, observing child participants have to predict where he will look, and children aged 3 to 5 years are divided in how they answer. Some correctly say that he will look in the last place where he saw the chocolate, namely the green drawer which, ironically, is empty at the present time. Other children say that he will search in the blue drawer where the chocolate is at present, but where Maxi has not seen it previously within the story. The children are categorized by age in how they tend to answer, with the younger children pointing to the current location of the chocolate (the blue drawer) and the older ones pointing to the place where Maxi last saw it (the green drawer). Wimmer and Perner's (1983) explanation for the younger children's inclination to point to the current location is that they must be constrained to do that if they have no conception of Maxi's beliefs. Apparently they do not grasp that Maxi's behaviour is a product of his belief, which in this case is false and will therefore lead him to search in the wrong place.

Siegal and Beattie (1991) offered a different explanation for the age trend. They suggested that the younger children probably do know about other people's beliefs, including Maxi's, but that they differ from older children in failing to interpret the test question appropriately. They assume quite sensibly, according to Siegal and Beattie, that the story is about Maxi finally obtaining his chocolate. They also assume, again quite sensibly, that they are allowed to contribute to the information in the story, and not just to limit their judgement of where Maxi will search strictly to the information presented in the story. After all, in real life people do all kinds of things that we cannot predict specifically on the basis of the information we have at our disposal, for the simple reason that the information we have is nearly always incomplete. For example, although this is not stated in the story, perhaps Maxi's mother had somehow communicated to Maxi before, when or after she moved the chocolate, that this is what she had done.

More importantly, why should the child's judgement of where Maxi will search be confined to the time period immediately following his arrival in the kitchen? Evidently the older children take the question to mean, 'Where will Maxi search as soon as he arrives in the kitchen?' That is, where will he search first of all? In contrast, for all we know it could be that the younger children interpret the question to mean, 'Where will Maxi search for his chocolate an hour or a day or a week after he has arrived in the kitchen?'. It is certain that Maxi would not persist indefinitely in searching in the green drawer where he left his chocolate. In essence, Siegal and Beattie (1991) made the highly plausible suggestion that the younger children may differ from the older ones not in their ability to comprehend mental states, but in their conversational skills which, in particular, cause the younger children to misunderstand what the experimenter means by the test question.

Having conducted that analysis of the unexpected transfer task, the remedy Siegal and Beattie (1991) came up with was simple and highly consistent with that of Lewis and Osborne (1990). They presented the unexpected transfer task to children aged 3 and 4 years, but divided the sample into two groups. Half the children were asked to predict where Maxi would look for his chocolate, and the rest were asked to predict where he would look for his chocolate first of all. The results were clear, and are shown in Figure 7.1. Those children who were asked the question suffixed with 'first of all' were much more likely to predict that Maxi would look in the place where he last saw his chocolate (the green drawer) and not where it was currently located. An improvement in the experimenter's communication with the child yielded an improvement in terms of the number of children who made a correct judgement, which cannot be explained by suggesting that

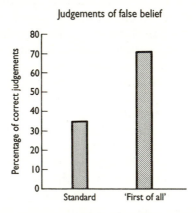

Judgements of false belief

FIGURE 7.1 Children find it easier to acknowledge false belief in an unexpected transfer test when asked where the protagonist will look *first of all*.

the younger children were ignorant of Maxi's beliefs. Instead, it seemed very much as though the point of difficulty was in the clash of conversational worlds between young children and adults.

Another problem facing young children is that they might have difficulty in comprehending and integrating the key elements of the unexpected transfer story. It might be their lack of ability in story comprehension that is responsible for their incorrect predictions of Maxi's search, rather than their failure to grasp his false belief. This point was investigated by Lewis *et al.* (1994), who dispensed with the customary play-people dolls and conveyed the unexpected transfer story by means of a picture-book they had composed. This allowed the researchers easily to go through the story again in order to highlight its main elements. This is precisely what they did, except that on going through the story a second time, the child did not sit passively, but was actively encouraged to relate the story back to the experimenter. There was considerable variation in the children's ability to succeed in this. Some 3-year-old children showed very good comprehension when they repeated the story, while others showed very poor comprehension, with many actually failing altogether to explain what it was about.

Those who showed good comprehension were also very effective in predicting that Maxi would search for his chocolate in the place where he last saw it. Those with poor comprehension tended to judge that Maxi would search for his chocolate in its current location (see Figure 7.2). The relationship between comprehension and correct judgements of false belief was maintained independently of the age of the child. In other words, children aged 3 years had no difficulty in acknowledging Maxi's false belief so long as they had shown proficiency in understanding the story. Contrary to the views of many researchers (e.g. Wimmer and Perner, 1983), it was not the age of the child that mattered, but the ability to comprehend the story.

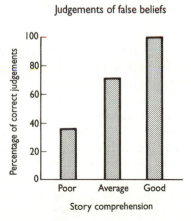

Judgements of false beliefs

FIGURE 7.2 Children who are good at comprehending stories stand a much better chance of acknowledging false belief in an unexpected transfer test than those who have poor comprehension.

Lewis *et al.* (1994) further assumed that getting the child to relate the story back to the experimenter not only served as a check on the child's comprehension but actually assisted comprehension. This led them to predict that children who told the story back to the experimenter would be more likely to acknowledge Maxi's false belief than children who went through the story a second time passively, as the experimenter told it once more. This expectation was supported. Having the children relate the story back to the experimenter helped them to acknowledge Maxi's false belief. It did appear that the limiting factor in children's ability to acknowledge false belief was their comprehension of the story, rather than whether or not they had acquired a concept of false belief. It seemed that the children already possessed that concept, but were unable to demonstrate this competence if they were struggling to comprehend the story.

We are left with the need to explain the children's difficulty in acknowledging false belief in the deceptive box task, especially failure to acknowledge their own prior false belief. There is actually a rather mundane reason why young children might fail in this task. They may be very reluctant to admit that they had been so silly as not to have realized that this particular tube had been tampered with! Perhaps they judged that they had known it contained a pencil all along just because they were trying to save face and deny that they had been duped in the first place. If so, the children's claim that they had thought the tube contained a pencil is related to their embarrassment at being wrong in the first place, rather than their inability to acknowledge that they or anyone else could hold a false belief. In other words, perhaps they knew that they had held a false belief, but felt loath to admit it.

THE IMPORTANCE OF DECEPTIVE BOX AND STATE CHANGE

Children have difficulty in acknowledging false belief in the deceptive box procedure that does not depend on the ability to comprehend a story. Therefore, it makes sense to focus on this when trying to establish whether young children really do have a basic difficulty with the concept of mind. We have looked at two factors that might result in children giving incorrect judgements in the deceptive box task without having to make reference to an immature conception of mind. One is that young children fail to acknowledge their own prior false beliefs because they do not like to admit that they had been mistaken, so they try to save face by pretending that they had known the truth all along. The other is that young children fail to comprehend the time reference in the test question, and assume that the experimenter is asking what another person will think is in the tube after he or she has opened the lid, looked inside and seen the pencil. Similarly, they may assume that when asked about their own false belief, the experimenter wants to know what they think is inside at present, not what they used to think.

Both of these problems were dealt with in one of the most powerful yet surprisingly rarely cited articles in this entire area of psychological investigation. It was conducted by Wimmer and Hartl (1991), and their first priority was to determine whether children fail to acknowledge their own prior false belief because they are loath to admit that they had been mistaken initially. The Austrian children who participated were first introduced to Kasperl, a puppet well known to them on television. His fame on television arises from his knack of getting everything wrong. An equivalent on UK television is Sweep, from the *Sooty and Sweep* show. Given Kasperl's tendency to get everything wrong, if there is anyone who is going to have a false belief, it is likely to be Kasperl!

Kasperl sat alongside the child participant and both were shown a Smarties tube, and both declared at this initial stage that they thought it contained Smarties. The experimenter proceeded to open the tube, unexpectedly reveal a pencil, then return this to the tube and close the lid. Finally, the child participants were asked what Kasperl had thought was in the tube first of all, and also what they themselves had thought was in there. The great majority of children aged 3 years claimed that they had thought there was a pencil in the tube, and they also claimed that Kasperl had thought there was a pencil in there. Their failure to acknowledge Kasperl's false belief was striking in the sense that they would not have experienced any personal embarrassment in saying that Kasperl had been mistaken, and should actually have anticipated that he would think something incorrect even in circumstances most favourable to him. Their failure to acknowledge a past false belief therefore does not seem to be explained by a sense of personal embarrassment in having been so silly as to think that a Smarties tube would contain Smarties!

In that case, it appears that we must resort to explaining the young child's difficulty in acknowledging false belief by suggesting that he or she simply assumed that the experimenter meant not 'What did you/Kasperl think first of all. . .?' but 'What do you/Kasperl think right now. . .?' – unless we are to concede that young children really do have a serious problem with false belief. To tackle this problem, Wimmer and Hartl (1991) devised the state change procedure, which is ingenious in its elegant simplicity. Wimmer and Hartl suggested that if young children have no conception of belief, then that will limit how they can interpret the test question. They will be constrained to answer the question 'what did you think was inside?' as 'what was inside?'. Hence, children's difficulty with the test question is not incompatible with their difficulty in understanding belief, and could actually be explained by their failure to understand belief. Thus their improved ability to comprehend the question at the age of 4 years is not directly due to greater insight into conversation, but to greater insight into mind. There is a very simple way of arbitrating between the conversational hypothesis and the cognitive hypothesis (the latter positing that the child lacks a conception of belief), and this is the state change procedure.

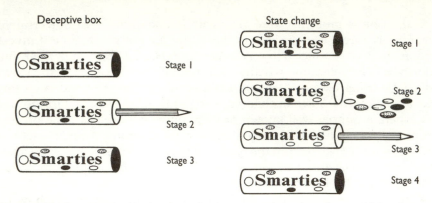

FIGURE 7.3 Compared with the deceptive box procedure, there is an additional stage in state change. In this, the child's initial belief is confirmed as being true when the experimenter opens the tube to reveal that it does contain Smarties, as anticipated.

The state change procedure, shown in Figure 7.3, works as follows. The child is shown a Smarties tube and as usual is asked what is inside it. When the child has replied 'Smarties', the experimenter opens the lid to reveal that there are indeed Smarties in the tube. The experimenter proceeds to remove the Smarties right away from the scene and replaces them with a pencil, all of this while the child watches. The experimenter then closes the lid with the pencil inside the tube and asks the usual test question, 'when you first saw the tube, what did you think was inside?'. According to Wimmer and Hartl (1991), the 3-year-old children, who lack a conception of belief, will be limited to interpreting this question as 'when you first saw the tube, what was inside?'. Therefore, they should give a correct answer in the state change procedure because, first of all, there were in fact Smarties in the tube. However, their correct judgement would not be a report of their prior belief but of the prior reality; they would give the right answer for the wrong reason. Meanwhile, in the standard deceptive box task, if the child interpreted the question in exactly the same way ('when you first saw the tube, what did you think was inside?' as 'when you first saw the tube what was inside?'), then they would answer wrongly with 'pencil', because this is what was in the tube initially. It is only coincidental that a pencil is in there at present, according to Wimmer and Hartl.

Wimmer and Hartl's (1991) analysis of how the question might be tackled by a child who does not understand about belief allows them to make a specific prediction about the pattern of judgements across the state change and deceptive box task. They predict correct judgements in the state change (for the wrong reason) and incorrect judgements in the deceptive box task. In contrast, the conversational hypothesis might predict that the child simply does not understand the time reference in the test question, and thinks that the experimenter is asking what is inside the box at present. If so, surely the child would display the same misunderstanding in the state change task as in the deceptive box task, and would therefore report the present content of both (a pencil). The results provided very strong support for Wimmer and

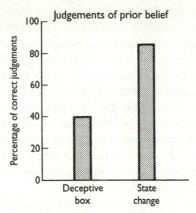

FIGURE 7.4 Children find it easier to make a correct judgement in state change than in a standard deceptive box task, but they might be giving the right answer for the wrong reason.

Hartl's (1991) hypothesis, with over 80 per cent of children aged 3 years giving a correct judgement of 'Smarties' in the state change (but perhaps for the wrong reason), while about two-thirds gave an incorrect judgement of 'pencil' in the standard deceptive box task. This striking pattern of judgements across tasks is illustrated graphically in Figure 7.4.

In summary, however we explain the child's success or failure in the unexpected transfer story task, young children's difficulty with false belief in the deceptive box task does not seem to be explainable by reference to their failure to comprehend the test question or their feeling of embarrassment in admitting that they had initially been mistaken. Any attempt to conclude that children have been underestimated with regard to what they understand about mind will have not only to demonstrate success in their performance in a test of false belief, but also to explain the distinctive profile of children's judgements across the state change and deceptive box tasks. It is for this reason that we can regard Wimmer and Hartl's (1991) study as one of the most important investigations conducted on this aspect of development.

CHILDREN'S UNDERSTANDING OF SOURCES OF KNOWLEDGE

The next step is to begin to explore what it is about false belief that presents difficulties for young children. According to Wimmer *et al.* (1988a), it is the ability to understand that information does not imprint itself directly on the mind, but rather is something that has to be perceived. Information arriving via the sensory organs has to be transduced into knowledge, a process that appears to be remarkably accurate but certainly not foolproof. For example, illusions can lead us to think something that is untrue. If abandoned in the desert, we might see in front of us something that looks like an oasis paradise, only to discover that it is a mirage. In an example closer to home, on seeing a Smarties tube, the familiar exterior may fool us into thinking that it contains Smarties when really it contains only a pencil. To understand that beliefs can be false is to understand that people can fall victim to misleading information. Wimmer *et al.* suspected that young children may not understand that beliefs can be false because they do not grasp the relationship between information arriving via the senses and the consequent state of belief – a belief state that could be at odds with what exists in reality. Children's failure to acknowledge false belief qualifies as evidence that they do not understand the precarious route from perception through to knowledge. What Wimmer *et al.* needed now in order to clinch their argument was a direct demonstration that young children do not understand, for example, that seeing leads to believing.

Wimmer *et al.* (1988a) approached this by asking children to judge whether another person knew the mystery content of a box. In some cases this other person had looked in the box, while in others she had not. Similarly, some of the participating children had themselves looked in the box, while others had not. The children were asked if the other person had looked in the box and if she knew what was inside. Even 3-year-old children had no difficulty in reliably and appropriately judging whether the other person had looked in the box. In stark contrast, their judgements of whether the other person knew what was inside the box were strikingly inconsistent. They frequently judged that the other person knew what was in the box when she had not looked inside it but, conversely, they judged just as frequently that the other person did not know what was in the box when she had looked inside it! Whether or not they themselves knew what was inside the box made no difference; the children were not just saying that the other person knew what was inside when they themselves knew. Meanwhile, most children aged 4 and 5 years made a link between seeing and knowing. If they judged that the other person had seen inside the box, then they judged that she knew what was inside it. If they judged that the other person had not seen inside the box, then they judged that she did not know.

Gopnik and Graf (1988) reported a related finding. They allowed children to discover the content of a box by one of three routes. The experimenter either gave them a clue (you can write with it – a pen) or told them explicitly, or they themselves saw what was inside the box. Subsequently, the children were asked to report what was inside the box, which they did without trouble, and then they were asked how they knew what was inside. Did they look inside, were they told, or did they receive a clue? The children aged about 3 years appeared to select one of the three available options at random. However bizarre it might seem, many of these young children would judge, for example, that they knew because they had looked, when in fact they had been told. In contrast, children aged 4 and 5 years reliably answered correctly, that they had seen if that was in fact the case, or that they had been told if that was the case. Gopnik and Graf concluded that young children have so little insight into the connection between informational access and knowledge that they do not even encode the source of their own knowledge.

A consistent finding was reported by Povinelli and DeBlois (1992), and was mentioned in Chapter 3 in connection with studies on chimps' understanding about mind. There were two upturned cups, and the children knew that one of them would have treasure hidden underneath it. They witnessed an experimenter hide the treasure, but a screen partially obscured their view such that they could not see under which particular cup the treasure was hidden. However, there were two other experimental assistants present in the room. One stood by and was able to see exactly where the treasure was hidden, while the other could not see, owing to the fact that he had a bag over his head. Subsequently, the child was able to see both cups in full view, and the assistant who had been wearing a bag over his head now discarded it. Both assistants pointed, but to different cups. The observing child participant then had the task of deciding which assistant's advice she should take – the one who had observed the hiding of the treasure, or the one who had not observed it. Most children aged 3 years seemed to answer at random. They were just as likely to search under the cup indicated by the assistant who had watched the hiding of treasure as under the other cup. They did not appear to grasp that the assistant who saw where the treasure was hidden was the person who knew where it was hidden. In contrast, the children aged 4 and 5 years reliably searched specifically under the cup indicated by the assistant who had witnessed the hiding of the treasure.

All of these findings are consistent with the view put forward by Wimmer et al. (1988b), stating that what distinguishes a 3-year-old from a 4-year-old, with regard to understanding minds, is the insight that informational access leads to knowledge, while lack of informational access leaves the individual in a state of ignorance. In other words, the older children understand that seeing is believing. These researchers even went so far as to make a rather intriguing prediction about an error which the older children might make that would betray their reliance upon a seeing-believing rule. They suggested that 4- and 5-year-olds might rely on the seeing-believing rule so heavily that they would overlook other ways in which people might acquire knowledge. Consequently, according to the prediction, children of this age might even deny that another person knew a fact when that person could have acquired the knowledge in question not by seeing but by making an inference.

Sodian and Wimmer (1987) tested this hypothesis in the following way. The experimenter allowed the child participant to look inside a bag, and when he did so, he learned that it contained choconuts – and only choconuts. The experimenter also showed the child a plain box, which was visibly empty. Subsequently, the experimenter asked the child participant to look away while she moved one of the objects from the bag into the box. Since there was only one kind of object in the bag (choconuts), and since the box had previously been empty, the child could thus infer that there was now a choconut inside the box. The experimenter confirmed that the child had made this inference when she asked the child to say what was inside the box, and children aged 4 to 6 years had no difficulty in replying that the box contained a choconut. It proved to be unnecessary for the child to look inside the box in order to answer correctly in this way, showing that the child could make a simple inference on the basis of the experimenter's clue.

There was nothing remarkable in itself about the fact that children of this age could make a simple inference. However, having established this, Sodian and Wimmer (1987) were able to test an intriguing hypothesis that they had formulated. They postulated that children aged 4 and 5 years would rely too heavily on what another person had seen when judging what they believed. They predicted, therefore, that children would judge that another person would know a fact if she had visual access to the relevant evidence, but that she would not know a fact if she lacked that experience. Sodian and Wimmer even went so far as to predict that children would deny that another person had knowledge of a critical fact when that person lacked visual access but otherwise had all the information necessary to make exactly the same inference that the child himself or herself had just made.

In Sodian and Wimmer's (1987) study, children were introduced to Susie, the experimenter's assistant, and had to judge whether Susie knew what was inside the box. They judged correctly that she did know when she looked inside it, and that she did not know when she did not look and had no other information. However, when Susie was given the clue, just like the child participant, that one of the objects in the bag had been moved to the box, children aged 4 and 5 years tended to deny that Susie knew what was inside the box. It made no difference that these children could use the clue for themselves to infer that there was a choconut in the box. Indeed, the children's judgements of what Susie knew were generally independent of what they themselves knew to be inside the box. This striking phenomenon is something that Sodian and Wimmer call 'inference neglect', and its presence

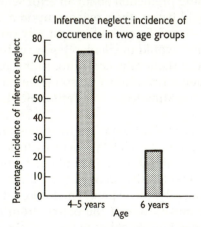

FIGURE 7.5 At the age of 4 or 5 years many children can acknowledge false belief, but they tend to deny that another person can know a fact by making an inference. They seem to assume that it is necessary to have direct information in order to know something.

in 4 and 5-year-olds is contrasted with the situation in 6-year-olds, as shown in Figure 7.5, which illustrates the combined data from the three studies.

Perner and Davies (1991) obtained a finding consistent with Sodian and Wimmer's (1987) report of inference neglect. They told children a story about John, who was depicted as seeing his football in the garden, but who then went inside his house to watch television. Subsequently, Jane arrived and announced to John that his football was in the garage. Hence John became a victim of conflicting information – what he had seen (the ball in the garden) and what he was told (the ball in the garage). Under one condition, the observing child participants knew, independently of the information available to John, that Jane's message was in fact true, whereas under another condition they knew that the message was false. Children then had the task of judging what John believed. In other words, they had to judge whether he would believe or disbelieve Jane's message. Children aged 4 and 5 years tended to judge that John would believe what he had seen previously in preference to what he was told subsequently; they judged that he would attach more weight to what he had seen directly than to what he was told.

Just on the basis of this finding, it might appear that children of the age tested assume that people (in this case, John) are generally mistrusting of verbally reported information (in this case, Jane's message). However, the results of a further condition showed that this was not the case. John was depicted as not seeing his football anywhere, so he was in a state of ignorance regarding the whereabouts of the ball. Subsequently, Jane announced to John that his football was in the garage, a message which the observing child participants (but not John) knew was false. Under this condition, children aged 4 and 5 years judged that John would believe the false message. Integrating this with Perner and Davies' (1991) other findings, we can conclude that children aged 4 and 5 years understand that how a person treats a message (whether to believe or disbelieve it) will depend upon what that person already believes, based on seeing directly. If the message contradicts prior knowledge based on seeing, children judge that the person will disbelieve the message. If, on the other hand, the message does not contradict prior knowledge, then children judge that the person will believe it. Whether the child participant knows independently that the message is true or false is irrelevant to the way they make their judgements.

Perner and Davies (1991) concluded that children aged 4 and 5 years understand that people actively interpret and integrate information. They understand that people evaluate information, such as a message, in the context of knowledge which they already possess. They also understand that people do not believe everything they hear, and neither do they disregard everything they hear. Rather, children appear to comprehend that whether or not a person will believe a given message depends on what that person already believes.

Apart from allowing Perner and Davies (1991) to draw an interesting conclusion, the results which they report contribute in another way to our

understanding of what children of this age understand about the relationship between seeing and knowing. In fact, it seems slightly odd that the
child should have been so willing to judge that John would disbelieve a
message that contradicted what he had seen previously. For all John knows,
Jane could have moved the ball from the garden to the garage, thus making
her message true. Indeed, her purpose in announcing that the ball is in the
garage could have been to update John's knowledge in accordance with the
change in situation. More generally, it would be strange if people were
unwilling to alter their beliefs in the light of an informative message from
another individual. If that were so, then messages would become virtually
redundant as a source of information. Although Perner and Davies presented their results as a celebration of the 4- and 5-year-old's understanding
that people interpret and evaluate verbal information, in another respect
their results appear to betray a misunderstanding about people's willingness to be informed by messages.

What kind of misunderstanding might the children have laboured
under? Perhaps they assume that other people are informed by what they
see to a much greater extent than they assume that people are informed by
what they are told. In Sodian and Wimmer's (1987) study, children aged 4
and 5 years effectively judged that Susie would not be informed by the
experimenter's message announcing that she had transferred an item from
the bag to the box. In Perner and Davies' (1991) study, children of the same
age judged that John would not be informed by Jane's message when he
held a prior belief based on what he had seen. Perhaps the children subscribe to a seeing-believing rule to the effect that people believe what they
see. In the case of Perner and Davies' results, the children were perhaps
judging that John believes what he sees so firmly that he will reject a conflicting message because it is merely a message. On the other hand, in
Sodian and Wimmer's study, perhaps the children judged that Susie would
not know that there was a choconut in the box because she had merely
been given a vague verbal clue and had not seen it directly. In summary,
perhaps the results of these different studies are united in demonstrating
the process whereby children aged 4 and 5 years ascribe beliefs to people.
They have acquired and then apply a seeing-believing rule, and sometimes
even over-apply that rule.

THE TROUBLE WITH SEEING-BELIEVING

Despite the evidence which suggests that children aged 4 and 5 years
strongly associate seeing with believing, ultimately it does not make sense
to say that children aged 3 years have difficulty in acknowledging false
belief because they have yet to construct a rule that links seeing with believing. The argument with regard to explaining failure to acknowledge false
belief would be that children do not yet realize that it is essential for an
individual to have the appropriate informational access if that person is to

be credited with a true belief; if they have misleading or outdated information, then we should ascribe a false belief to them. However, young children's difficulty in acknowledging false belief is not confined to their judgements about other people's beliefs, but can be generalized to judgements of their own prior belief. In judging that they had wrongly believed that a Smarties tube contained Smarties, it is unnecessary to recall what they had or had not seen. Making a judgement of their own prior belief need not require any such process of inference. Rather, they only have to recall what they used to think. Yet most children aged 3 years still fail to acknowledge their own prior false belief. Their difficulty must lie in the demands of acknowledging a belief as false, rather than in making a link between seeing and believing.

Apart from that argument, two studies have cast serious doubt on the claim that children aged 3 years cannot make a link between seeing and knowing. Pratt and Bryant (1990) noted that Wimmer *et al.* (1988a) asked a rather long and difficult question of their children. They asked them whether another person knew what was inside a box or whether she did not know. Pratt and Bryant replicated the procedure, but simply asked children whether the other person knew what was inside the box. With the simpler wording, children aged 3 years were much more likely to attribute knowledge to the other person in accordance with her visual access to the critical information. Indeed, the children's attribution of knowledge was strongly linked with their judgement of whether the other person had looked inside the box. As a matter of interest, Pratt and Bryant repeated the procedure, this time using the more convoluted question asked by Wimmer *et al.*, in order to investigate what kind of effect that would have. They found that children would tend to give their judgement before the experimenter had finished articulating the question. If the experimenter ignored the child's interjection, and just soldiered on regardless to the end of the question, then the children sometimes changed their answer. It seems that the children may have assumed that, because the experimenter ignored their first response, it was a sign that they were not judging as required and so thought it appropriate to give a different answer. Ironically, it seems that this may have led the children to answer incorrectly.

The possibility that 3-year-olds really do grasp the link between seeing and knowing was corroborated by Pillow (1989). In his study, children judged which of two puppets knew what was inside a box. One of the puppets stood on the box and the other opened the lid and looked inside (see Figure 7.6). Children reliably and without difficulty judged that the puppet who looked in the box was the one who knew what was inside. Evidently the children grasped that simply standing on the box was not sufficient for the puppet to know what was inside, but looking in it was. However, Pillow (1993) reports that children of the same age do appear to be confused about the link between the quality of information and the quality of the ensuing knowledge. For example, children sometimes

FIGURE 7.6 Even children aged 3 years understand that it is the person who looked in the box who knows what is inside it, rather than the person who stood on the box.

wrongly judged that touching (but not seeing) an object would inform a person about its colour.

CONCLUSIONS

We have established in this chapter that, at around 4 or 5 years of age, clinically normal children begin to acknowledge that beliefs can be false. They acknowledge their own prior false beliefs as well as the false beliefs of other people. In contrast, younger children seem to have serious difficulty in acknowledging false belief. The dominant view of this developmental trend seems to be that at approximately 4 years of age, children negotiate a radical conceptual shift that equips them with a basic but broad understanding of mind. Young children's difficulty in acknowledging false belief cannot be explained entirely by their misunderstanding of what the experimenter is asking them. Their success in Wimmer and Hartl's (1991) state change experiment testifies to this. Neither can their difficulty be explained as a failure to understand the link between seeing and knowing, although it does appear that slightly older children rely too heavily on their observation of what a person has seen when judging what that person knows. In the next chapter, we shall evaluate the claim that children profit from a radical shift in their thinking at around the age of 4 years.

8

A RADICAL SHIFT IN THE CHILD'S UNDERSTANDING?

INTRODUCTION

In the previous chapter, we were left with the impression that, at about 4 years of age, children negotiate a mysterious shift in their thinking that allows them to acknowledge that beliefs can be false. In this chapter, I shall challenge that view. In doing so, I shall argue that the development in children's ability to acknowledge false belief is a gradual process, a process that owes as much to an ability to resist reporting current reality as it does to understanding that people have minds which hold beliefs. On the face of things, this may seem an unprofitable approach to the problem on account of the findings of Wimmer and Hartl (1991), discussed in the previous chapter. In their state change task, children succeeded in resisting current reality. However, in this chapter I shall argue that, when interpreted differently, Wimmer and Hartl's results actually provide powerful support for a theory of gradual development, ironic as that may seem.

AGE TREND IN ACKNOWLEDGING FALSE BELIEF: A SECOND LOOK

It does seem rather suspicious that most 3-year-olds fail to acknowledge false belief while most 4- and 5-year-olds succeed. Surely this suggests that the older child has acquired a new insight, and in this case, what could it be other than a completely new conceptualization of mind? Either one takes into account another person's false belief or one does not – there can be no intermediate shades of success that fall between those two possibilities. Thus at first sight it seems to make no sense even to begin thinking that development could be gradual. However, just because the child either gives an incorrect or a correct judgement of false belief, it does not necessarily follow that the child's growing understanding of mind is stage-like. Perhaps, after all, we are just gaining the misleading impression that development is stage-like because the test of false belief as it is commonly formulated only allows a correct or incorrect answer. If it were possible for the child to be partially correct, then perhaps we would see that development is gradual. Maybe a defining characteristic of acknowledging false belief is that one is either correct or incorrect. That may be so, but it is still possible to proceed on the assumption that development of the child's understanding is gradual.

In that case, how do we make progress? We need to begin with a complete reconsideration of what is involved in making a judgement of false belief. Consider a 5-year-old child who correctly acknowledges her prior false belief about the contents of a Smarties tube. If we ask the child about her thoughts in connection with the contents of the tube, she could respond with either 'Smarties' or 'pencils'. How she answers in fact depends very much on how we ask the question. If we ask the child what she used to think, this will bias her to respond with 'Smarties', whereas if we ask her what she thinks right now, this will bias her to answer 'pencil'. If instead this child was aged 3 years, then she might answer 'pencil' to both questions. While the older child can shift her attention between current knowledge (pencil) and prior belief (Smarties), it seems that the younger child's attention is dominated by current knowledge. It might be not so much that the younger child lacks any understanding of false belief, but rather that her attention is simply dominated by current knowledge.

This is all very well, but why should the younger child's attention be dominated by current knowledge? One answer is as follows. The storage in memory of the prior belief could actually be extremely flimsy, since strictly speaking it never enjoyed the status of 'current knowledge'. Rather, it was just a guess that the child might have expected to be correct given prior experience of Smarties tubes, but it was unconfirmed at the time when the child articulated her initial belief. Opening the box to reveal the pencil demonstrated that the guess was wrong. In contrast, current knowledge is confirmed as true, and it is not surprising that it dominates the child's attention. So when the child says that she used to think there were pencils in the tube, perhaps this happens just because, in this context, the pencils compete more successfully for the child's attention as a candidate for judging what she used to think, owing to their physically tangible existence (unlike Smarties).

This may seem fine in theory, but how can we determine if it is really what is happening when a 3-year-old fails to acknowledge her own prior false belief? One way would be to embody the child's initial belief in a physical reality, and then perhaps it could compete with her knowledge of current reality on equal terms when she is asked what she used to think was inside the tube. We (Mitchell and Lacohee, 1991) proposed this idea, and our solution to the problem was to test children in the following way. We showed the child a Smarties tube and asked her to guess what was inside it. When she responded with 'Smarties', we asked her to identify a picture of

Smarties from a set of pictures presented to her. We then asked the child to post this into a special post-box where it remained out of sight until the end of the procedure. We opened the lid of the tube to reveal that in fact it contained a pencil, we returned the pencil to the tube and finally asked the child what she had thought was in the tube when she posted the picture into the post-box. Figure 8.1 shows the important steps in the procedure.

We conducted three experiments along these lines, and the results of all of them suggested that posting a picture of their prior belief helped the children to acknowledge it. The effect is illustrated in Figure 8.2, which shows the data from our second experiment of the series. For about 63 per cent of the time children aged 3 and 4 years correctly acknowledged that they had thought the tube contained Smarties after they had posted a picture of their initial belief. In contrast, children successfully acknowledged their prior false belief only about 23 per cent of the time in a standard version of the task.

Although the results supported our hypothesis, perhaps they could be explained in another way. It might be that, as other authors have suggested (e.g. Lewis and Osborne, 1990; Siegal and Beattie, 1991), children were more likely to succeed in acknowledging their prior false belief after they had posted a picture of Smarties not because the act of doing so provided a physical embodiment of their prior belief, but because the question was easier for children to understand. Other authors had suggested that young children get confused about the point in time to which the experimenter is referring – before or after we opened the lid and discovered the pencil inside. The wording of the posting question actually makes a very precise time reference ('What did you think when you posted your picture?'), so it might have been this that helped the children to give a correct judgement,

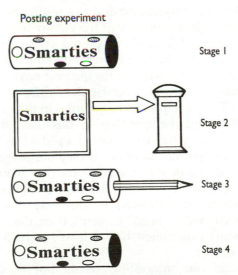

FIGURE 8.1 Children posted a picture of their belief that the box contained Smarties prior to discovering that in fact it contained a pencil.

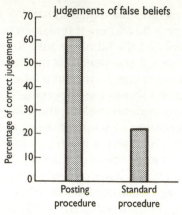

FIGURE 8.2 More children were able to acknowledge false belief in the posting procedure than in a standard procedure.

rather than the content of the picture. Fortunately, we were able to eliminate this competing explanation with the aid of a control condition, in which children still posted a picture, but it was of their favourite cartoon character (e.g. Mickey Mouse) instead of what they believed the tube contained. Finally, the children answered exactly the same question, but incorrect judgements were very frequent. In fact, they were just as frequent as incorrect judgements in a sample of children tested under the standard procedure. Evidently, it was not the wording of the question that mattered, but the image on the picture.

There remains yet another reason why the wording of the posting question might have affected the children. Perhaps the young children found the question difficult to comprehend and as a result misinterpreted it as not being about their prior belief, but about the picture that resided in the postbox. Perhaps when asked 'When you posted your picture, what did you think was inside . . . ?', the children thought that the experimenter was asking 'What is the picture you posted into the post box?', so the child's reply of 'Smarties' would not be a genuine recall of prior false belief, but just a statement of fact ('There is a picture of Smarties in the post box'). If the children did misunderstand the question in this way, then tell-tale errors would become apparent when they posted a picture of their favourite cartoon character in the control condition. If they misinterpreted the question to be asking about the content of the post-box, they would answer 'Mickey Mouse' because there was a picture of Mickey Mouse inside it. In fact, however, the children never answered in this way. Instead, they usually responded incorrectly with 'pencil'. It seems, then, that the conclusion arising from our posting experiment has at least survived an initial wave of searching questions.

Lacohee pursued our interesting result, but in collaboration with Freeman (Freeman and Lacohee, 1995). These researchers investigated whether there was something peculiar to pictures that helps young children to acknowledge their false belief. All we had said (Mitchell and Lacohee, 1991) was that the picture helps because it has a tangible physical existence. If that is correct, then an item other than a picture that also serves as a counterpart to a false belief should help to the same extent. To find out whether this is the case, Freeman and Lacohee persuaded children to post a picture in one condition and a sample in another. For example, the children were shown an egg box and quite sensibly guessed that it contained eggs initially. They then either posted an egg into a post-box (in the novel sample posting condition), or they posted a picture of an egg. Under both posting conditions, children were more likely to acknowledge their own prior false belief than in a standard test that did not involve posting. However, correct judgements of false belief were even more common among children who posted a picture of their belief rather than a sample of their belief (i.e. if they posted a picture of an egg rather than an actual egg).

Freeman and Lacohee (1995) formulated an intriguing conclusion with which I disagree, and I shall explain why shortly. They concluded that pictures have a special quality which makes them well suited as an *aide-mémoire* to beliefs. Effectively, they were suggesting that beliefs resemble pictures, and that seeing a picture of what one believes is unusually effective in alerting one to the fact that one is holding a belief about this. Hence, posting a picture in particular helps young children to acknowledge their prior beliefs.

The reason I disagree with this charming conclusion is to do with the evidence which suggests that children are not helped by a non-pictorial physical counterpart. Strictly speaking, children could not have been posting a sample of what they believed that the egg box contained. The sample egg cannot be in the egg box and in the post-box at the same time. Therefore, the sample egg that the child posted into the post-box is definitely not a physical counterpart to what the child believed was in the egg box. At the very least, it is not one and the same egg.

This argument may seem a little weak, but I hope to persuade you otherwise with a reminder about state change. The child sees a Smarties tube which is opened to reveal that it actually contains Smarties. These are removed and then replaced by a pencil. Now in this case, the child's initial belief really does have a physical counterpart, namely the Smarties that the experimenter removed from the tube. These are the very Smarties of the child's belief. In Freeman and Lacohee's (1995) procedure, by contrast, the egg that is posted is not the very egg of the child's belief. When we view things in this way, the state change procedure assumes a whole new significance, not just in relation to Freeman and Lacohee's study, but also centrally in relation to the theory I wish to propose. What is beginning to emerge here is the idea that children might be giving a correct judgement in state change because their initial belief was shown to have a physical counterpart.

ANOTHER LOOK AT STATE CHANGE

Wimmer and Hartl (1991) argue very cleverly that children aged 3 years have no understanding of belief and are therefore confined to interpreting the experimenter's question as though there was no reference to belief in it. So when the experimenter asks, 'When you first saw the tube, what did you think was inside it?', the child will interpret this as, 'When you first saw the tube, what was inside it?'. My account is different. It is that the child acknowledges his prior belief as a belief, and is helped to do that on having seen that the initial belief had a physical counterpart in reality (the tube contained Smarties). It is irrelevant that the prior belief happens to be true; all that matters is that it was seen to be anchored in a physical reality. In contrast, it matters enormously that the belief was true in Wimmer and Hartl's account, because it is only under such a condition that the child's supposed interpretation of the question ('What was inside the tube?') could lead him to give a correct answer for the wrong reason.

Now we can begin to arbitrate between the two explanations put forward to account for children's correct judgements in state change. If, as Wimmer and Hartl (1991) suggest, young children interpret the question as 'What was inside?', then a tell-tale error would become apparent in a novel task that is illustrated in Figure 8.3. As the figure indicates, we show the child a Smarties tube and ask her to guess what is inside it. After the child has responded with 'Smarties', we open the lid to reveal unexpectedly that it contains a door key. We then remove the key as the child watches patiently and replace it with a pencil. Finally, we ask the usual question, namely 'When you first saw the tube, what did you think was inside?', which Wimmer and Hartl suggest the child will interpret as 'When you first

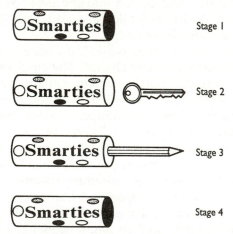

FIGURE 8.3 A deceptive box with a succession of two unexpected contents. Children were asked either what they thought was in the box (correct answer = 'Smarties') or what was in the box (correct answer = 'key').

saw the tube, what was inside?'. If they do interpret the question in that peculiar way, then they will respond with 'key', since that was the object inside the tube first of all. Indeed, children should answer 'key' just as often as members of a control group asked explicitly to report what was in the box first of all. In contrast, my prediction is that children will tend to report current reality when judging belief in a context where the belief has no physical counterpart, so I predict that they will respond with 'pencil'.

The suggested study was duly conducted by Saltmarsh *et al.* (1995). Each child was shown a box whose atypical content was exchanged for another atypical content while the child watched. Finally, half of the children were asked what was inside the box first of all, while the rest were asked what they thought was inside the box first of all. The data are shown in Figure 8.4. Unfortunately for Wimmer and Hartl (1991), the findings were not at all as they would have predicted. It was common for children to report the current content when asked what they had thought was in the box first of all; indeed, that was the most popular reply. In contrast, when asked what was inside the box first of all, the vast majority of children correctly reported the initial content; certainly it was uncommon for them wrongly to report the current content. Frankly, Wimmer and Hartl were wrong in their predictions.

It is one thing to show that they were wrong, but quite another to show that children give a correct judgement of belief as a judgement of belief. Evidently children do not give a correct judgement for the wrong reason, as Wimmer and Hartl (1991) suggest, but is their judgement to be construed as a genuinely correct one for the reason I state? Remember that I suggested that in principle it should make no difference whether the belief the child has to judge is true or false. It is similarly incidental that the child is making a judgement about his or her own prior belief instead of another person's

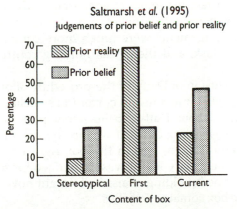

Saltmarsh *et al.* (1995)
Judgements of prior belief and prior reality

FIGURE 8.4 When asked what was inside the box, children tended to respond correctly with 'key', which was the initial content (lined bars). When asked what they thought was inside, children tended to respond incorrectly with 'pencil', which was the current content (dotted bars).

prior, present or future belief. If the state change procedure could be used to elicit a correct judgement of false belief, then that would suggest that they give the right judgement for the right reason. So we are assuming that the child's success in state change stems not from the belief having been true initially, or from it being personal to the child participant, but from the child having seen a physical counterpart to that belief.

We (Saltmarsh *et al.*, 1995) devised a test of 'false belief state change' to solve the problem. In following this line of inquiry, we had to take the preliminary step of showing that just as the child is helped to recall her own prior true belief in state change, so she is helped to recall the prior true belief of another individual. This is not controversial, and certainly Wimmer and Hartl (1991) would have no problem in accepting that suggestion. The full importance of our introduction of another person to the equation will become apparent shortly. The child participant sat alongside Daffy and both guessed that a Smarties tube contained Smarties. Daffy then left the scene and, in his absence, the child's (and Daffy's) belief was confirmed to be true – the tube did contain Smarties. The experimenter proceeded to replace the Smarties with a pencil. Finally, Daffy returned, and the children judged both what they themselves had thought was in the box first of all, and also what Daffy had thought was there first of all. So the children made judgements in an ordinary state change task about their own and Daffy's prior true belief.

We all (including Wimmer and Hartl, 1991) predict that children would find it easier to acknowledge their own and Daffy's prior true belief in this than to acknowledge their own or Daffy's prior false belief in a standard deceptive box task. According to Wimmer and Hartl, of course, children would be interpreting the question as 'What was inside the box?', whether they were being asked about themselves or about Daffy, and therefore they would give the right answer for the wrong reason. As predicted, the children did give correct judgements very frequently in the state change concerning their own prior true belief and also concerning Daffy's prior true belief; correct judgements were much more common than in a standard deceptive box task, and there was nothing controversial about this finding.

However, the inclusion of Daffy in the procedure allows us to transform a test of prior true belief into a test of current false belief. All we did was to change the question about Daffy's belief from past to present tense, so instead of asking what Daffy thought was in the box first of all, we asked the child what Daffy thought was in the box right now. Since Daffy had been absent when the usual content was exchanged for something atypical, we can assume that he is holding a false belief right now. Presumably Daffy still thinks that the box contains Smarties.

Let us pause to consider how 5- or 6-year-old children would answer the question about current belief with regard to the content of the box. If the child was asked about her own current belief she would respond with 'pencils', whereas if she was asked about Daffy's current belief she would respond with 'Smarties'. Effectively, there are two possibilities which the child could consider when judging belief in this context, and altering the topic of the question (Daffy or self) is sufficient to direct the child to choose one possibility in preference to the other. In contrast, I am supposing that a 3-year-old child would not find it so easy to switch between those two possibilities. Instead, no matter how the question is worded, she might be heavily biased to report belief as something that was seen to have a physical and tangible existence. However, in this procedure in which the child makes a judgement about Daffy's current false belief, it so happens that the correct response (Smarties) was seen to have a physically tangible existence. Putting it simply, it should be easy for the child to acknowledge that Daffy believes the tube contained Smarties because the child herself (it need not be Daffy) had seen that the tube contained Smarties. So 'Smarties' becomes an accessible candidate for the child when judging Daffy's current false belief. The child's knowledge of the current content of the box (pencil) would not be overwhelming in this context because its physical status is matched by the prior content.

In contrast to all of this, Wimmer and Hartl (1991) predict quite simply that children would interpret 'What does Daffy think is inside the box now?' as 'What is inside the box now?'. They predict, then, that realist errors would be just as common in our novel procedure as they are in a standard deceptive box task. They would also predict that children would give more correct judgements with regard to Daffy's prior true belief than with regard to his current false belief. This follows because if children give a correct answer for the wrong reason, that could only work for prior true belief and not for current false belief.

The results were entirely in support of the hypothesis I favour, but completely inconsistent with that of Wimmer and Hartl (1991). When judging Daffy's current false belief, children were much more likely to respond correctly with 'Smarties' if they had seen this content in the box previously (state change) than if they had not (standard deceptive box). Moreover, correct judgements about Daffy's current false belief were just as common as correct judgements about his prior true belief. Hence it was not the truth of the belief that mattered, but whether it was seen by the child participant to have had a physically tangible existence. Therefore, when children give a correct judgement of their own or Daffy's prior true belief in state change, it seems most likely that they are acknowledging this as a belief and not just as a prior reality, contrary to the view of Wimmer and Hartl. Ultimately, then, the results reported by those researchers do not provide evidence against an early understanding of false belief, but ironically provide evidence in support of such understanding. The results also offer an insight into the kind of difficulty young children face in acknowledging false belief. It seems that they can easily acknowledge beliefs that have a grounding in reality, but cannot so easily acknowledge beliefs that are devoid of that quality.

Explaining behaviour

People's behaviour provides a clue about their beliefs. We might say that beliefs can be read off behaviour. For example, if Maxi were to go so far as to search in the green drawer where he left his chocolate, that gives us a further clue that he is holding a false belief. This is a rather interesting clue to belief, because we might say that Maxi's search behaviour is a physical counterpart to his false belief, and accordingly predict that observing child participants will find it easy to acknowledge that Maxi is holding a false belief in this context. This is precisely the manipulation introduced by Bartsch and Wellman (1989). In a preliminary phase of the procedure, the child participants witnessed the experimenter remove Band-aids from a Band-aids box and place them instead into a plain white box. Subsequently, a puppet in a story that the experimenter enacted before the child was depicted as needing a Band-aid to dress the wound of another person. The puppet then went to the Band-aids box, and at this point the experimenter asked the child participant to judge where the puppet thought the Band-aids were. It was very common for children aged 3 years to judge correctly that the puppet thought (wrongly) that there were Band-aids in the Band-aids box. In contrast, when children did not see the puppet search in the Band-aids box, they wrongly ascribed a true belief to the puppet. They committed the classic error of answering that he thought the Band-aids were in the plain white box.

A superficially similar study produced equivocal results. Moses and Flavell (1990) showed a video to children about a girl called Cathy, who deposited crayons in a bag and then left the room. In her absence, a clown arrived and replaced her crayons with rocks. Finally, Cathy returned to get her crayons and approached the bag. Child viewers were asked to judge what she thought was inside the bag. Although children were more likely to judge that she (wrongly) thought that there were crayons in the bag than under a condition in which they did not see Cathy approach the bag, incorrect judgements ('She thinks there are rocks') were very common.

There are two ways of reconciling the results of these two studies. One is to conclude that Moses and Flavell (1990) underestimated children, and the other is to conclude that Bartsch and Wellman (1989) overestimated them. First, we shall consider how Moses and Flavell may have underestimated children. Cathy's behaviour alone actually provides no clue about what she thinks is in the bag. Because she is looking in the bag, it does not mean that she thinks there are crayons inside it. The exterior of the bag in no way advertised its contents as 'crayons'. In contrast, there is a clue to belief in the behaviour of the puppet in Bartsch and Wellman's study. Because it is a Band-aids box in which the puppet is looking, presumably he believed there were Band-aids inside. The belief can be inferred from the behaviour in Bartsch and Wellman's study but not in that of Moses and Flavell. In that case, perhaps we can say that the behaviour in question in Bartsch and

Wellman's study served as a salient physical counterpart to the puppet's belief, but that it did not do so in Moses and Flavell's study.

As mentioned previously, however, perhaps Bartsch and Wellman's (1989) results give too flattering an impression of what young children understand about false belief. According to Perner (1991), children in Bartsch and Wellman's procedure may have been judging not that the puppet thinks (wrongly) that there are Band-aids in the box, but that he is thinking about Band-aids in the box. In other words, perhaps the children were judging that the puppet was day-dreaming about Band-aids, and day-dreams are neither correct nor incorrect, they are just day-dreams. In contrast, beliefs are held as being true, but ironically they can in fact be false. Perner suggests that it is specifically this characteristic of beliefs that poses a problem for young children – the understanding that people hold their beliefs with the assumption that they are true. If Perner's suggestion (which is rather implausible in my view, incidentally) were true, then children were not acknowledging false belief in Bartsch and Wellman's procedure, but only the fact that people can day-dream – which Perner thinks is not a very impressive achievement.

Robinson and I (Robinson and Mitchell, 1995) set out to clarify this issue. We composed a story about identical twins called Joe and Steve, which is shown in Figure 8.5. They have a ball which they put in the drawer on the left-hand side of the scene, and Joe then leaves. In his absence, Steve moves the ball from the left-hand drawer to the right-hand drawer, and then he leaves the scene as well. In the next scene, both twins have returned with their mother, who asks them to get the ball. Under one condition, the children finally see the twins go to a drawer, but they each go to different drawers. One goes to the place where the ball used to be and the other goes to the place where the ball is at present. We cannot tell which twin is which, owing to their identical appearance. The task presented to the observing child participant is to infer the identity of the twin who went to the empty location. Is it Joe who went outside, or is it Steve who stayed inside? Many children aged 3 years correctly answered that it was Joe who went outside. Their good performance contrasted sharply with that in a control condition under which observed children did not see the final picture. Instead Joe was singled out and children were reminded that he was the one that went outside. Children then had to judge where Joe would look for the ball first of all. A substantial majority of the children wrongly answered that he would look in the place where the ball was at present. Thus when explaining behaviour that had already happened, young children succeeded in making a link between the twin who went outside and searching in the empty location. However, when predicting where that same twin would search for the ball, the children wrongly predicted that he would look in the place where the ball was at present.

We suggested that the children's success in inferring that the twin who searched in the wrong place was the one who went outside stemmed from the twin's false belief having a counterpart in his behaviour. This physical

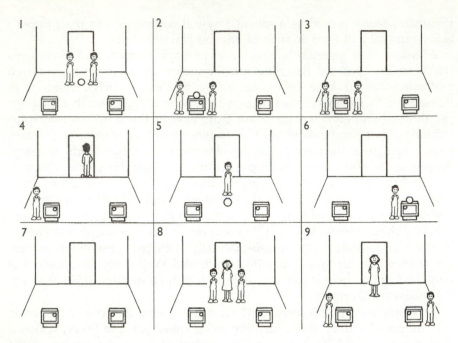

FIGURE 8.5 Only one of the twins sees the ball being transferred from the left to the right drawer. When Mum asks them to fetch the ball, one twin goes to the drawer where the ball is currently, and the other goes to the drawer where the ball used to be. Observing children were able to infer that the twin who went to the empty drawer is the one who went outside at the critical moment.

embodiment of the false belief seemed to make it easier for young children to understand. Moreover, we argued that the children could not have been assuming merely that the twin looking in the empty drawer was thinking about the ball in there (day-dreaming), rather than thinking that the ball was in there. Day-dreaming is detached from reality, and one can easily day-dream that a ball is in an empty location without having seen it there. If the children thought that the twin looking in the empty drawer was day-dreaming, there is no reason to suppose that this was Joe, who had been outside; the day-dreamer could equally well have been Steve, who stayed inside. Since the children preferentially judged that the twin at the empty drawer was Joe who went outside, it seems they were assuming that Joe's absence at a critical moment in time meant that he was holding a false belief regarding the whereabouts of the ball. Hence it seems that children's ability to identify correctly the twin as Joe demonstrated that they were genuinely acknowledging that he was holding a false belief. Perner's day-dreaming argument simply does not make sense in this context.

In summary, then, there is ample evidence to suggest that children can be helped to acknowledge a belief (true or false, self or other) when the belief in question is seen to have a counterpart in physical reality. However, this does not mean that young children find it easy to acknowledge false belief after all. On the contrary, the evidence strongly suggests that young children have considerable difficulty in acknowledging false belief. I am not trying to convince you that in fact false belief is easy for young children – rather, my purpose is to suggest why it might be difficult. Acknowledging false belief is difficult because the young child pays a little too much attention to current reality. Older children find it easier to acknowledge false belief because they are not so heavily locked into current reality. So I am in agreement with researchers such as Perner (1991) and Gopnik (1993) who say that false belief is difficult for young children, but I disagree with them as to why that is so. According to those researchers, young children lack a concept of belief, whereas older children possess such a concept. In my view, the two age groups differ by a matter of degree, and in particular they differ in how much they rely on reality when making their judgements. What we have seen so far is that my prediction is supported by the finding that young children can be helped to acknowledge false belief if the belief is endorsed by a counterpart in reality. An equally important prediction from my account is that older children, and even adults, share the same process for judging beliefs as young children, and therefore they may also be susceptible to a realist bias in some contexts. That is a view we shall now explore.

DIFFICULTY IN ACKNOWLEDGING FALSE BELIEF IN OLDER CHILDREN

A research student studying with me (Steverson, 1996) investigated the effect of suggestion on children's ability to acknowledge false belief. We suspected that suggestion presented an opportunity to reveal correct judgements in young children, but that it could also be used to elicit immature realist judgements from older children. Steverson showed children a Smarties tube and asked them what they thought was inside it. After they had guessed 'Smarties', she opened the tube to reveal only a pencil. She returned it to the tube, closed the lid and then suggested to the child, 'When you first saw this tube, you thought there were Smarties inside, didn't you?'. Very many children agreed with this suggestion, even those who failed to acknowledge their own prior false belief in a standard procedure.

However, we cannot tell just from that result whether the children agreed with the suggestion because they were generally compliant, or because the suggestion was true and they knew this. To help discriminate between these competing possibilities, Steverson (1996) introduced a control condition in which she suggested falsely that children had thought there were jelly babies in the tube. If they were generally compliant, then the children would accept this control suggestion, but in fact they very seldom did so. It seems that when they agreed with the suggestion that they had thought the tube contained Smarties, this was not due to general compliance, but to the fact that they knew the suggestion was true.

On the other side of the coin, we predicted that older children, aged 5 and 6 years, might be willing to accept a suggestion that they had believed a Smarties tube contained pencils. That expectation was confirmed, and once again the children correctly rejected a control suggestion that they had believed the tube contained jelly babies. However, this case is slightly different. Here it was being suggested to the children that they had known the true content of the tube all along, and perhaps they felt loath to contradict the experimenter's apparently favourable impression of their knowledge of things. In other words, perhaps there is some potential investment for children in accepting the suggestion that they had known the truth all along. To test for this possibility, Steverson (1996) took a lesson from Wimmer and Hartl (1991) and introduced Sweep to the procedure. Sweep is notorious for getting things wrong, so presumably the child would have the prior expectation that he would think the wrong thing in this context. As it happens, this was confirmed when Sweep judged that the tube contained Smarties but it turned out that really there was only a pencil inside. However, the experimenter suggested to the child that when Sweep first saw the tube, he thought there was a pencil inside. Children aged 5 and 6 years were highly inclined to agree with this, whilst rejecting a control suggestion. It seems that the children's acceptance of the suggestion had nothing to do with involvement of their ego but rather they accepted it because this meant that they would not have to acknowledge a false belief.

Altogether, then, it seems that children below the age of 4 years can succeed in acknowledging false belief if assisted, while children above that age can fail if hindered. These findings are consistent with children aged 6 years and below having difficulty with false belief. It is not the case, apparently, that 4-year-olds have acquired a new concept and that being the end of the story. Rather, it remains tempting for them to judge all beliefs to be true, and this can be demonstrated through suggestion. The older children do find it easier to acknowledge false belief than the younger ones, but an all-or-nothing stage does not appear to be at issue here. What would be really dramatic is a demonstration that adults seem to find it hard to resist reporting what they know of reality when judging another person's (or their own) belief. This is the provocative idea that we shall explore next.

DIFFICULTY IN ACKNOWLEDGING FALSE BELIEF IN ADULTS

We have known for a couple of decades that adults suffer from a 'hindsight bias'. The seminal study was conducted by Fischhoff (1975), who told participants some details of a historical event concerning a battle between British and Ghurkha armies that took place a couple of centuries ago. The participants were informed about factors that might favour one side or the other. For example, the British were well organized, had excellent weapons, ample supplies and good tactics. On the other hand, the Ghurkhas were intimately familiar with the terrain, they were highly motivated to defend their own territory, and they enjoyed numerical superiority. The participants' task was to weigh up the evidence and then to decide which army stood a better chance of clinching victory. They were also told incidentally of the outcome, but were asked to ignore this when making their decision. Thus they had to decide which army they thought would win, as if they had not actually known the outcome. Another crucial factor was that half the participants were told that in fact the British had won, while the rest were told that in fact the Ghurkhas had won. This was presented as though it was factual information, but it varied between experimental conditions.

The participants showed a hindsight bias in the sense that they tended to judge that the odds were in favour of the army they were told had actually won. The participants showed what we might call a 'knew it all along' effect. Under another condition, the participants made a slightly different kind of judgement. Instead of having to judge what they would have thought as if they did not know the actual outcome, they were asked to judge what another group of people, who had not been told the actual outcome, would predict. A similar effect occurred in the sense that participants were inclined to judge that another group of people would predict an outcome that the participants themselves had been told was true. This seems to be different to a hindsight bias, and more like an inclination to report what one assumes to be true oneself when asked to judge what another person believes. In other words, it appeared that the participants were having some trouble with false belief!

My colleagues and I set about trying to shed some light on the matter (Mitchell *et al.*, 1996a). We told adults a story, adapted from Perner and Davies (1991), which was described in the previous chapter, and is illustrated in Figure 8.6. In Scene 1, Kevin stood on a chair and looked into a jug that was on the shelf, and he saw orange juice in the jug. In Scene 2 he left the room. In Scene 3, Kevin returned to the room with Rebecca, who announced that there was milk in the jug. At this point, participants are asked to judge what Kevin thinks is in the jug. Kevin is a victim of conflicting information, and there is no way of telling whether he would choose to believe what he saw with his own eyes some time ago, or whether he would believe what Rebecca had told him more recently. All things being equal, he would probably believe what he saw in preference to what he was told. On the other hand, all things being equal, he would probably believe more recent information (in this case, the message) in preference to earlier information. We thought that, under these conditions, where there is no right or wrong answer regarding what Kevin would believe, there would be opportunity for the participants' own belief about the content of the jug to contaminate their judgement of what Kevin would believe. Therefore, we informed some of the participants in an aside that Rebecca had poured out the orange juice and replaced it with milk, which meant that her message was unequivocally true. We call this false belief true message (FBTM), because Kevin's prior belief is false and Rebecca's message is true. Under another condition, we supplied no additional information, and called this

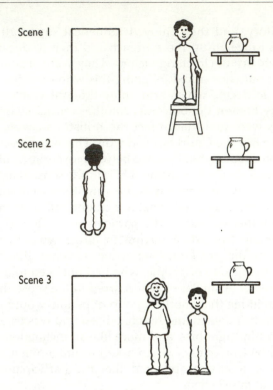

Scene 1

Scene 2

Scene 3

FIGURE 8.6 Kevin sees orange juice in the jug (Scene 1) and then leaves (Scene 2). Finally, Kevin returns with Rebecca, who announces that there is milk in the jug (Scene 3). Participants judge what Kevin believes, what he saw or what he was told. Under one condition, participants know that what Kevin saw remains true, while in another they know that the message is true. Kevin receives the same information under both conditions.

true belief false message (TBFM). Pilot studies had revealed that observing participants were highly inclined to disbelieve Rebecca's message themselves when no additional information was provided. They assumed that Kevin had a true belief based on what he had seen in the jug, and that Rebecca simply told him something that was untrue. We also included a control condition with a slightly different set of pictures. In this, Kevin was not depicted as looking in the jug initially, so he had no prior belief. However, observing participants were told that the jug contained orange juice. Subsequently, Kevin was the recipient of a false message, when Rebecca announced that there was milk in the jug. We labelled this no belief false message (NBFM). We asked both adults and children aged 5 and 8 years to judge what Kevin thought was in the jug at the end of the story.

The children's judgements did not differ with age, so we combined the data from the two age groups. The data from the children were highly consistent with the data reported by Perner and Davies (1991), in that children as a group showed a slight preference for judging that Kevin would retain his prior belief based on what he saw in the jug, and therefore that he would reject Rebecca's message. The participants judged in the same way whether they knew that Rebecca's message was true or false. In other words, their own knowledge of the truth of the message did not influence how believable they thought Kevin would perceive it to be – their judgements did not differ between FBTM and TBFM. It might have been that children were generally inclined to judge that Kevin did not believe any kind of message, but the control condition (NBFM) disproved that possibility. When Kevin was depicted as having no prior belief, the children judged that he would believe a false message. Again, this is consistent with the findings of Perner and Davies. The pattern of children's judgements across story conditions is depicted in the dotted bars in Figure 8.7.

The adults judged differently, and in a manner that was at the same time striking and entirely in support of our hypothesis. Their judgements across story conditions are depicted in the lined bars of Figure 8.7. The bars of special interest are TBFM and FBTM, which show that when Kevin the story protagonist was the victim of conflicting input, the participants were inclined to judge that he would believe the message if they (the observing participants, not Kevin) knew independently that it was true (FBTM), but that he would disbelieve the message if they knew it was false (TBFM). In other words, the adult participants differed from the children in allowing their privileged knowledge of reality to contaminate their judgement of Kevin's belief – in circumstances where Kevin was a recipient of partial and conflicting information. It is remarkable to find that adults are prone to a realist bias under circumstances where children are not.

It might be that, as we considered in the previous chapter, the children had latched on to a simple rule for judging belief. Apparently they were simply judging that Kevin will base his beliefs on what he sees, and that

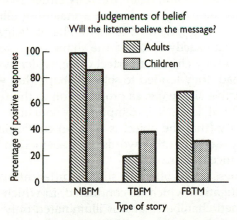

FIGURE 8.7 Children tended to judge that Kevin would believe what he saw, whether that meant attributing a true or false belief to him. In contrast, adults judged that Kevin would believe whatever they themselves knew to be true. The adults were thus susceptible to a realist bias, whereas the children were not.

those beliefs will be held so firmly that they are resistant to updating by a subsequent conflicting message, uttered in this case by Rebecca. Ultimately, it is no use relying exclusively on that kind of seeing-believing rule in order to infer other people's beliefs, so it appears that the adults had quite sensibly dispensed with it, at least to an extent. Ironically, it seems that once we no longer rely so heavily on a simple seeing-believing rule, a realist bias once again surfaces. It is an intriguing possibility that the realist bias that dominates 3-year-olds' judgements of belief vanishes in middle childhood, only to return in adulthood in a more subtle form. Evidently, being able to acknowledge false belief requires the capacity to resist a realist bias, and even adults are not ideally equipped in this respect. In the light of these findings, it is no longer sensible to persist in saying that an understanding of belief is acquired in a single step at the age of 4 years.

ADULTS' DIFFICULTY WITH APPEARANCE AND REALITY

Young children have a further difficulty that is related to failure to acknowledge false belief. Not only do they report reality when asked about belief, but they also tend to report reality when asked about the appearance of an object. This is evident when the appearance and the reality of an object differ, as in a sponge that is painted so that it appears like a rock (see previous chapter). Surely adults experience no similar difficulty in distinguishing between appearance and reality? Amazingly, once again a survey of the existing literature suggests that adults may well have such a problem. The classic research on this issue was conducted by Thouless in the 1930s.

Thouless (1931) placed a circular disc on a table, and then asked participants to regard it from one end of the table and report how it looked from their particular vantage point. They did this either by drawing how the ellipse appeared to them, or by selecting a matching ellipse from a set of alternatives that Thouless presented to them. The participants tended not to choose an ellipse that exactly matched the shape projected on to their retinas, but neither did they choose a perfect circle, which was the 'real' shape of the object. Instead, they tended to select a shape that was a compromise between the projective shape (i.e. as projected on to the retina) and the real shape. Superficially at least, it is tempting to conclude that participants' knowledge of reality (that the object is a circle) contaminated their judgement of how it appeared. In other words, they seemed to be having trouble separating appearance from reality.

However, Thouless (1931) offered a slightly different interpretation based on a further investigation which he conducted, in which the disc was presented in a darkened chamber that was illuminated only to the extent that the white surface of the circle was visible though a peep-hole. As before, because the circle was viewed obliquely, it appeared elliptical, but in this case there were no perspective cues to put the apparent shape into the visual context of a circle viewed at a slant. Under these conditions, Thouless reports that participants judged the shape accurately, and were able to resist exaggerating its circularity. None the less, the participants did know that the elliptical shape arose from a circle which they were viewing obliquely.

Taylor and I (Taylor and Mitchell, 1996) had reason to doubt Thouless' (1931) suggestion that exaggeration of circularity owed nothing to knowledge that the shape under inspection was really a circle. Thouless' testing was understandably primitive, and might not have been sensitive to a subtle exaggeration that arises purely from knowledge that the object is an ellipse, and independently of any perspective cues suggesting the same. We conducted an experiment to find out whether this was the case, and constructed the apparatus shown in Figure 8.8. The disc was mounted on a rod that allowed it to be swivelled. When the box was closed, the disc could be viewed through a peep-hole in the side. The interior of the box was completely dark, but the disc remained visible on account of the luminous material of which it was composed. Participants looked at the disc through the peep-hole and then looked through a peep-hole on to a computer screen. On the screen, they saw a circle which they could compress along the vertical axis in order to match the shape to the one they could see through the peep-hole in the box. Crucially, one group of participants saw the box in its opened state prior to the trial, and so knew that they were seeing a slanted circle when they looked through the peep-hole. Another group of participants had not had that experience, and were allowed to believe that the shape they could see through the peep-hole was just an ellipse and nothing more.

The findings were that participants who were ignorant of the real shape of the object made accurate judgements about its shape. The shape that they created on the computer screen accurately matched the shape they could see in the box through the peep-hole. In contrast, participants who knew that the shape was really a circle tended to exaggerate its circularity to a small but reliable extent. Figure 8.9 shows the difference between the shape as projected on to the retina (shaded area) and the shape which most participants judged it to be (outer line). There were no perspective cues to suggest that the shape was really a circle, so these could not have been responsible for the exaggeration of circularity. If there had been such cues, then presumably participants who did not see that the object was really a circle prior to the trial would also have exaggerated the circularity. Rather, it seems that merely knowledge of the reality that the object was a circle was sufficient for participants to exaggerate its circularity when judging its shape. In other words, knowledge of reality contaminated judgements of appearance. Just as young children seem to find it difficult to ignore reality when judging appearance, the same appears to be true of adults.

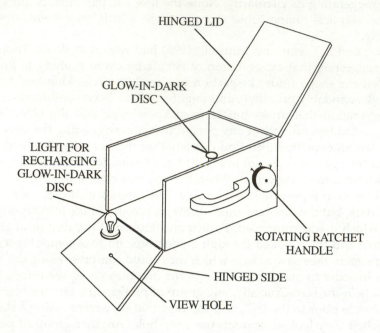

HINGED LID

GLOW-IN-DARK DISC

LIGHT FOR RECHARGING GLOW-IN-DARK DISC

ROTATING RATCHET HANDLE

HINGED SIDE

VIEW HOLE

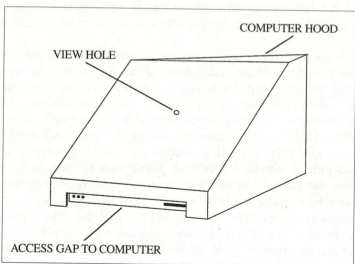

COMPUTER HOOD

VIEW HOLE

ACCESS GAP TO COMPUTER

FIGURE 8.8 Participants viewed a circle situated inside a box presented at a slant and then tried to match the shape on a computer screen that they inspected through a peep-hole. Under one condition, participants knew that the object in the box was a circle, while in the other they were allowed to believe that it was an ellipse, as it appeared.

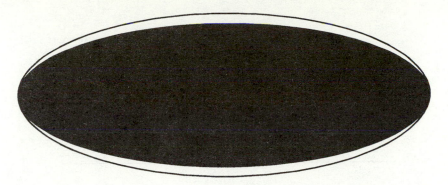

FIGURE 8.9 Participants exaggerated the circularity of the shape they could see to a small but reliable extent. The shaded area shows the actual shape projected on to the retina, and the outer line shows the shape that participants judged it to be.

CONCLUSIONS

The impression arising from the previous chapter was that, beyond 4 years of age, children come to rely (too heavily) on a rule that links seeing with believing. That view also seems to be confirmed in the present chapter. However, apart from that, much of the view that was explored in the previous chapter appears to be incorrect. It seems that the reason why young children report reality when asked about belief is primarily because reality holds an attentional magnetism for them. If beliefs can be embedded in a reality, then they will be easier for the young child to acknowledge, so acknowledging false belief is not an all-or-nothing concept, which the 4-year-old has but the 3-year-old does not. Rather, it seems that reality is more engaging for a young child than for an older child, and the age groups differ by a matter of degree in this respect, rather than qualitatively. Indeed, it might be that a realist bias never disappears, in which case we can expect to see realist errors in adults as well in some unusual circumstances. That is precisely what we found, not only in the context of judging beliefs but also in the context of differentiating between appearance and reality. Seemingly, development is much more gradual and complex than had been realized until recently. In the final two chapters, we shall look once again at young children in order to explore the various ways in which they use their understanding of mind. In particular, we shall examine how effective they are in deceiving other people, and we shall consider their capacity for pretence and their communication skills.

9

DECEPTION

There is a very special reason why we should be interested in the ability to deceive. It is to do with the utility of a conception of mind. Possessing an understanding of mind is not just a superfluous intellectual gift that we are blessed with for no good reason, but is vital for ensuring that we thrive as humans. It is not politically correct to celebrate our aptitude for misleading other people, but if we are realistic, we surely must acknowledge that it is a phenomenon that pervades much human interaction. We can only hope that people's remarkable capacity for deception is moderated by a moral conscience to use the faculty fairly and wisely.

An ability to deceive is a special ability which humans possess that contributes to basic survival. We are able to appreciate that we can lead someone or something off the scent if we can leave a false trail or other false clues that will allow our pursuer to think something contrary to the truth. For example, a malicious killer who is trying to find where we are hiding will be looking and listening for clues. The sound of a breaking twig or rustling leaves might betray our position. To mislead this individual, we could throw a stone some distance, so that the pursuer will hear it land and wrongly think that is the place of hiding. As the pursuer goes off in the wrong direction, this might give us vital seconds to make a getaway.

Deception is very common in nature, and certainly not unique to humans. For example, stick insects are disguised as plants, while certain orchids resemble female bees so strongly that male members of the species can be lured into an act of pollination by the irresistible temptation of mating. Humans are special, though, because to deceive another human one has to go about the task very intelligently. Humans are not easily duped, and frequently are on guard in anticipation of being misled. Anyone who succeeds under those conditions must be highly attuned to the kind of thought processes possessed by other people. The level of skill required is demonstrated by the rather cute and naïve attempts young children can make to deceive. For example, a child may approach her mother unexpectedly, announcing that she has not just stolen a biscuit, whilst holding her hands behind her back. Her mother will probably question why the child should suddenly be saying this, noting that she is pleading too strongly, and assume ironically that the child has stolen a biscuit and is actually holding it behind her back at this very moment!

We might suppose, then, that the ability to deceive is both a very primitive utilization of our understanding of mind and also a skill that could be deployed to achieve various personal ambitions within a social context. The child who pleads innocence too much, and is identified as being dishonest as a conesquence, will face the wrath of others and perhaps lose some status as a result. The child who carries off the deception successfully might get what she wants and maintain a good image. Although I would not want to praise anyone who is skilful at deception, I cannot help but observe that any person who is good at deception is likely to have advantages over people who are not so good. Indeed, political thrillers would hardly be so plausible or appealing if they were devoid of characters in high office who deceive and manipulate other people.

In short, we can assume that a capacity for deception is basic, and also that an individual with a refined and sophisticated skill in deception would probably go far in society, however repulsive that may seem to people who try to remain honest for moral reasons. We can make two predictions. One is that people who are able to dominate others might achieve this not so much by brute aggression, as by a willingness and skill in deceiving others. Despot political leaders have a bad record in that department. For example, Hitler promised Chamberlain that if Britain made concessions over the Nazi occupation of Czechoslovakia, then he would display no further territorial ambitions. Chamberlain naïvely claimed a political victory at the apparent appeasement of Hitler, which cost the Czech people their freedom (this was a dark moment in British diplomacy), only to find that Hitler invaded Poland the following year. Incidentally, this was only possible as a result of another deception, this time involving Russia, which was that Germany and Russia would have a pact of friendship, such that Russia would not leap to Poland's defence. Of course, Hitler, in his infinite treachery, had every intention of launching a full-scale surprise attack against Russia when the time suited him.

Fortunately for the human race, people like Hitler are in a tiny minority, and most are identified as having a psychiatric disorder. However, if they are not, there is a danger that such individuals would deceive others so skilfully and convincingly that they would swiftly be able to assume a position of power. On a more down-to-earth note, anybody who was not so evil as Hitler might still assume a position of influence if he or she were able to carry off deceptions plausibly. Politicians who make grand promises fall under suspicion in this context. We shall begin, then, by looking at the relationship between deception and leadership, and we shall then go on to examine how developmentally primitive is the ability to deceive.

DOMINANCE AND DECEPTION

Keating and Heltman (1994) investigated the relationship between dominance and deception in children aged 3 to 6 years, as well as in adults. Dominance was determined in the children by observing their routine behaviour in a school setting. The children under observation varied widely in their dominance behaviour. While some children were meek and submissive, others terrorized the playground with their shoving, hitting and verbal abuse. Some children who excelled in dominance also engaged in aggressive pointing, aggressive staring and verbal assertiveness. Is it sensible to ask whether these children would also be the ones most skilful in deception?

We can expect dominant children to be effective in deception for a variety of reasons. One is that their inclination to be antisocial means that they do not respect the rights or feelings of other people. Consequently, this could be expressed as a willingness to intimidate others as well as a willingness to allow others to be misled. Indeed, part of the dominance could take the form of deception – a monopoly on knowledge amounts to a monopoly on power, so to speak. If that is so, we might suppose that dominant children who cheat others are unpopular with their peers owing to their renowned antisocial acts. Effectively, they would be social outcasts displaying self-centred behaviour in a willingness to trample all over other people's feelings. The price they pay is social isolation, which might create a vicious circle because it makes them more alienated and antisocial.

On the other side of the coin, ironically, it could be that people who cheat and bully others are popular. It might be that people who have great social insight from an early age have yet to acquire the moral values that urge them to treat others fairly and with respect. Their psychological insights may make them attractive to others because they are sensitive to others' moods and thoughts. However, because they find themselves popular with hardly any effort, they may lapse into abusing the friendship of others by cheating or bullying them. Effectively, they would not be respecting others who are handicapped by having less social insight. Putting it crudely, these individuals may be so psychologically insightful and socially skilled that they can retain their privileged station of popularity whilst abusing their followers. Whichever way we look at it, then, it would not be surprising if children (or people in general) who were dominant were also skilful in carrying out acts of deception.

Having rated the children by determining their dominant tendencies, Keating and Heltman (1994) proceeded to investigate how skilled they were in carrying off an act of deception. They presented the children with two drinks of orange juice, one of which was laced with quinine flavour and therefore tasted repulsive. After the children had tasted the two drinks and recovered from their bout of shivering at the objectionable taste of one of them, they had no difficulty in indicating which was nice and which was nasty. Subsequently, the children were cajoled into sipping them again and then trying to persuade the experimenter's assistant that both drinks tasted nice. Not surprisingly, many children were only able to do this with a cringing facial expression, and despite what they were saying, it was patently obvious that they were telling lies. However, some children seemed able to carry off a convincing deception, and had their facial muscles surprisingly well under control.

The researchers filmed the children informing the assistant that both drinks tasted nice, and then showed the resulting footage to a panel of judges, but with the sound-track dubbed out. On the basis of the children's facial expressions, the judges had to rate whether they thought the children were being honest or telling lies. These judges had already been briefed that one of the drinks actually tasted nasty, so their task was to figure out which drink was laced from clues in the children's behaviour. The judges' ratings enabled Keating and Heltman to assign a score to each child on how effective they were in carrying out an act of deception. As predicted, it turned out that those who were judged to be honest, when in fact they were lying, were also the children who were most dominant over others. Those children who terrorized the playground tended to be the same individuals who had sufficient control over themselves to wear a happy expression when tasting a repulsive drink.

In a closer analysis of the judges' ratings with regard to the films of the children, Keating and Heltman (1994) asked what it was about the children's lying that the adults found so plausible. The factor that the researchers isolated was the ability to say that the nasty drink tasted nice whilst at the same time smiling. The natural reaction to a bitter taste is a contorted face, but dominant children in particular were able to overcome this and present a semblance of having an enjoyable experience.

Before proceeding further, we should first question the basis of the relationship between dominance and deception. Given the wide age range, it might be predominantly the older children who have sufficient control over themselves to wear a pleasant expression whilst having a nasty sensory experience. Of course, common sense suggests that it would not be at all surprising to find that the older members of a group of children tend to be the ones who dominate. Age and seniority seem to be closely linked in childhood as well as at other times in life. To explore this possibility, Keating and Heltman (1994) checked whether the relationship between deception and dominance was maintained even when age was statistically controlled as a variable, and they found that it was. It was not just the older children who tended to be both dominant and deceptive – the relationship seemed to be genuine rather than spurious, at least in this respect.

Another possibility is that dominance is one expression of social confidence and a willingness to deceive is another. Perhaps timid children fall victim to the aggression of others and also do not have the self-confidence to carry off a convincing act of deception. Fortunately, Keating and Heltman (1994) had an independent measure of social confidence. If children had a generally socially confident style, that would be apparent not only when they were being deceitful, but also when they were being honest about the pleasant taste of the untainted drink. They asked the adult judges who viewed the films to rate how socially confident the children appeared, and they then isolated the judgements made about the children communicating honestly that the untainted drink tasted nice. Hence they created an assessment of each child's level of social confidence, taken from a context in which they were not being deceitful. The researchers proceeded to control statistically for children's rating of social confidence when examining the relationship between dominance and deception. In short, the results showed that the children who were socially dominant and deceitful were not just the individuals who tended to be socially confident generally. The relationship between dominance and deception was maintained even when social confidence was statistically partialled out. Altogether, then, the relationship between dominance and deception in children appears to be genuine rather than spurious.

What about adults? Does the relationship between dominance and deception that we see in children extend right into adulthood? Keating and Heltman (1994) asked adult participants to carry out the same task of drinking orange juice from two different glasses, one of which tasted nice and the other nasty. They were asked to communicate to a video camera that both drinks tasted nice. The researchers had to find another method of assessing dominance, and they did this by placing participants in small groups. They were then told that they had to imagine – and role play – a scenario in which they were members of an expedition exploring the Arctic wastes in a light aircraft. The aircraft crashed, but they survived, only to find themselves in a wilderness that was 40 degrees below freezing. They were told that they had a very limited range of provisions and had to work out a solution for survival. Ostensibly, the task is about how to be resourceful, but it is also a valuable tool for establishing who seeks to take the lead and dominate the situation. People tend to compete, some more than others, to have their own ideas adopted by the group. Following this episode, the members of each group rated one another on dominance in the situation. This allowed the researchers to compile a dominance score for each of their participants.

As with child participants, Keating and Heltman (1994) found that the adults who tended to be most dominant were the same individuals who were capable of carrying out convincing acts of deception. They were the same people who a panel judged to be telling the truth about the nice taste of a drink when in fact they were telling lies. However, a closer inspection of the films and the judges' ratings revealed that the adults achieved their deception in a different manner to the children. While the children would smile as they experienced the bitter taste, the adults maintained an unflinching expression and a steady gaze. They looked right into the lens of the camera, with a 'straight' expression, and told a whopping great lie! In contrast, those who were correctly identified as telling lies tended to shift their gaze and 'grin nervously'.

This seems rather ironic, because the children would smile and look sincere, while the adults would smile and seem mendacious. Perhaps the children who were convincing as liars owed their success (if we can call it that) to an adult assumption that children are naïve, innocent and not fully in control of their emotional expressions. Perhaps they were assuming that if a young child tastes something nasty, you can depend on him or her to make that fact known very plainly. Young children are not well known for concealing their distaste – or are they? It seems from Keating and Heltman's (1994) study that, while many children may not be skilful in that respect, some are. And those who are tend to be the same children who dominate others.

The study by Keating and Heltman (1994) provides some intriguing findings about the relationship between dominance and deception. For various reasons, it is hardly surprising that people who dominate are also the same individuals who are skilful in deceiving others. Further research is needed to find out more precisely how the two aspects are linked. None the less, on a more general level we can see how deception is an aspect of an understanding of mind that people can use to their advantage in social situations. An understanding of mind is a faculty that serves an important purpose which individuals might use in a way that they suppose is to their personal advantage – in this case, perhaps as a tool of dominance and manipulation of others. So far, we have considered prowess in deception as a feature of personality. On a more general level we might suppose that, because the capacity for deception is of such obvious usefulness, it would emerge as one of the earliest signs of an understanding of mind.

EARLY UNDERSTANDING OF DECEPTION

One of the special qualities of Keating and Heltman's (1994) study is that it is not too heavily contrived and therefore not too far removed from real life. A study that shares the same virtue, conducted by Lewis et al. (1989), was inspired by the familiar experience of young children disobeying rules and then telling lies about it. Parents typically feel highly sceptical about experimenters who say that young children are very feeble at deception when in fact they are frequently confronted with their own child doing something that is forbidden and then denying it. Lewis et al. traded on this common experience by introducing children who were 3 years old or just under to an attractive toy zoo that was covered with a sheet. The experimenter said to each child that they were not allowed to touch the toy yet, but would be able to play with it shortly. It was explained that the child just had to be patient while the experimenter went into another room to attend to something important. The experimenter then departed, leaving the child alone in the room.

The researchers had the hunch that the temptation would be too great for these young children. They guessed, accurately as it turned out, that the children would be unable to resist at least peeping at the toy zoo under the sheet. In total 29 of 33 children who were tested did peep under the cloth, but unknown to them the researchers were able to spy on the children by means of a strategically placed but inconspicuous camera in the testing room. When the experimenter returned, she asked the children directly if they had peeped at the toy. Of the 29 children who did actually peep, 18 children appeared to attempt to conceal the fact that they had done so. Seven of the children told a straight lie that they had not peeped, and 11 refused to answer the question.

Lewis *et al*. (1989) went on to investigate whether the children who told lies did so in a convincing manner. They showed videos of the children who denied that they had peeped to a panel of adults. Some of the children were telling the truth and had not actually peeped, while others were telling lies and had in fact peeped. Would a panel of adults be able to classify the children accurately according to who was and who was not telling lies? Most of us think that we can detect when other sophisticated adults are telling lies, so surely it should not pose too great a problem to figure out when a 2-year-old child is lying. Counter to common sense, though, the adult judges were at a complete loss when it came to sorting out the liars from the honest children. On reflection, perhaps this is not so surprising. If one (whether child or adult) is to tell lies, one needs to be convincing about it. If one tells lies and is found out, that could lead to more trouble than if one had owned up and been truthful from the start. People hate the thought of being cheated.

Lewis *et al*. (1989) also questioned how the children managed to carry off such a convincing deception. Their analyses yielded data which were entirely consistent with the findings of Keating and Heltman (1994). It seems that the children who were judged to be telling the truth when they were actually telling lies maintained relaxed and smiling expressions as they did so. In telling a lie, it would be no good wearing one's guilt on one's face. It seems that at least some of the children observed by Lewis *et al*. knew enough about deception to understand that one should speak a non-truth as though one was speaking the truth. Further study of the video evidence revealed that the children who did not confess but remained mute tended to wear very nervous facial expressions. It seems as if they may have been attempting to conceal their misdeed but lacked either the nerve or the know-how, or both, to do so in a convincing manner.

Another study demonstrating an early capacity for deception was conducted by Chandler *et al*. (1989). They reasoned that one of the most primitive forms of deception is the destruction of incriminating evidence. A more sophisticated form is the fabrication of false evidence. If an individual understood about the mind as a receptacle of information and misinformation, then they ought to have an understanding of deception. For example, a person could not know that treasure is hidden in a particular vessel if they had not seen it in there and had no clues as to its whereabouts. If they had not seen it there, then they would be depending on clues. If the clues are destroyed, they will remain in a state of ignorance. If they are supplied with false clues, then they will formulate a belief as to the whereabouts of the treasure, but one that is false. Hence, being able to destroy evidence and fabricate false evidence tells us something about the child's competence in understanding how information is essential to the mind and how the mind can be host to misinformation.

Chandler *et al.* (1989) proceeded to formulate a task in which children had ample opportunity to destroy extant evidence and fabricate false evidence. The apparatus is illustrated in Figure 9.1, and featured a doll with multiple legs that radiated from a central pivot, like the spokes of a wheel. As the experimenter (or child) pushed the doll along, her legs rotated. Her journey was to one of four miniature dustbins, with the purpose of depositing treasure in one of them. Her mission was shrouded in secrecy, however, at least with regard to the experimenter's assistant, who had left the room temporarily. The experimenter and the child conspired to trick the assistant by getting the doll to navigate to one of the bins and hide the treasure therein. The plan was ruined, however, on account of a trail of tell-tale inky footprints which the doll left in her wake. This happened because the doll set out from an ink pad, which resulted in the dye being absorbed into the soles of her shoes.

Fortunately for the experimenter and the child, the damning evidence of the footprints could be removed owing to the washable quality of the ink. The doll navigated across a smooth plastic board, which allowed the footprints to be wiped away easily. The experimenter had demonstrated to the child participant previously that stains made by the ink could be erased with a cloth that was available nearby. The children practised doing this before the doll set out to hide the treasure. After the treasure had been hidden, the experimenter drew the child's attention to the footprints and asked her if she could think of any way in which they could prevent the assistant from finding the treasure. Nearly all of the children, including those aged only 2 years, responded by taking the cloth and wiping away the footprints. The experimenter congratulated the child on having such a good idea and

FIGURE 9.1 The doll approached one of the bins where she deposited treasure, but left tell-tale footprints in her wake. Observing children had the opportunity to engage in deception by erasing the footprints with a cloth.

then enquired whether there was anything else she could do to prevent the assistant from finding the treasure. Very many children, including the youngest ones, took hold of the doll and led her from the ink pad to a bin that did not house the treasure! Subsequently, the assistant returned and asked the child participant where the treasure was. Many children, once again including the very youngest, either remained silent or pointed to a bin that did not house the treasure.

This imaginatively conceived study appeared to succeed in demonstrating that, from as early as 2 years of age, children are aware that people's knowledge and beliefs depend critically on a supply-line of information. If the information is tampered with, then a person exposed to that could at best remain in a state of ignorance concerning the truth, and at worst be host to an entirely false belief. It is difficult to explain why children would tamper with evidence if they did not have some insight into the effect it would have on belief. Apart from suggesting that an early understanding of mind is apparent in the province of deception, Chandler et al.'s (1989) study is to be applauded for their concern to devise a child-based procedure. The game of hide-and-seek is well known to virtually all children, and the procedure devised by these researchers appears to succeed in creating a framework that would be familiar to them.

HAS CHILDREN'S COMPETENCE BEEN OVERESTIMATED?

Sodian et al. (1991) took a more sceptical view, as they felt that the findings of Chandler et al. (1989) were a little too good to be true. Basically, they were saying that two questions of the utmost importance were not addressed by those researchers' procedure. The first question concerns the children's eagerness to erase the trails to the baited bin. We cannot actually tell whether the children erased these trails in order to prevent the assistant from knowing the true location of the treasure, or whether they were just enjoying wiping away the trails for fun because they could not think of anything else to do with the cloth that the experimenter seemed so anxious to press upon them. At the very least, we would want to be sure that children confine their erasing of trails to a condition under which they are supposed to be deceiving rather than truthfully informing the assistant. The other question that remained unaddressed concerned the children's understanding of the effect of fabricated evidence. If children understand that false evidence leads to a false belief, then they ought to judge that the assistant thinks the treasure is in the (empty) bin that has footprints leading to it. If they actually judged that the assistant believes the treasure is not there but in the bin where the child knows it is really located, we would have very good reason for being suspicious of what the child understands about deception.

Sodian et al. (1991) devised a variant of the procedure of Chandler et al. (1989), in which a lorry trundled across a tray of sand. The driver dismounted from his cab and hid under one of several cups. The lorry was then removed, but the tell-tale tracks remained, giving away the driver's hiding place. Observing child participants had the opportunity to erase the tyre tracks with a rake that was issued to them. They were also encouraged to create false tracks by pushing the lorry to a cup that did not conceal the driver. Under one condition, a nasty burglar was in pursuit of the driver, so it was important for the driver's hiding place to remain a secret from the burglar, who might inflict harm on the driver. Under another condition, a benign king was in pursuit of the driver in order to offer a reward to him, so the driver would profit from being found by the king.

Sodian *et al.* (1991) found a considerable difference between children younger than 4 years and those older. The younger children seemed to find it very difficult indeed to latch on to the idea of erasing the tyre tracks by raking over the sand. When the experimenter eventually cajoled them into doing this, they did it indiscriminately. They were just as likely to erase the trails when they were supposed to be assisting the king to find the driver as when they were supposed to be obstructing the nasty burglar. If children were persuaded with heavy prompting to lay a false trail specifically when the burglar was in pursuit, they still showed signs that they did not grasp the implications of this misinformation for the burglar's state of belief. When asked where the burglar would think the driver was hidden, they tended to point to the place where he really was hidden. Moreover, when the burglar arrived on the scene and demanded to be told by the children where the driver was hiding, they usually yielded to his request by pointing to the cup that actually concealed the driver.

The older children were quite different. They seemed to have little difficulty in understanding that they should rake away the tyre tracks when the burglar was in pursuit. When the king was in pursuit, they refrained from erasing the tracks, but instead were inclined to reinforce the strength of them by leading the lorry out to the cup that concealed the driver once again. In short, they easily discriminated between the king and the burglar in the manner in which they manipulated information about the driver's location. When asked where the burglar would think the driver was hidden, they usually pointed to the cup that had false tracks leading to it. They were very different from the younger children in another respect. When the burglar demanded to know the whereabouts of the driver, the older children tended to point to a cup that did not conceal him. When the king requested this information, the children were willing and eager to disclose the driver's location.

These findings certainly do not inspire confidence in the possibility that young children really do understand about mind in the context of deception, but Hala *et al.* (1991) retaliated with their own criticisms of the procedure of Sodian *et al.* (1991). They said that the tyre tracks in sand are not particularly conspicuous, unlike the inky footprints in their original study, so the children may not have grasped that they would be informative to another person. They also noted that it seems odd to expect the children to help the king by reinforcing existing clues. This appears to require an understanding of the strength of a clue, rather than the importance of a clue being present or absent. Apart from that, there was a very substantial amount of make-believe involved, which required the child to enter into the spirit of accepting that the burglar really was nasty and the king really was nice, and that it made some kind of sense for a lorry driver to hide under a cup. . .for a reason that remains unclear.

Hala *et al.* (1991) conducted their own replication. Under a co-operative condition, there were no inky footprints leading to the bin that housed the treasure, but the children had the opportunity to create these in the usual way by leading the doll out from the ink pad. Under a competitive condition, the footprints were present, and the children had the opportunity to erase them. These researchers report that children under 4 years of age succeeded in erasing the tell-tale trail to the baited bin under the competitive condition, and thus successfully replicated their earlier finding. They also report that the children easily hit upon the idea of laying footprints to the baited bin under the co-operative condition. Moreover, when asked directly where the assistant would think the treasure was, they usually pointed to the bin that lay at the end of a trail of misleading footprints.

Despite Hala *et al.*'s valiant defence of their claims, further evidence was mounting to suggest that young children have very little understanding of deception in relation to mind. Sodian (1991) had an idea that was both ingenious and amusing with regard to investigating young children's understanding of deception. As Sodian correctly noted, one of the difficulties that we face in investigating children's understanding of deception is that it is difficult to be certain that children will be willing to deceive another person. After all, deception does not make for good etiquette, and this is a social rule that is probably drilled into children from the beginning. If children do not deceive another person, it might be because they think that to do so is bad manners, rather than because they fail to understand the effect that deception has on mind. Sodian then saw the problem in devising a test that would hinder another person from attaining his goal in a way that did not require any understanding of deception. Presumably, the bad manners is to do with obstructing another person from attaining his goal, and not to do with the actual mechanism whereby that obstruction is achieved.

As a control condition, therefore, Sodian (1991) came up with the idea of investigating young children's ability to indulge in sabotage! She created a context in which a nasty burglar was determined to steal some treasure which was stored inside a treasure chest. Under one condition, the child was issued with the key to the chest and had the opportunity to lock it to prevent the burglar from gaining access. Most children under 4 years of age exploited this opportunity and locked the treasure chest with glee. Under another condition, the children were not issued with the key and were unable to lock the treasure chest. However, they could effect the same outcome by telling lies to the burglar. The burglar enquired whether the chest was locked, and the children could effectively prevent him from getting the treasure by saying that the chest was locked when in fact it was not. It turned out, though, that only the children over 4 years of age succeeded in telling a blatant lie to the burglar. The younger children tended to report truthfully that the chest was not locked, thereby allowing the burglar to steal the treasure.

In this study, Sodian (1991) claimed that if children were reluctant to tell lies because they felt that it was bad manners to do so, then that concern should be equally in evidence in the sabotage condition. They should show just as much reluctance to indulge in sabotage as in deception, since both activities are socially disgraceful. However, the children's attempts to thwart the burglar were confined to the sabotage condition, which led Sodian to conclude that young children's failure to deceive is not due to social inhibition but to a lack of understanding that misinformation has the power to fool another person into thinking something counter to the truth.

There are many different ways of carrying out deception. A primitive form is to tell lies or tamper with evidence, while a more sophisticated form of deception is to tamper with evidence in a special kind of way – to frame another person! Just as it is possible to lead a person off the trail and direct them to an empty container by providing fabricated clues, as in the study by Chandler *et al.* (1989), so it is possible to fabricate evidence to make it appear that a misdeed was carried out by an innocent person. Ruffman *et al.* (1993) explored children's understanding of that situation using an imaginative procedure which they had devised themselves.

Ruffman *et al.* (1993) told children a story about a naughty boy called John. He was forbidden from eating food between meals, but he paid no heed to this rule and decided to raid the larder. However, on realizing that his father would see that some of the food had vanished, John had to concoct a scheme that would allow him to avoid becoming the focus of suspicion, and so escape blame. His plan was to wear his big sister's outsize shoes while sneaking across the kitchen on his mission to purloin food. As in Chandler *et al.*'s (1989) procedure, the shoes left tell-tale footprints which had the distinctive and unmistakable shape of the soles of Katy's extra large shoes, as shown in Figure 9.2. Having completed his sinister deed, John

FIGURE 9.2 John donned Katy's large shoes, apparently in an attempt to frame her. Observing children had to judge who an adult would think had stolen the food – John or Katy.

returned to a place of safety and gobbled up his loot contentedly. Later, John's father arrived on the scene, noticed that food had been stolen from the larder and then turned his attention to the incriminating footprints. At this point, observing child participants were asked to judge who the father thought had stolen the food. The researchers presented the task to children aged around 3 and 4 years, and they discovered a clear age trend in the children's judgements. The older children correctly judged that the father thought that Katy was the culprit, while the younger children seemed unable to appreciate the significance of the footprints left by Katy's shoes. They judged that the father would think that it was John who had stolen the food.

Although the younger children usually gave incorrect answers, it seems perhaps even more remarkable that many of the children aged 4 years should have succeeded in giving a correct answer. Surely the process of framing another person is rather complex, and requires a sophisticated understanding of how deception can be used intelligently. The children were judging not just that the father remained ignorant of John's miscreant behaviour, but also that he would suspect an innocent person. Surely an acceptance of this injustice must depend on a level of understanding of human action that goes substantially beyond the usual stories that young children experience, in which it is inevitable that the protagonist who carries out a heinous deed finally receives the punishment he deserves. If children aged 4 years can grasp the complex deception contrived by Ruffman *et al.* (1993), then perhaps this is a sign that even younger children would have some comprehension of simpler forms of deception. The research reviewed earlier, by Chandler *et al.* (1989) and Lewis *et al.* (1989), suggests that such circumstances do exist. Perhaps we have not been posing the research question appropriately. Instead of asking whether or not children below the age of 4 years understand about deception, perhaps we should be asking what forms of deception they understand about, or under what circumstances they show insight into deception.

ARE CHILDREN BEING UNDERESTIMATED?

This was the approach adopted by Chandler and Hala (1994). The experimenter persuaded the child participant to enter into a conspiracy to play a trick on the experimenter's assistant. The assistant had a box of cookies, which she left in the room with the experimenter and the child as she departed momentarily, ostensibly to speak with the headteacher. In the assistant's absence, the experimenter suggested that they should play a trick on her assistant by removing the cookies. The experimenter reminded the child that they wanted to play a really good trick on the assistant and then encouraged the child to suggest something that they could put inside the box in place of the cookies, so as to give the assistant a big surprise. The experimenter had a variety of nasty objects with her, such as a giant rubber spider of authentic appearance. The children were especially eager to choose this as an item to replace the cookies! Finally, the experimenter asked the child to judge what the assistant would think was inside the box. Of the children aged 3 years who participated, around 75 per cent answered correctly and with some glee that the assistant would think the box contained cookies.

Apart from the striking quality of the replacement objects, Chandler and Hala (1994) suspected that one of the main reasons why these young children apparently found it so easy to grasp that the assistant was being deceived was because they had an active role in instigating the deception. Instead of simply being passive observers of a deception engineered by another individual, they had a direct stake in the act, by choosing which item to put in the box in order to replace the usual content of cookies. Chandler and Hala pursued this hunch by introducing two small modifications to their procedure. Under one novel condition, the children instigated the deception, by suggesting to the experimenter which replacement item to put in the box. Under another novel variant, the experimenter suggested the replacement item and the child was to carry out the deed. Chandler and Hala found that if children were responsible for instigating and planning the deception, they tended to acknowledge that the assistant would be host to a false belief, even if they were not directly instrumental in putting the replacement content into the box. On the other hand, if the children did not plan the deception, but simply followed the experimenter's suggestion in replacing the content of the box, then they were less likely to acknowledge the experimenter's false belief. In short, it seems that when children were required to figure out the plan of deception, this served to highlight for them the prospect of the assistant holding a misapprehension.

Yet another study reports early ability to acknowledge false belief in the context of deception. Sullivan and Winner (1993) showed children a box, such as a Smarties tube, and then elaborately removed the usual content (Smarties) and replaced it with a pencil with the stated aim of tricking the assistant who had left the room temporarily. Children aged 3 years stood a good chance of judging that the assistant would entertain a false belief by wrongly thinking that the box contained its usual content, namely Smarties. Indeed, they were more likely to acknowledge the false belief in this context of deception, compared with a control condition based on a standard deceptive box procedure in which a Smarties tube contained the atypical content of a pencil all along. On discovering the pencil in the tube, the children proceeded to ascribe a true belief to the assistant. Sullivan and Winner concluded that simply alerting the children to the idea that a deception was being carried out was sufficient to help them to acknowledge false belief. If they are right, then perhaps there was no need for Chandler and Hala (1994) to stress the importance of children being involved in instigating the deception for them to succeed in acknowledging false belief.

However, there are very good reasons for questioning Sullivan and Winner's (1993) conclusion. The deception and standard conditions differed not only in the presence or absence of a deceptive framework, but also in the way in which the box was presented to the child participant. In the deceptive condition, the box first had its usual content (Smarties), which was subsequently replaced by an atypical content while the child watched. Under the standard condition, the box contained an atypical content (pencils) all along. It might be that in the deception condition, merely seeing the Smarties in the tube initially was sufficient to help the children to acknowledge false belief. It should be recalled from the previous chapter that young children stand a better chance of acknowledging false belief if that belief is seen by the child participant to have some basis in reality (Saltmarsh *et al.*, 1995).

Saltmarsh and I (Saltmarsh and Mitchell, 1996) attempted to clarify matters. We shot a video that featured real people, called John and Ness. John left the scene and, in his absence, Ness opened a Smarties tube to reveal that it contained Smarties, as expected, but she then replaced these with a spoon. In another version, the tube contained a spoon all along. In one version, Ness behaved in a theatrically deceptive manner by looking around furtively and laughing behind her hand. Under another condition, she played the script in a neutral non-deceptive manner. Each version of the box (with or without the usual content inside initially) was presented in either the deceptive or the neutral framework. This would allow us to determine whether it was Ness' deceptive manner that helped children to acknowledge John's false belief, or the fact that the box first contained its usual content under one of the conditions.

The results were inconsistent with Sullivan and Winner's (1993) expectation, but consistent both with what we expected and also with what Chandler and Hala (1994) would have predicted. Whether Ness played her part in a deceptive or neutral manner in itself made no difference to the ability of observing children to acknowledge John's false belief about the box. On the other hand, whether or not observing children saw or did not see the usual content in the box made a substantial difference. If the children saw that the box contained Smarties initially, which were then replaced by a spoon as they watched, then they stood a good chance of acknowledging John's false belief. If the box contained the spoon all along, then they stood little chance of acknowledging John's false belief.

In Sullivan and Winner's (1993) study, and also in ours, children did not instigate a deception but were passive observers, so from Chandler and Hala's (1994) perspective we would not expect an increase in their correct judgements of false belief. On the other hand, we would expect correct judgements on the basis that children are helped if they see that a belief to be judged has some physical basis. The appropriate conclusion seems to be that there is a good chance that young children will be able to acknowledge false belief in the context of deception, so long as they are actively involved in planning the deception. If they are 'the brains behind the act', they will probably grasp the significance of the misinformation for the victim, but if they are 'the brawn behind the act' they will probably not appreciate this significance. Moreover, it appears that being actively involved in the planning helps young children to acknowledge false belief over and above any benefit they may have received from seeing that the false belief under consideration has some physical basis.

Conclusions

The ability to deceive intelligently is made possible by an understanding of mind. Having a conception of mind is not just a superfluous luxury, but rather it is something available to us because it has an important function. For that reason, we might expect to find the earliest signs of an insight into mind in the context of deception. Putting it most simply, it would not be surprising if young children who are novices in most matters are experts in deception. The research into understanding of deception has yielded mixed results. Some studies suggest that below 4 years of age children understand very little about deception, so they appear naïvely honest. On the other hand, some studies suggest that a sophisticated grasp of deception is present from an early age. The studies that report early success appear to fall into two categories. One category is the more naturalistic kind of research, as conducted by Lewis *et al.* (1989), while the other category is research that encourages the child to scheme about the deception, as conducted by Chandler and Hala (1994). Meanwhile, research which suggests that understanding of deception emerges later in development tends to assign a more passive role, intellectually speaking, to the child participant. The moral of this is surely that there is always a danger that inflicting weird and wonderfully contrived procedures on children in experimental settings runs the risk of underestimating their competence. In the next chapter, we shall explore some other ways in which young children might use their understanding of mind.

10

PRETENCE AND COMMUNICATION

At about 18 months of age, quite spontaneously children begin to exhibit an astonishing symbolic capacity. This is evident in two ways. First, the child begins to engage in symbolic pretend play. In the child's imagination, ordinary mundane objects are transformed into completely different things at a whim. The child can create a make-believe world populated by people who are in fact just wooden playing bricks. These 'people' will be assigned different roles, such as a baby being cared for by a mother. Other objects that are conveniently to hand will be drawn into the drama, so an ordinary household cushion might now become a bed for the baby, a crayon could become the baby's feeding bottle, and playing beads could become food. A capacity for pretence shows that the child's thinking is not strictly confined to things that are in the immediate vicinity and impinging on his or her senses. For the child to think about how a mother and baby behave together, their physical absence need not be an impediment. All the child does to solve the problem is to assign these identities to whatever objects are available, such as wooden playing bricks. Quite simply, the child can explore a hypothetical world via symbolism, and this is a peculiarly well-developed ability in humans. Although there is sometimes talk of chimps showing pretence, the creativity of the human infant totally eclipses anything we see in chimps.

Note, incidentally, that the pretence we witness in human infants is unlike the behaviour in cats that we might be tempted to call 'pretence'. Cats chase a ball of string, and it is fair to say that they are 'playing', but perhaps it is going a little too far to say that they are 'pretending'. The cat might be acting as if the ball of string is a mouse, but it probably does not make any sense to say that the cat is pretending that the ball is a mouse in the way that we might say that a toddler is pretending that a brick is a baby.

The difference between the cat and the toddler is to do with creativity. The cat's behaviour is highly predictable, and we could almost say that it is elicited by a moving ball of string. Perhaps the cat's behaviour is merely triggered by a stimulus, and the animal might even be helpless to do anything other than chase around frantically. In contrast, the toddler's pretence seems to be more of a creative and voluntary act. The toddler is not at the mercy of a stimulus; if she were, then maybe she would react to the stimulus in a stereotypical way (as does the cat) that is suited to whatever object is presented. For example, playing bricks are ostensibly for building, so if the behaviour of toddlers was dictated by whatever stimuli were presented, we would see them using the bricks only for this purpose. We could still say that the toddler is playing, since the child would only be building a model structure, but it would probably not be correct to say that they are pretending. Accordingly, perhaps we can say that a cat chasing a ball of string is playing but not pretending.

The other kind of symbolism that burgeons in toddlers is the capacity for language as a tool of communication. Generally, infants begin to utter their first words at about 12 months of age, but it is not until 6 months or so later that they begin to string together words according to primitive rules of syntax which make an elementary conversation between the toddler and another person possible. Prior to this, the baby uses language in a way that is no more impressive than what we see in linguistic apes – and it is disputed whether they really are linguistic! Perhaps the baby's single word utterances are better thought of as instrumental vocalizations. The baby might get what he or she wants by mouthing an appropriate word, but not yet grasp that language is a symbolic code capable of encapsulating 'meaning' as we understand it. To say that a couple of people are holding a conversation with each other is to imply that they are, for example, experiencing an exchange of ideas that is encoded symbolically through language. Hence, an infant could not begin to participate in a genuine conversation if he or she were not able to treat language as a symbolic encoding of states of affairs that exist in the world, or ideas that a person might want to convey. Perhaps a developing symbolic competence at the age of around 18 months is expressed in two primary ways, namely pretence and verbal communication.

THE SIGNIFICANCE OF PRETENCE

According to Leslie (1987), the advent of pretence in the toddler's development heralds the dawning of an ability to apprehend other people's minds. This suggestion makes sense on a superficial level as well as when we delve more deeply into the idea. On the face of things, the first point we should note is that minds cannot be perceived directly. To acknowledge the existence of mind requires a leap of the imagination. Pretence shows that the child has the necessary imaginative credentials for conceiving of such a hypothetical concept as the mind. More specifically, when the child pre-tends that one wooden brick is the mother and another is the baby, the child might be said to be simulating the existence of other minds in this context. Seemingly, the toddler knows enough about what people are (and implicit in that is the idea that people have minds) to be able to create a rich and rounded simulation of the behaviour of mother and baby. Obviously, these simulated individuals might not be any person in particular, but none the less the example appears to show that the toddler has the capacity, in principle, to contemplate other minds through pretence.

Leslie (1987) argues that pretence implies an understanding of mind in a further and much deeper respect. He makes the very important point that, when pretending, toddlers have a remarkable capacity for keeping track of what actually maintains in reality. In pretence, the toddler is not confused about reality, as the person with schizophrenia is confused when experiencing delusions. Apparently the toddler is able to venture into the world of make-believe without risk of losing touch with reality, unlike a person with schizophrenia. For example, the toddler never confuses the brick with a real baby, in which case he or she might try to feed real baby food to the inanimate object! Toddlers are patently aware that their pretence is non-real and non-serious. Indeed, fun and animation typically shine from the toddler's face as he or she engages in pretence.

Consequently, Leslie (1987) suggested that toddlers must be able to quarantine the pretend identity that they have assigned to a mundane object from its real identity, and are somehow able to tolerate the difference between these two conflicting identities. Indeed, toddlers might even compare and contrast the two identities. Now that is sufficient, according to Leslie, for the toddler to understand that the contents of minds and what maintains in reality need not be one and the same thing. This suggestion seems similar to that advanced by Gopnik and Astington (1988) and also by Flavell *et al.* (1983). They suggest that when children begin to distinguish between the appearance and reality of an object, this signals an understanding that minds can conceive of things in various and even conflicting ways. Putting it another way, children appear to understand that there is nothing inevitable about how an object is represented by a mind. Rather, it is a peculiarity (or perhaps a privilege in the case of pretence) of mind that objects can be represented as they are or as something else.

PRETENCE AND SOCIAL SENSITIVITY

Some children engage in pretence more than others. If Leslie (1987) is right to suppose that pretence is an expression of the capacity to understand mind, then it should follow that those children who display more aptitude for pretence also demonstrate proficiency in understanding mind in other respects. One manifestation of a refined understanding of mind is a well-cultivated skill in interacting with other people. As has been amply demonstrated by the sad case of autism, a lack of insight into mind not surprisingly seems to go hand in hand with social incompetence. On the other side of the coin, it might be that people who have an unusually good understanding of mind can excel in their social interactions. However, it does not necessarily follow that a person with a refined understanding of mind would always be the life and soul of the party. Having a good understanding of mind does not equate with possession of an extroverted personality. In other words, an individual with a good understanding of mind can be expected to show great social skill and sensitivity without necessarily being socially flamboyant.

Connolly and Doyle (1984) investigated the relationship between pretence and social competence in children aged 3, 4 and 5 years. They observed children's spontaneous pretence in the natural setting of their preschool. Two different kinds of pretence were conspicuous. One was the assigning of pretend identities to mundane objects. For example, children playing 'cops and robbers' would pick up suitably elongated playing bricks and chase around whilst aiming these at each other with suitably vocalized sound-effects. Another form of pretence was children's role-playing, in which case one child would be Mum, another Dad and yet another would be Baby. The children would enact their various roles according to stereotyped patterns of behaviour appropriate for the character concerned. That should not be taken to imply that the children assumed their respective roles in a robotic and rigid manner. Rather, they were flexible and creative in their roles, in the sense that they would adapt to others and co-ordinate their behaviour appropriately. The scene that emerged was thus a product of the various contributions. It amounted to much more than what would have been a mere aggregation of children acting out their own roles in isolation.

Although pretence is a typical feature of early childhood, some of the children observed by Connolly and Doyle appeared to have more of a flair for this activity than others. Some children seemed more proficient than others in suspending disbelief and entering into their roles in a creative manner. The researchers rated the children according to how flexible they appeared when playing roles through pretence, especially in terms of the variety of different roles. They also rated how imaginative the children were in assigning pretend identities to objects and generally how creative their pretence appeared to be. From this, the researchers formulated a general rating of proficiency in pretence for each of the children that they observed.

Connolly and Doyle (1984) also formulated an impression of how socially skilled the children appeared to be. This rating was a composite of what the teacher said about each child, and how each child was observed to behave when interacting with peers in the natural setting of the preschool. The teachers rated how socially skilled they thought each child was, and they also ranked each of the children in terms of their popularity among other children. With regard to social skill, the researchers were keen to observe the children's verbal fluency and inclination to engage other children in a conversation. Apart from this, the researchers asked each child to select an appropriate gift from a set for various people. The set included such things as a tie, a toy truck, a doll and perfume. The people they were to select for were a boy of their own age, a girl of their own age, their father and their mother. Some children would choose the toy truck for their mother, while others showed more insight by selecting the perfume. The researchers were thus able to assemble a profile of social skill for each child, based on their rated popularity, their ability to select gifts appropriately for other people, and their skill when interacting with peers. It turned out that the children who showed most aptitude for entering into the spirit of pretence in a fully creative manner tended to be the very same children who were judged to have the greatest social skill.

On the face of things, this relationship between pretence and manifest understanding of mind (social competence) is precisely what we would expect if Leslie (1987) is correct to argue that pretence signals insight into mind. However, there are some alternative explanations which we need to eliminate. One is that it might just be the older children who show proficiency in both pretence and social competence. If so, it is not so much the understanding of mind that unites pretence and social competence, as general maturity. To investigate this possibility, Connolly and Doyle (1984) statistically partialled out the age of the children, and found that the relationship between pretence and social competence survived none the less. Another possible explanation is that, since we can expect general intelligence to coincide with proficiency in pretence and social competence, it might be that abilities in pretence and social competence are united by their mutual link with intelligence (rather than a more specific understanding of mind). Thankfully, this possibility can also be ruled out. The researchers included a test of general intelligence in their battery of tasks which the children performed. When their tested intelligence was partialled out of the relationship between proficiency in pretence and social competence, the relationship between the latter two factors still remained. Hence children who are proficient in pretence also show good insight into mind as demonstrated by their social competence. The findings reported by Connolly and Doyle offer powerful support for the link between pretence and understanding of mind that Leslie formulated in principle.

HAVE CHILDREN BEEN OVERESTIMATED?

The recurring theme that we are in danger of overestimating young children arises once again here. Lillard (1993) proposes that, with regard to what pretence signals for an understanding of mind, young children's activity is only meaningful if they can recognize pretence for what it is. As I mentioned previously, genuine pretence is not 'acting as if', like a cat acting as if a ball of string is a mouse. There is an additional quality, which is the attitude that accompanies the behaviour. It is not correct to say that a cat has an attitude of pretence when chasing the ball of string. As we considered previously, the cat's behaviour is perhaps largely automated, in which case the cat presumably has no attitude towards it, just as we have no attitude towards other automatic behaviours such as breathing. In contrast, the toddler who pretends that a wooden brick is a baby perhaps does hold an appropriate pretend attitude, which is that the brick is only a baby in the realm of make-believe. The toddler holds a pretend attitude as opposed to a serious one.

However, Lillard (1993) was suspicious that toddlers are in fact oblivious to the attitude involved in pretence, in which case they lack genuine understanding. To find out whether this was the case, she introduced participating children to a troll doll called Moe. She explained to children that, because he was a troll, Moe lived on a different planet that had no birds. Because Moe's planet was not inhabited by birds, Lillard explained, he had never seen a bird and had no idea what they were. Lillard then extended Moe's arm horizontally and made him glide around the table in front of the child participant. She then asked the children if Moe looked like a bird, and nearly all of the children tested concurred that he did. She then asked them if he was pretending to be a bird. Those above the age of 6 years denied that he was, while the younger children agreed that he was indeed pretending to be a bird.

It seems that the older children recognized that it would be incorrect to say that Moe was pretending to be a bird if he had no idea what a bird was. His behaviour might resemble that of a bird in some remote way, but to qualify as pretending to be a bird, he must first know what a bird is. This helps to illustrate how the attitude that accompanies the behaviour is all-important in pretence. The behaviour alone is not sufficient. In that case, Lillard (1993) was inclined to suggest that children below the age of 6 years understand pretence differently from older children. Specifically, they only construe pretence as 'acting as if' and not as a state of mind. This led her to argue that Leslie (1987) was quite wrong to suggest that the behavioural expression of pretence alone is sufficient to credit the toddler with a primitive understanding of mind. The child must also show understanding of pretence as an attitude of mind, and when they are probed on this, genuine understanding only becomes apparent at 6 years and older. Effectively, Lillard is suggesting that younger children understand pretence as 'acting as if'.

This view was corroborated by Perner *et al.* (1994), who told children a story about a girl called Jane who was depicted as feeding her rabbit. It so happened that the rabbit had vacated its hutch, so Jane was feeding it in vain. In one version of the story, which half the participating children heard, Jane knew that there was no rabbit in the hutch, while the other children heard a variant of the story in which Jane was depicted as being ignorant of the rabbit's absence. The children were then asked if Jane was pretending that her rabbit was in the hutch, or whether she really thought it was there. Perner *et al.* reasoned that if Jane was ignorant of the rabbit's absence, then the fact that she was putting out food implies that she thought it really was there. On the other hand, if she was fully aware of the rabbit's absence but still put out food, that would be a sign that she was pretending it was there.

Perner *et al.* (1994) report that children aged 5 years and older correctly judged that Jane really thought the rabbit was in the hutch when she was putting out food, but that she was ignorant of its absence. On the other hand, they judged that she was just pretending if she put food out whilst being fully aware of the rabbit's absence. In contrast, the young children did not discriminate in this way, but instead tended to judge that Jane was pretending in both versions of the story. This failure to discriminate seems to be entirely consistent with the view expressed by Lillard (1993). The older children appeared to regard pretence as a state of mind that can be contrasted with other states of mind, such as belief. They seemed to understand that in one story Jane's act of feeding signalled pretence, while in another it signalled belief. It is not the act itself that counts, but the accompanying state of mind, which only the older children appeared to apprehend. In contrast, the younger children seemed to offer the gloss 'pretend' to mean 'acting as if'. In both versions of the story, Jane was acting as if the rabbit was present (when in fact it was absent). In summary, perhaps below the age of 5 or 6 years, children do not understand pretence as a state of mind, in which case possibly Leslie (1987) was wrong to suggest that the emergence of pretence in toddlers portends an incipient understanding of mind.

ARE TODDLERS BEING UNDERESTIMATED?

Just as it is a recurring theme to question whether we are overestimating children, so it is also a recurring theme to question whether we are underestimating them. If pretence in toddlers does not signal any insight into mind, then what are we to make of their appetite for pretence? Surely we must conclude that what we have called pretence in toddlers is actually no more deserving of that label than the cat's chasing after a ball of string. We had taken it for granted that toddlers have something more to offer in the sense that their pretence is creative. Perhaps that is not so after all – perhaps toddlers are simply imitating the behaviour of other people they see around them in a non-creative manner, in which case they are not pretending as such, but merely 'acting as if'. One way to distinguish between genuine pretence and 'acting as if' is to focus on creativity. 'Acting as if' as in pure imitation is non-creative and non-flexible, but genuine pretence is supposed to be different. Hence we can test whether the toddler's pretence is insightful and meaningful by investigating the child's capacity for flexibility and creativity – to go beyond what is seen in the behaviour of other people. This was the objective Harris and Kavanaugh (1993) set for themselves.

Harris and Kavanaugh (1993) engaged toddlers in a pretend scenario that revolved around the familiar routine of afternoon tea. This involved laying the table, pouring the tea and sipping sedately. One possibility is that the children would enact this as a familiar script in a rather rigid and stereotyped manner, which is what would happen if they did not have a genuine grasp of pretence. On the other hand, if they were pretending in the sense of creative make-believe, their behaviour should be more flexible. To investigate this, the researchers introduced a bizarre and presumably completely unexpected element to the episode. Suddenly, Naughty Teddy appeared (controlled by the experimenter), who proceeded to wreak havoc by pretend pouring out the pretend contents of the tea cups all over the floor. Moreover, he brought long a pretend tube of toothpaste and pretend squeezed it all over one of the innocent protagonists who was a bystander!

After Naughty Teddy had departed and everyone had caught their breath, the participating toddlers were urged to help pretend clean up the pretend mess. They had no difficulty in entering into the spirit of this diversion, and were entirely animated in commenting with disgust on the mess Teddy had caused. This was reflected not just in their actions, but in their language too. For example, one toddler described the protagonist who had become a victim of Teddy's malice as 'toothpasty'. In helping to clean up the pretend mess with pretend cloths, the children did not just make a token gesture with their wrists, but were highly concerned to do a thorough job in the appropriate location of the pretend spillage. In short, there was an abundance of evidence to show that the toddlers who participated were remarkably creative and flexible in their pretence. The evidence strongly suggested that the children were temporarily inhabiting a make-believe world rather than just enacting a routine script. If the latter had been the case, it is difficult to see how the children could have sustained their script behaviour in the face of such a bizarre diversion.

We are left with the need to explain why the children appeared to have a serious lack of understanding of pretence in the studies reported by both Lillard (1993) and Perner et al. (1994). An obvious difference between these and the views expressed by both Leslie (1987) and Harris and Kavanaugh (1993) is that the latter authors were concerned with what we can conclude from the fact that toddlers engage in pretence. According to Leslie (1987) in particular, the ability to engage in pretence is sufficient evidence to support the claim that the pretending child has insight into mind. In contrast, Lillard (1993) and Perner et al. (1994) required additional evidence. They wanted to see positive evidence that toddlers have a reflective understanding of pretence, but they were unable to obtain such evidence, which led them to conclude that early pretence does not add up to much. However, the level of competence which Lillard and Perner et al. sought was very much in advance of what Leslie specified as a demonstration of insight into mind. The failure to obtain positive evidence is difficult to interpret. After all, in both studies the children were asked rather silly questions. For example, in Lillard's study the children first had to accept that Moe was from a different planet, that he had never seen a bird before, and that none the less he was gliding around just like a bird. There are several levels of pretence here, indeed pretence within pretence, and it is not surprising that the children had difficulty in answering questions about pretence. In the study by Perner *et al.* (1994) it is actually debatable whether Jane was pretending at all. She was just putting food in the rabbit's hutch, and it is quite possible that pretence would not have entered the children's heads if the experimenter had not pressed the idea upon them with the test question.

It is reasonable, then, to consider the studies by Lillard (1993) and Perner *et al.* (1994) in a light that makes children's poor performance understandable. Apart from that, no matter how children perform on various contrived tasks, all that matters is that they engage in pretence. That is the appropriate level of analysis, according to Leslie (1987). If we accept Leslie's theory, then the kind of data presented by Lillard and Perner *et al.* poses no threat to Leslie's theory in principle. Some researchers do question Leslie's analysis on his own terms, including Harris and Kavanaugh (1993), but even if we did not accept every detail of his argument, it does seem worth considering the possibility that early pretence is a symbolic activity which heralds the arrival of a primitive understanding of mind.

EARLY COMMUNICATION

Pretence might signify a primitive understanding of mind in itself, but it does more than that. It allows the child to sample other people's perspectives through role play. Similarly, communication in itself is an impressive symbolic activity, and its development opens a route into other minds that is surely much richer in content than could be experienced by any non-linguistic animal. Speech opens a window on the mind, as illustrated in Figure 10.1. The easiest and most reliable way to find out what someone is think-

FIGURE 10.1 There is a sense in which speech is deeply informative about the mind of the person articulating the utterance. Metaphorically, speech opens a window on the mind of the person doing the talking. Through the window of speech, we are able to perceive the mind behind the message.

ing is to ask them! 'Tell me what you are thinking' is a common phrase, which is used at least between people who are intimate. When the response comes, this is treated seriously, and we feel enlightened not just about the content of the other person's mind, but also about what kind of person they are. We gain a feel for the things that preoccupy them, what amuses them and what delights them. Without language as a channel of communication between minds, we would remain very much in the dark about the psychology of those around us. Effectively, we read minds when we comprehend speech.

Obviously we must treat speech with caution, because there are very many reasons why verbal reports could be misleading. As we saw in the previous chapter, people sometimes tell lies. Even if the person who spoke to us was entirely sincere, there is always a risk that they would misinform due to being badly informed themselves, or simply because of a verbal slip. Speech opens a window on the mind but, to extend the metaphor, it is a window paned with frosted glass. Speech is a rich source of information about other minds, but it would be a serious mistake to treat that information as though it were as reliable as information that arises from direct sources such as seeing. With regard to development, we should expect children to learn a great deal about minds once they are able to hold a conversation. The more proficient their conversation, and the greater their willingness to penetrate beyond mere pleasantries, the greater should be their insight into mind. Surely our insight into mind continues to develop throughout life, and much of this knowledge is gained as a result of our ability to speak with other people. For example, the high office of statesman or ambassador must require a deeply refined understanding of people, and accordingly it would not make sense for a young adult to be offered such a position.

As with pretence, the starting point is at about 18 months of age, when the first signs of meaningful conversation emerge. This is where a strange paradox surrounding verbal communication is most conspicuous. The paradox is that on the one hand the child as listener has to assign meaning to the words that constitute the message, yet on the other hand he has to appreciate that meaning ultimately is the prerogative of the person uttering the message. This paradox highlights the distinction between the meaning of the message and the meaning of the speaker – the two are not necessarily the same thing. From the very earliest experience of using language, it is essential that the child should recognize that meaning is the privilege of the speaker.

This is evident from a seminal study conducted by Baldwin (1993), who noted that toddlers potentially face a serious problem in learning vocabulary. Although for some of the time the toddler and adult will be looking at the same thing when the adult names it or talks about it, for much of the time they will be looking at different things. So, for example, the toddler might be gazing at the cat when the adult starts to talk about the health of the house plants. The toddler thus hears the word 'geranium' mentioned as he is looking at the cat. Will he then wrongly call the cat a geranium? This is most unlikely, so there is a mystery concerning the child's ability to avoid labelling things wrongly. How does he do it?

The answer seems to lie in the fact that the toddler has an astonishing aptitude for attending to the adult's line of regard. Baldwin (1993) observed that when the adult named an object, or just started talking generally, the toddler would typically shift his gaze to the adult's eyes and then calculate the geometry of the adult's line of sight to find whatever was at the end of it. The toddler would shift his gaze back and forth between the adult's eyes and the target of the adult's vision, so if the adult shifted his or her gaze to another object, the toddler would not be far behind in shifting his gaze to that object as well. This capacity for tracking gaze, which seems to border on the miraculous, offers the solution to the toddler's acquisition of an accurate vocabulary. Seemingly, the toddler does not assume by default that the object of his own attention is the same thing that the adult is talking about. When the adult speaks, it appears that the child's gaze is subordinate to the adult's in defining the topic.

Intuitively, and at first sight, this remarkable aptitude seems to suggest that toddlers are attuned to differences between their own and other people's attentional focus. It also suggests that toddlers appreciate that meaning is the privilege of the person uttering the words. It would not do for the child to insist stubbornly that what the adult is talking about is the thing that the child is looking at. Rather, the child has to defer and yield with regard to the topic of attention and mental contemplation. Another mind is thus imposing itself on the toddler, and in turn the toddler rises to the occasion by being most accommodating. Whatever the constraints on the conclusions we might wish to draw from this example, at the very least it can be said that toddlers are able to work with other minds and to profit from the appropriate give and take.

Evidently, toddlers are highly receptive to the meaning that the adult is trying to convey. It would not be surprising, then, if there is a link between the quality of parental conversation with the child and what the child understands about minds. As I said previously, verbal communication opens a window on the mind, and it must therefore be the case that what the child understands about mind will hinge substantially on the quality of communication from the parent. An impressive study by Dunn *et al.* (1991) confirmed that this is the case. These authors conducted a longitudinal study in which they first observed children aged about 33 months, and then paid another visit to the home 6 months later. During the first visit, the researchers observed the characteristics of talk from the mother addressed to the child. Six months later, the researchers tested the children for their understanding of mental states.

An intriguing relationship emerged, such that elements of the mother's speech addressed to the child at 33 months predicted the child's level of insight into mind at 39 months. Specifically, mothers who explained behaviour by reference to mental state had children who were better equipped to reason about mental states 6 months later. For example, the mothers of children who were later to show a precocious understanding of mind would explain that Jane could not find her coat in the school cloakroom because she had forgotten where she put it. Children who had the beneficial experience of conversation from such mothers were later able to explain that a protagonist looked in an empty Band-aids box for Band-aids because he wrongly thought it was full.

Although Dunn *et al.* (1991) stress the positive features of their results, there is a rather obvious negative side to them, which is that mothers who did not have the patience or skill to explain to their children why people acted as they did tended to have children who showed considerable ignorance about mind 6 months later. It might be that parental skill in communicating to toddlers nurtures insight into mind, while a lack of skill is detrimental to the child's understanding. Clearly, there are sobering ramifications for parental style to be drawn from the work of these researchers.

ASSIGNING A TENTATIVE STATUS TO VERBAL MESSAGES

It would not do to accord the same status to information presented in a verbal report as to information acquired via a primary sense, such as seeing. This is recognized in legal circles, given that hearsay does not qualify as admissible evidence in a court of law. For example, suppose the prosecution is trying to establish from a witness at what time the accused was standing at the bus stop. Suppose the barrister asked, 'What time was he (the accused) at the bus stop?' and the witness replied, '9 pm, m'lud.' Suppose the barrister persevered, asking, 'are you absolutely sure?' to be met with, 'yes, absolutely.' Then, 'how do you know?', and the witness offered the clarification, 'well, he (the accused) told me he was there at 9 pm!' This would be very silly, since it would make no sense for the witness to express certainty of a fact if its basis was a verbal report from another person (in this case the accused). On the other hand, if the witness had said she saw the accused at 9 pm, that would make a huge difference.

After all, it is only common sense that we should accord a tentative status to information presented in a verbal report. It is information from another mind, which could be invaluable, but it still has to be recognized as having a potential for unreliability. Quite simply, it is not as trustworthy as information from a direct source. Children could only be encoding verbal information as the product of another mind if they assigned a tentative status to it. If they treated verbal information as being factually true, on a par with what they see directly, then they would not be treating verbal information as the product of another mind. One of the definitions of a mind is that it runs the risk of being misinformed and therefore passing on misinformation in verbal communication. Essentially, then, we should ask whether young children assign a tentative status to information offered to them in a verbal report.

This is precisely the question asked by my colleagues and I (Mitchell *et al.*, 1996b), in a sister study of work discussed in Chapter 8 (Mitchell *et al.*,

1996a). We told children a story about a protagonist called Kevin, who was inquisitive about the content of a jug, so he looked inside and saw orange juice in the jug. Subsequently, Rebecca appeared on the scene and announced that the jug contained milk (see Figure 8.6). Observing child participants had to judge what Kevin would think was inside the jug after receiving this conflicting information, and the vast majority of even the youngest children tested, who were 3 years of age, judged that he thought the jug contained orange juice. In other words, the children judged that Kevin would rely more heavily on what he had seen than on what he was told when the two sources of information were in conflict.

Under a different circumstance, children of the same age showed good understanding that Kevin would be informed by a message when that was appropriate. In this story, Kevin did not look in the jug, but either he hoped that the jug contained orange juice, or he pretended that it did. Subsequently, as before, Rebecca arrived and announced that the jug contained milk. This time, the children had no difficulty in judging that Kevin would believe that the jug contained milk, as he had been told. Evidently the children understood that verbal messages are taken as being informative, and count much more than mere hope or pretence when it comes to deciding the state of reality (what Kevin really believes is inside the jug). Despite that, there was a limit to the degree to which children regard verbal messages as informative. They judged that Kevin would not believe the message in preference to what he had seen with his own eyes. It seems that even children as young as 3 years understand that seeing is believing. Putting it another way, they apparently understand that verbal messages are typically assigned a tentative status.

UNDERSTANDING THAT MESSAGES ARISE FROM MINDS

It is one thing to treat messages tentatively, and yet another to demonstrate an explicit understanding that messages are a product of the mind. Children might have a healthy mistrust of verbal messages, yet without being able to trace the meaning of the message explicitly to the mind of the speaker. This issue was investigated by Elizabeth Robinson and myself (Robinson and Mitchell, 1992, 1994). We told children a story that is illustrated schematically in Figure 5.6. In Scene 1, Mum is putting away two bags of wool. Each bag contains a different ball of wool, but otherwise the bags are fairly similar. She puts one bag in the drawer and the other in the cupboard, and then departs. Later, as shown in Scene 2, John arrives and gets the bags out to play with them. When he has finished playing, he returns the bags, but the funny thing is that he gets them mixed up by swapping the bags round, so the bag that Mum put in the drawer is now in the cupboard, and the bag Mum put in the cupboard is now in the drawer. Mum did not witness this, due to her absence, so she assumes that the bags remain where she left them. Finally, still ignorant of the fact that John has tampered with the bags, Mum requests one of the bags by location. She shouts her request from the adjacent room, saying that she wants the bag in the cupboard. It is very important that she gets the correct bag, otherwise the dress she is making will look silly. At this point, observing child participants are asked which bag Mum really wants.

We can infer that the bag Mum really wants is the one that is currently in the drawer. The only way that we can infer this is by interpreting Mum's request as referring to the bag that resides in the cupboard *in her mind's eye*. There is no way in which we could have gathered that prior to hearing Mum's request. In making this inference, we show that we understand that Mum's message arises from her mind and refers to a state of the world that exists in her mind. It is a state of the world that is at odds with current reality. Would children also show this kind of insight, or would they interpret her request too literally? It turned out that although children aged 3 years showed little inclination to interpret non-literally, many children aged 4 years did succeed. It seemed that children as young as 4 years discriminate between the literal meaning of the message and the meaning intended by the speaker. The message stated 'cupboard' but, in a sense, the speaker meant 'drawer', or at least that is how the children appeared to interpret it.

Before getting carried away with celebrating the young child's considerable insight into the mind that resides behind the message, we should pause to eliminate an alternative explanation for the children's success. Perhaps the children's correct judgements were actually false positives. What we require is a closely matched control condition in which children correctly interpret the request literally. The control we devised involved a story that was almost identical, except that John returned the bags to exactly the same places where Mum had left them after he had finished playing. When Mum finally requested the bag in the cupboard, it would be correct to interpret this literally by judging that she really wanted the bag in the cupboard. If the children wrongly interpreted Mum's request non-literally in this story, then we should be very suspicious about their non-literal interpretations in the story in which the bags were swapped round. It turned out that children aged 4 years very seldom offered an incorrect non-literal interpretation in the control story; their non-literal interpretations were confined to the story in which the bags were swapped round.

It seems as if we are able to conclude that, from about 4 years of age, children perceive verbal messages as a product of mind and therefore as a window on the mind. When they hear somebody speaking to them, they are treating this not just as being informative about reality, but as being informative about the mind of the person who is doing the speaking. It is most likely, then, that from about 4 years of age children are accumulating information about the distinctive minds of those people who enter their sphere of interaction. If children lacked this ability, or if they experienced only impoverished communication with others, then presumably their understanding of mind would be seriously impaired.

UNDERSTANDING THAT UTTERANCES HAVE TO BE INTERPRETED

Although children show a surprising insight into the relationship between message and mind from a very early age, development does not end there. A further level of understanding is that messages are subject to interpretation. One and the same message can be interpreted differently by different people. This is perhaps most apparent in the case of ambiguous messages. The classic research on this topic was conducted by Elizabeth Robinson (see Robinson and Whittaker, 1987, for a review). In a typical procedure the child has three cards, each displaying a comical male figure, two of them wearing hats, as shown in Figure 10.2. The experimenter has an identical set

FIGURE 10.2 The experimenter announces that she has chosen a man wearing a hat and a child participant is invited to try to identify this chosen figure. Children of 6 years and below tend to insist that they have chosen correctly, while slightly older children correctly express reservations on the grounds that the message is ambiguous.

of cards, and the purpose of the game is for one of the players to select a card and then to describe it so as to enable the other player to select exactly the same card from her own set. A screen is erected between the experimenter and the child, so that the message assumes great importance in ensuring that the two players have the same card.

When it is the experimenter's turn to describe the card, she will say that the card she has chosen shows a man wearing a hat. Children then select what they think is the same card from their own set. Children aged about 6 years and younger are extremely eager to choose one of the cards showing a man with a hat, and having done so are inclined to insist that they are sure that they have chosen correctly and that the experimenter gave them enough information. If the screen is then removed, the two players can compare their chosen cards and, in the event of an ambiguous message, the experimenter rigs the game so that her card is different from that of the child. The experimenter will then ask whose fault it is that they have chosen different cards, and those children aged below 6 years tend to blame the listener, in this case themselves. Children still blame the listener if that person happens to be the experimenter, and it was the child who inadvertently gave an ambiguous message (which is very common in children of that age).

The older children, on the other hand, tend to judge that they are not sure which man with a hat the experimenter has chosen, and that the experimenter has not told them enough. In the event of the child and the experimenter having chosen different cards following an ambiguous message, the older children tend to blame the person who gave the message for the failure of communication. The older children seem to understand that the message has to be interpreted – and that it can therefore be misinterpreted. In the case of ambiguity, this understanding is evident when the children acknowledge that the message could be interpreted in a way other than that which the speaker intended.

It seems likely, then, that when children are about 6 or 7 years of age they begin to appreciate that utterances have to be interpreted and can be misinterpreted. Prior to that age, they appear to assume that comprehension of intended meaning is a mere formality – which in most cases it is, of course. Why should there be a lag in the development of understanding that messages are a product of mind and understanding that messages are subject to interpretation? One possibility is that children find it difficult to evaluate utterances, and do not regard language in general as something to be scrutinized and assessed. It might be that a certain level of literacy is required for the child to regard language itself as something that can be contemplated. Perhaps only when the child gets used to seeing language as something tangible and enduring on the written page will he or she begin to realize that it is available for consideration (Olson and Torrance, 1983).

If that view is correct, then children have not so much a specific problem with ambiguity as a more general one with evaluating utterances (whether these are ambiguous or otherwise). We (Mitchell and Robinson, 1994) set out to investigate this matter by formulating a rather interesting prediction.

We presented the story about Mum and her bags of wool that are swapped round. Instead of asking 5- and 6-year-old children to judge which bag Mum really wants, they were asked to judge whether Mum said the right thing to get the bag she wants. In this case, children were asked not to interpret but to evaluate the message. The intriguing prediction was that if children could make an interpretation of the message as arising from mind, but were unable to reflect on messages as things that can be good or bad (and tended to judge that they are good no matter what), they might appear to contradict themselves. They might judge that Mum does not want the bag in the place that she mentioned, yet judge that she said the right thing for the bag she really wants.

It turned out, however, that the children were just as effective in judging that Mum said the wrong thing as they were in judging that she wanted the bag in the non-mentioned location. On the other hand, if Mum gave an ambiguous utterance, by requesting the bag in the drawer when there were two bags in the drawer, they tended to judge that her message was good. Consequently, it seems that the children have a specific problem with ambiguity and not a more general difficulty with the concept of evaluating utterances. We concluded that, although children aged 5 years might be able to reflect on utterances to an extent, they do not seem to realize that an ambiguous message is prone to misinterpretation. Perhaps they do not appreciate that it is possible for two different minds, for example, to interpret one and the same piece of information differently. Precisely that view was put forward by Chandler and Helm (1984) in relation to ambiguous visual information.

EVEN LATER DEVELOPMENTS

Understanding that messages can be interpreted differently by different minds is fine in principle, but there is yet another step in understanding how minds might process degraded utterances. This was a topic I investigated for my doctorate (Mitchell *et al.*, 1991). I composed stories in which a protagonist incorrectly described the item they intended to refer to. For example, John wanted Mary to fetch his reading book, and he asked her to get the yellow book with the word 'reading' and a picture of a cat on the front cover. In fact, the book was as described in every detail except it had a picture of a dog on the cover. In other words, John gave a slightly incorrect description of the object he wanted. Under another condition, John was depicted as significantly misdescribing the book (he gave the wrong colour among other things).

Observing child participants were then asked to judge whether Mary knew which book John wanted. A clear age trend emerged between 6 and 9 years. The older children judged that Mary did know which book John wanted when he gave a slightly incorrect description, but that she did not know when his description was grossly inaccurate. In contrast, the younger children made no such distinction. It seems that the older children had come to appreciate how utterances serve as clues to meaning, with some utterances functioning better in that respect than others. It appears that although the younger children might understand that different people can interpret the same message differently, as the research into ambiguity testifies, they have yet to grasp what minds make of messages as clues, and what constitutes a good verbal clue and what constitutes a bad clue. They have yet to acquire a finer appreciation of the link between the content of the message and the kind of interpretation that is likely to be made.

CONCLUSIONS

The evidence presented in this chapter illustrates the two sides of development. On the one hand, children have a remarkable symbolic competence from a very early age, as demonstrated by their pretence and early linguistic capacities. It certainly does not follow that little development occurs beyond the early years. On the contrary, a huge amount of development takes place in understanding that messages arise from minds, in understanding that messages are subject to interpretation and in understanding that messages can provide good or bad clues to the meaning intended by the speaker. These developments extend well into middle childhood, and probably well beyond that into the relatively uncharted waters of adolescence – but research on this is sparse.

On a more general note, what we learn from this book is that there is no simple story of development. It is not the case, in my view, that children suddenly acquire an insight into mind at 4 years of age. Rather, the child has very important insights from an earlier age, but some aspects of development take place over many years, presumably throughout childhood. Another point we should not forget is that an understanding of mind is not compartmentalized and isolated, but depends on other aspects of development, especially the skills in language and communication that burgeon during the first 7 years of life.

Development is surprisingly reliable, but the acquisition of a sound insight into mind cannot be taken for granted. The unfortunate case of autism is testament to this. It is probably no coincidence that children with autism appear to lack understanding of mind and also have conspicuously impaired communication. There is no firm evidence to indicate the direction in which the causality lies, but it is entirely plausible that children with autism are limited in what they can know about minds because they are denied access to the most direct route to other minds – via verbal communication.

When we look at animals other than humans, a consistent picture emerges. Humans are uniquely linguistic and they have the greatest insight into mind. However, there are glimmers of insight into mind in apes, just as there are glimmers of an embryonic capacity for language. Development should be considered between species as well as within them, and in that context we see humans as highly evolved social animals. The organ under-lying this, of course, is the brain, which has become specialized in under-standing minds and communicating between them. Apes have many impressive abilities, but in evolutionary terms humans have progressed very much further.

REFERENCES

Argyle, M. 1978: *The psychology of interpersonal behaviour*, 2nd edn. Harmondsworth: Penguin Books.

Avis, J. and Harris, P. 1991: Belief-desire reasoning among Baka children: evidence for a universal conception of mind. *Child Development* **62**, 460–67.

Baldwin, D.A. 1993: Infants' ability to consult the speaker for clues to word reference. *Journal of Child Language* **20**, 395–418.

Baron-Cohen, S. 1989a: Perceptual role taking and protodeclarative pointing in autism. *British Journal of Developmental Psychology* **7**, 113–27.

Baron-Cohen, S. 1989b: Are autistic children 'behaviourists'? An examination of their mental-physical and appearance-reality distinctions. *Journal of Autism and Developmental Disorders* **19**, 579–600.

Baron-Cohen, S. 1989c: The autistic child's theory of mind: a case of specific developmental delay. *Journal of Child Psychology and Psychiatry* **30**, 285–97.

Baron-Cohen, S. 1991a: The development of a theory of mind in autism: deviance and delay? *Psychiatric Clinics of North America* **14**, 33–50.

Baron-Cohen, S. 1991b: Do children with autism understand what causes emotion? *Child Development* **62**, 385–95.

Baron-Cohen, S., Leslie, A.M. and Frith, U. 1985: Does the autistic child have a 'theory of mind'? *Cognition* **21**, 37–46.

Baron-Cohen, S. and Ring, H. 1994: A model of the mind-reading system: neuropsychological and neurobiological perspectives. In Lewis, C. and Mitchell, P. (eds), *Children's early understanding of mind: origins and development.* Hove: Erlbaum, 183–207.

Bartsch, K. and Wellman, H. 1989: Young children's attribution of action to beliefs and desires. *Child Development* **60**, 946–64.

Bauman, M.L. and Kemper, T.L. 1994: Neuroanatomic observations of the brain in autism. In Bauman, M.L. and Kemper, T.L. (eds), *The neurobiology of autism.* Baltimore: The John Hopkins University Press, 119–45.

Blair, R.J.R. 1995: A cognitive developmental approach to morality: investigating the psychopath. *Cognition* **57**, 1–29.

Bowler, D.M. 1992: 'Theory of mind' in Asperger's syndrome. *Journal of Child Psychology and Psychiatry* **33**, 877–93.

Boysen, S.T. 1993: Counting in chimpanzees: non-human principles and emergent properties of number. In Boysen, S.T. and Capaldi, E.J. (eds), *The development of numerical competence: animal and human models.* Hove: Lawrence Erlbaum Associates, 39–59.

Brown, R. 1973: *A first language.* Cambridge, MA: Harvard University Press.

Bruner, J.S. 1983: *Child's talk: learning to use language.* New York: W.W. Norton.

Butterworth, G. and Jarrett, N.L.M. 1991: What minds share in common is space: spatial mechanisms serving joint visual attention in infancy. *British Journal of Developmental Psychology* **9**, 55–72.

Chandler, M., Fritz, A.S. and Hala, S. 1989: Small-scale deceit: deception as a marker of 2-, 3-, and 4-year-olds' early theories of mind. *Child Development* **60**, 1263–77.

Chandler, M. and Hala, S. 1994: The role of personal involvement in the assessment of early false belief skills. In Lewis, C. and Mitchell, P. (eds), *Children's early understanding of mind: origins and development*. Hove: Erlbaum, 403–25.

Chandler, M. and Helm, D. 1984: Developmental changes in the contribution of shared experience to social role taking competence. *International Journal of Behavioral Development* **7**, 145–56.

Chomsky, N. 1975: *Reflections on language*. New York: Pantheon Books.

Connolly, J.A. and Doyle, A. 1984: Relation of social fantasy play to social competence in preschoolers. *Developmental Psychology* **20**, 797–806.

Courchesne, E., Yeung-Courchesne, R., Press, G.A., Hesselink, J.R. and Jernigan, T.L. 1988: Hypoplasia of cerebellar vermal lobules VI and VII in infantile autism. *New England Journal of Medicine* **318**, 1349–54.

Crook, J.H. 1980: *The evolution of human consciousness*. Oxford: Clarendon Press.

Davidson, I. 1991: The archaeology of language origins: a review. *Antiquity* **65**, 39–48.

de Gelder, B. 1987: On not having a theory of mind. *Cognition* **27**, 285–90.

Dennett, D.C. 1978: Beliefs about beliefs. *Behavioural and Brain Sciences* **1**, 568–70.

de Waal, F.B.M. 1995: Bonobo, sex and society. *Scientific American* **272**, 58–64.

Dunn, J. 1994: Changing minds and changing relationships. In Lewis, C. and Mitchell, P. (eds), *Children's early understanding of mind: origins and development*. Hove: Erlbaum, 297–310.

Dunn, J., Brown, J., Slomkowski, C., Tesla, C. and Youngblade, L. 1991: Young children's understanding of other people's feelings and beliefs: individual differences and their antecedents. *Child Development* **62**, 1352–66.

Elkind, D. 1967: Egocentrism in adolescence. *Child Development* **38**, 1025–34.

Fischhoff, B. 1975: Hindsight is not equal to foresight: the effect of outcome knowledge on judgment under uncertainty. *Journal of Experimental Psychology: Human Perception and Performance* **1**, 288–99.

Flavell, J.H., Flavell, E.R. and Green, F.L. 1983: Development of the appearance-reality distinction. *Cognitive Psychology* **15**, 95–120.

Fodor, J.A. 1992: A theory of the child's theory of mind. *Cognition* **44**, 283–96.

Freeman, N.H. and Lacohee, H. 1995: Making explicit 3-year-olds' implicit competence with their own false beliefs. *Cognition* **56**, 31–60.

Frith, C.D. and Corcoran, R. 1996: Exploring 'theory of mind' in people with schizophrenia. *Psychological Medicine* (in press).

Frith, U. 1989: *Autism: explaining the enigma*. Oxford: Basil Blackwell.

Gallup, G.G. 1970: Chimpanzees: self-recognition. *Science* **167**, 86–7.

Gopnik, A. 1993: How we know our minds: the illusion of first-person knowledge of intentionality. *Behavioral and Brain Sciences* **16**, 1–14.

Gopnik, A. and Astington, J.W. 1988: Children's understanding of representational change, and its relation to the understanding of false belief and the appearance-reality distinction. *Child Development* **59**, 26–37.

Gopnik, A. and Graf, P. 1988: Knowing how you know: young children's ability to identify and remember the sources of their beliefs. *Child Development* **59**, 1366–71.

Grice, H.P. 1975: Logic and conversation. In Cole, P. and Morgan, J. (eds), *Syntax and semantics 3: speech acts*. New York: Academic Press, 41–58.

Hala, S., Chandler, M. and Fritz, A.S. 1991: Fledgeling theories of mind: deception as a marker of 3-year-olds' understanding of false belief. *Child Development* **61**, 83–97.

Happe, F. 1994: *Autism: an introduction to psychological theory*. London: UCL Press.

Harris, P.L. and Gross, D. 1988: Children's understanding of real and apparent emotion. In Astington, J.W., Harris, P.L. and Olson, D.R. (eds), *Developing theories of mind*. Cambridge: Cambridge University Press, 295–314.

Harris, P.L. and Kavanaugh, R.D. 1993: Young children's understanding of pretence. *Monographs of the Society for Research in Child Development* **58**, Serial No. 231.

Hobson, R.P. 1995: *Blindness and psychological development 0–10 years*. Paper presented at the Mary Kitzinger Trust Symposium, September 1995, University of Warwick.

Hobson, R.P., Ouston, J. and Lee, A. 1988: What's in a face? The case of autism. *British Journal of Psychology* **79**, 441–53.

Hobson, R.P., Ouston, J. and Lee, A. 1989: Naming emotion in faces and voices: abilities and disabilities in autism and mental retardation. *British Journal of Developmental Psychology* **7**, 237–50.

Horwitz, B. and Rumsey, J.M. 1994: Positron emission tomography: implications for cerebral dysfunction in autism. In Bauman, M.L. and Kemper, T.L. (eds), *The neurobiology of autism*. Baltimore: The John Hopkins University Press, 102–18.

Hughes, C.H. and Russell, J. 1993: Autistic children's difficulty with mental disengagement from an object: its implications for theories of autism. *Developmental Psychology* **29**, 498–510.

Humphrey, N.K. 1986: *The inner eye*. London: Faber and Faber.

Huxley, A. 1950: *Brave new world: a novel*. London: Chatto and Windus.

Kanner, L. 1943: Autistic disturbances of affective contact. *Nervous Child* **12**, 17–50.

Kanner, L. and Eisenberg, L. 1956: Early infantile autism 1943–1955. *American Journal of Orthopsychiatry* **26**, 55–65.

Keating, C.F. and Heltman, K.R. 1994: Dominance and deception in children and adults: are leaders the best misleaders? *Personality and Social Psychology Bulletin* **20**, 312–21.

Klin, A., Volkmar, F.R. and Sparrow, S.S. 1992: Autistic social dysfunction: some limitations of the theory of mind hypothesis. *Journal of Child Psychology and Psychiatry* **33**, 861–76.

Lapsley, D.N. 1985: Elkind on egocentrism. *Developmental Review* **5**, 227–36.

Lapsley, D.K. and Murphy, M.N. 1985: Another look at the theoretical assumptions of adolescent egocentrism. *Developmental Review* **5**, 201–17.

Leekam, S.R. and Perner, J. 1991. Does the autistic child have a metarepresentational deficit? *Cognition* **40**, 203–18.

Leslie, A.M. 1987: Pretense and representation: the origins of 'theory of mind'. *Psychological Review* **94**, 412–26.

Leslie, A.M. 1994: Pretending and believing: issues in the theory of ToMM. *Cognition* **50**, 211–38.

Leslie, A.M. and Frith, U. 1988: Autistic children's understanding of seeing, knowing and believing. *British Journal of Developmental Psychology* **6**, 315–24.

Leslie, A.M. and Thaiss, L. 1992: Domain specificity in conceptual development: neuropsychological evidence from autism. *Cognition* **43**, 225–51.

Lewis, C. 1994: Episodes, events and narratives in the child's understanding of mind. In Lewis, C. and Mitchell, P. (eds), *Children's early understanding of mind: origins and development*. Hove: Erlbaum, 457–80.

Lewis, C., Freeman, N.H., Hagestadt, C. and Douglas, H. 1994: Narrative access and production in preschoolers' false belief reasoning. *Cognitive Development* **9**, 397–424.

Lewis, C. and Osborne, A. 1990: Three-year-olds' problems with false belief: conceptual deficit or linguistic artefact? *Child Development* **61**, 1514–19.

Lewis, M., Stanger, C. and Sullivan, M.W. 1989: Deception in 3-year-olds. *Developmental Psychology* **25**, 439–43.

Lillard, A.S. 1993: Young children's conceptualization of pretense: action or mental representational state? *Child Development* **64**, 372–86.

Lotter, V. 1966: Epidemiology of autistic conditions in young children. I. Prevalence. *Social Psychiatry* **1**, 124–37.

Maslow, A.H. 1954: *Motivation and personality.* New York: Harper.

Mitchell, P. 1994: Realism and early conception of mind: a synthesis of phylogenetic and ontogenetic issues. In Lewis, C. and Mitchell, P. (eds), *Children's early understanding of mind: origins and development.* Hove: Erlbaum, 19–45.

Mitchell, P and Isaacs, J.E. 1994: Understanding of verbal representation in children with autism: the case of referential opacity. *British Journal of Developmental Psychology* **12**, 439–54.

Mitchell, P. and Lacohee, H. 1991: Children's early understanding of false belief. *Cognition* **39**, 107–27.

Mitchell, P., Munno, A. and Russell, J. 1991: Children's understanding of the communicative value of discrepant verbal messages. *Cognitive Development* **6**, 279–99.

Mitchell, P. and Robinson, E.J. 1994: Discrepant utterances resulting from a false belief: children's evaluations. *Child Development* **65**, 1214–27.

Mitchell, P., Robinson, E.J., Isaacs, J.E. and Nye, R.M. 1996a: Contamination in reasoning about false belief: an instance of realist bias in adults but not children. *Cognition* **59**, 1–21.

Mitchell, P., Robinson, E.J., Nye, R.M. and Isaacs, J.E. 1996b: When speech conflicts with seeing: young children's understanding of informational priority. *Journal of Experimental Child Psychology* (in press).

Mitchell, P., Saltmarsh, R. and Russell, H. 1996c: Overly literal interpretations of speech in autism: understanding that messages arise from minds. (unpubl.) University of Birmingham.

Moses, L.J. and Flavell, J.H. 1990: Inferring false beliefs from actions and reactions. *Child Development* **61**, 929–45.

Mundy, P., Sigman, M. and Kasari, C. 1993: The theory of mind and joint attention deficits in autism. In Baron-Cohen, S., Tager-Flusberg, H. and Cohen, D. (eds), *Understanding other minds: perspectives from autism.* Oxford: Oxford University Press, 181–203.

Olson, D.R. and Torrance, N.G. 1983: Literacy and cognitive development: a conceptual transformation in the early school years. In Meadows, S. (ed.), *Developing thinking: approaches to children's cognitive development.* London: Methuen, 142–60.

Ozonoff, S., Pennington, B.F. and Rogers, S.J. 1991: Executive function deficits in high-functioning autistic individuals: relationship to theory of mind. *Journal of Child Psychology and Psychiatry* **32**, 1081–105.

Patterson, F. 1984: Self-recognition by *Gorilla gorilla gorilla. Gorilla* **7**, 2–3.

Perner, J. 1991: *Understanding the representational mind.* London: MIT Press.

Perner, J. Baker, S. and Hutton, D. 1994: Prelief: the conceptual origins of belief and pretence. In Lewis, C. and Mitchell, P. (eds), *Children's early understanding of mind: origins and development.* Hove: Lawrence Erlbaum Associates, 261–86.

Perner, J. and Davies, G. 1991: Understanding the mind as an active information processor: do young children have a 'copy theory of mind'? *Cognition* **39**, 51–69.

Perner, J., Frith, U., Leslie, A.M. and Leekam, S.R. 1989: Exploration of the autistic child's theory of mind: knowledge, belief and communication. *Child Development* **60**, 689–700.

Perner, J., Leekam, S. and Wimmer, H. 1987: Three-year-olds' difficulty with false belief: The case for a conceptual deficit. *British Journal of Developmental Psychology* **5**, 125–37.

Perner, J. and Wimmer, H. 1985: 'John thinks that Mary thinks that 'Attribution of second-order beliefs by 5–10 year old children. *Journal of Experimental Child Psychology* **39**, 437–71.

Peterson, C.C. and Siegal, M. 1995: Deafness, conversation and theory of mind. *Journal of Child Psychology and Psychiatry* **36**, 459–74.

Phillips, W., Gomez, J.C., Baron-Cohen, S., Laa, V. and Riviere, A. 1995: Treating people as objects, agents or 'subjects': how young children with and without autism make requests. *Journal of Child Psychology and Psychiatry* **36**, 1383–98.

Pillow, B.H. 1989: Early understanding of perception as a source of knowledge. *Journal of Experimental Child Psychology* **47**, 116–29.

Pillow, B.H. 1993: Preschool children's understanding of the relationship between modality of perceptual access and knowledge of perceptual properties. *British Journal of Developmental Psychology* **11**, 371–90.

Piven, J. and Folstein, S. 1994: The genetics of autism. In Bauman, M.L. and Kemper, T.L. (eds), *The neurobiology of autism*. Baltimore: The John Hopkins University Press, 18–44.

Povinelli, D.J. 1993: Reconstructing the evolution of mind. *American Psychologist* **48**, 493–509.

Povinelli, D.J. and DeBlois, S. 1992: Young children's (*Homo sapiens*) understanding of knowledge formation in themselves and others. *Journal of Comparative Psychology* **106**, 228–38.

Povinelli, D.J. and Eddy, T.J. 1996a: Chimpanzees: joint visual attention. *Psychological Science* (in press).

Povinelli, D.J. and Eddy, T.J. 1996b: What young chimpanzees know about seeing. *Monographs of the Society for Research in Child Development* (in press).

Povinelli, D.J., Nelson, K.E. and Boysen, S.T. 1990: Inferences about guessing and knowing in chimpanzees (*Pan troglodytes*). *Journal of Comparative Psychology* **104**, 203–10.

Povinelli, D.J., Nelson, K.E. and Boysen, S.T. 1992: Comprehension of role reversal by chimpanzees: evidence of empathy? *Animal Behaviour* **43**, 633–40.

Povinelli, D.J., Rulf, A.B., Landau, K.R. and Bierschwale, D.T. 1993: Self-recognition in chimpanzees (*Pan troglodytes*): distribution, ontogeny and patterns of emergence. *Journal of Comparative Behavioral Biology* **107**, 347–72.

Pratt, C. and Bryant, P. 1990: Young children understand that looking leads to knowing (so long as they are looking into a single barrel). *Child Development* **61**, 973–82.

Premack, D. and Woodruff, G. 1978: Does the chimpanzee have a theory of mind? *Behavioral and Brain Sciences* **4**, 515–26.

Robinson, E.J. and Mitchell, P. 1992: Children's interpretation of messages from a speaker with a false belief. *Child Development* **63**, 639–52.

Robinson, E.J. and Mitchell, P. 1994: Young children's false belief reasoning: interpretation of messages is no easier than the classic task. *Developmental Psychology* **30**, 67–72.

Robinson, E.J. and Mitchell, P. 1995: Masking of children's early understanding of the representational mind: backwards explanation versus prediction. *Child Development* **66**, 1022–39.

Robinson, E.J. and Whittaker, S.J. 1987: Children's conceptions of relations between messages, meanings and reality. *British Journal of Developmental Psychology* **5**, 81–90.

Ruffman, T., Olson, D.R., Ash, T. and Keenan, T. 1993: The ABCs of deception: do young children understand deception in the same way as adults? *Developmental Psychology* **29**, 74–87.

Russell, J., Mauthner, N., Sharpe, S. and Tidswell, T. 1991: The 'windows task' as a measure of strategic deception in preschoolers and autistic subjects. *British Journal of Developmental Psychology* **9**, 331–50.

Saltmarsh, R. and Mitchell, P. 1996: Childrens early ability to acknowledge false belief: realism versus deception. (unpubl.) University of Birmingham.

Saltmarsh, R., Mitchell, P. and Robinson, E. 1995: Realism and children's early grasp of mental representation: belief-based judgments in the State Change task. *Cognition* **57**, 297–325.

Savage-Rumbaugh, E.S., Murphy, J., Sevcik, R.A., Brakke, K.E., Williams, S.L. and Rumbaugh, D.M. 1993: Language comprehension in ape and child. *Monographs of the Society for Research in Child Development* **58**, No. 3–4.

Schmahmann, J.D. 1994: The cerebellum in autism: clinical and anatomic perspectives. In Bauman, M.L. and Kemper, T.L. (eds), *The neurobiology of autism*. Baltimore: The John Hopkins University Press, 195–226.

Siegal, M. and Beattie, K. 1991: Where to look first for children's knowledge of false beliefs. *Cognition* **38**, 1–12.

Siegal, M. and Peterson, C.C. 1994: Children's theory of mind and the conversational territory of cognitive development. In Lewis, C. and Mitchell, P. (eds), *Children's early understanding of mind: origins and development*. Hove: Erlbaum, 427–55.

Skinner, B.F. 1957: *Verbal behaviour*. New York: Appleton-Century-Crofts.

Skinner, B.F. 1976: *Walden two*. London: Collier Macmillan.

Sodian, B. 1991: The development of deception in young children. *British Journal of Developmental Psychology* **9**, 173–88.

Sodian, B. and Frith, U. 1992: Deception and sabotage in autistic, retarded and normal children. *Journal of Child Psychology and Psychiatry* **33**, 591–605.

Sodian, B., Taylor, C., Harris, P.L. and Perner, J. 1991: Early deception and the child's theory of mind: false trails and genuine markers. *Child Development* **62**, 468–83.

Sodian, B. and Wimmer, H. 1987: Children's understanding of inference as a source of knowledge. *Child Development* **58**, 424–33.

Steverson, E.J. 1996: *The malleability of the developing representational mind*. Ph.D. Thesis, University of Wales.

Sullivan, K. and Winner, E. 1993: Three-year-olds' understanding of mental states: the influence of trickery. *Journal of Experimental Child Psychology* **56**, 135–48.

Taylor, L.M. and Mitchell, P. 1996: Judgments of apparent shape contaminated by knowledge of reality: Viewing circles obliquely. (unpubl.) University of Birmingham.

Terrace, H.S., Petitto, C.A., Sanders, R.J. and Bever, T.G. 1979: Can an ape create a sentence? *Science* **206**, 891–902.

Thouless, R.H. 1931: Phenomenal regression to the real object. II. *British Journal of Psychology* **22**, 1–30.

Wellman, H.M. 1990: *The child's theory of mind.* Cambridge: MIT Press.

Welsh, M.C., Pennington, B.F., Ozonoff, S., Rouse, B. and McCabe, E.R.B. 1990: Neuropsychology of early-treated phenylketonuria: specific executive function deficits. *Child Development* **61**, 1697–713.

Whiten, A. and Byrne, R.W. 1988: Tactical deception in primates. *Behavioral and Brain Sciences* **11**, 233–73.

Wimmer, H. and Hartl, M. 1991: Against the Cartesian view on mind: young children's difficulty with own false beliefs. *British Journal of Developmental Psychology* **9**, 125–38.

Wimmer, H., Hogrefe, G.-J. and Perner, J. 1988a: Children's understanding of informational access as a source of knowledge. *Child Development* **59**, 386–96.

Wimmer, H., Hogrefe, G.-J. and Sodian, B. 1988b: A second stage in children's conception of mental life: Understanding sources of information. In Astington, J.W., Harris, P.L., and Olson, D.R., (eds), *Developing theories of mind.* Cambridge: Cambridge University Press, 173–92.

Wimmer, H. and Perner, J. 1983: Beliefs about beliefs: representation and constraining function of wrong beliefs in young children's understanding of deception. *Cognition* **13**, 103–128.

Wing, L. and Gould, J. 1979: Severe impairments of social interaction and associated abnormalities in children: epidemiology and classification. *Journal of Autism and Developmental Disorders* **9**, 11–29.

Woodruff, G. and Premack, D. 1979: Intentional communication in the chimpanzee: the development of deception. *Cognition* **7**, 333–62.

Zaitchik, D. 1990: When representations conflict with reality: the preschoolers' problem with false belief and 'false' photographs. *Cognition* **35**, 41–68.

Zelazo, P.D., Burack, J.A., Benedetto, E. and Frye, D. 1996: Theory of mind and rule use in individuals with Down syndrome: a test of the uniqueness and specificity claims. *Journal of Child Psychology and Psychiatry* (in press).

SUBJECT INDEX

AUTHOR INDEX